Charles Purser

Additional Information
and
Amendments to the

NORTH CAROLINA TROOPS
1861 – 1865

Seventeen Volume Roster

Compiled by

Charles E. Purser Jr.
Garner, North Carolina

2010

The Scuppernong Press

Wake Forest, NC

Additional Information and Amendments to the North Carolina Troops 1861-1865 Seventeen Volume Roster

©2010 Charles E. Purser, Jr.

First Printing

The Scuppernong Press
PO Box 1724
Wake Forest, NC 27588
www.scuppernongpress.com

Cover photo and book design by Frank B. Powell, III

Cover photo is the statue of Private Henry L. Wyatt on the Capitol grounds in Raleigh, North Carolina. Private Wyatt was the first Confederate soldier killed in battle.

International Standard Book Number ISBN 978-0-9845529-2-4

Library of Congress Control Number: 2010927476

Table of Contents

Additional Information and Amendments to the North Carolina Troops 1861-1865

Foreward

During the one hundredth anniversary of the American War Between the States, the North Carolina Department of Archives and History began an important project to research and print their findings on all North Carolinians who served during that war. Their first volume was published in 1966 and continues today in 2010 while researching data for Volume 18. The project is not done at this writing, but the Archives should be proud of the information which has helped thousands of descendants who are researching their North Carolina soldier. It is estimated another three volumes will complete this project.

It is probably hard for new and old researchers today to realize the tools the Archives research team had forty-three years ago in their search is now considered very archaic with today's Internet tools. If they were searching for a certain soldier the main sources were the Compiled Service Records and the census records on microfilm. A long and tedious job for the team, but they were able to produce a book about every two-and-half-years.

The advance of the Internet has greatly enhanced the materials for students of history to find new facts. This is how this publication came about. Using many sources on the Internet, but mainly the many items on Ancestry.com data can be found in lighting speed compared to the old cranking of microfilm machines. Another advantage to the current researcher is the ease of using computers in sorting and manipulating the data to see it at different angles.

This book is to help in adding a small, but important, piece of newly found information to the great work already done by the team of researchers at the North Carolina Archives.

Charles Purser
Garner, North Carolina
March 2010

Introduction

The data herein includes new information not found in the original entry in *North Carolina Troops – 1861-1865 A Roster.* You will note in each item that 'rost-'is usually first. This is the *North Carolina Troops* roster reference. Then you will have the source followed by the data on newly found information (CWPOWrec-, LMA, 1912 book-, etc.). Many will end with a 'note' for actions to be taken due to the new findings.

In many of the data are noted multifold 'rost'. A conclusion to the correct Roster entry will be in the notes section for most of the items. For instance, you will note that information as to place of birth, residence, when and where enlisted or other data would be entered in one Roster while the other Roster data in most cases will be a one line entry. In this case there is no doubt as to the correct soldier's data to keep and which to delete. In a few cases too many variables at this time precludes that consideration. Hopefully, in the future other researchers can figure the correct information.

Since there is a large number of new information on the cause of deaths of North Carolinians in prison, this data is included at the end of each volume for those soldiers of that volume.

There are more than 1,300 additional information and amendments in this document to the *North Carolina Troops 1861-1865,* seventeen volumes.

The Sources:

1850, 1860, 1870, 1880 census — Census data researched on Ancestry.com

1912 Book
Register of Confederate soldiers, sailors, and citizens who died in Federal prisons and military hospitals in the North. Published by the United States War Department in 1912 (see M918 in CWPOWrec.)
Microfilm series M918 contains a register of Confederate soldiers, sailors, and citizens who died in Federal prisons and military hospitals in the North between 1861 and 1865. The register is generally organized alphabetically by name of prison or hospital and then alphabetically by name of the deceased.

ADJ
General's Dept., Roll of Honor Office, Scrapbook 1861-1865 Microfilm S.1.108P, Asheville newspaper titled 'Some of our dead who died in Martinsburg.

American CW Soldiers
The project to date has digitized, indexed, and interlinked the roster records of 2,100,000 soldiers (out of approx. 4,000,000 who served), 2,719 regimental chronicles, 1,010 officer profiles, 3,343 battle synopses, and 1,012 soldier photographs. Historical Data Systems, Inc. P.O. Box 35 Duxbury, MA 02331. On Ancestry.com.

Ancestry.com —The main source for this report

BDL
Bucktrout Day book and ledger noted on Earl Gregg Swem Libray, William and Mary College Digital Archives…swem.wm.edu/archives/

City Point National Cemetery — Records on interment.net

Compiled Service records
The creation of compiled military service records for Confederate soldiers began in 1903 under the direction of Brig Gen Fred C. Ainsworth, head of the Record and Pension Office in the War Department. They are abstracts of original records found in the War Department Collection of Confederate Records and from documents borrowed by the War Department for the purpose of obtaining as full a service record as possible on these soldiers.

The compiled service records are arranged by unit, usually a regiment, and then alphabetically by soldiers' surname. Preceding the individual soldiers jacket-envelopes are empty envelopes which list the officers of the unit. Following these are jacket-envelopes that contain caption cards for muster-in and muster-out rolls, and record-of-events cards, indicating the activities of the unit during specific periods.

Confederate Veteran
Between the years of 1893 and 1932, the *Confederate Veteran* magazine was published. Each issue was filled with information, stories, and recollections of the Confederate armed forces during the War. Obituaries were often submitted by families or by UCV, SCV and UDC chapters for inclusion in the magazine when a veteran died. The personal accounts provided by veterans and other writers of the time concerning battles, military strategies, living conditions, supplies and food, medical treatments, prisoner-of-war camps, and other topics breathe life into the research of your Confederate ancestors, their wives, and their families. In 1988, Broadfoot Publishing Company reprinted all the issues of the *Confederate Veteran*, and these can be found in many larger libraries' genealogical and local history collections.

CWPOWrec
Civil War Prisoner of War Records, 1861-1865 (on Ancestry.com)
Source Information:
Ancestry.com. *Civil War Prisoner of War Records, 1861-1865* [database on-line]. Provo, UT, USA: The Generations Network, Inc., 2007. Original data:
Selected Records of the War Department Relating to Confederate Prisoners of War, 1861-1865; (National Archives Microfilm Publication M598, 145 rolls); War Department Collection of Confederate Records, Record Group 109; National Archives, Washington, DC.
Register of Confederate Soldiers, Sailors, and Citizens who Died in Federal Prisons and

Military Hospitals in the North, 1861-1865; (National Archives Microfilm Publication M918, 1 roll); Records of the Office of the Quartermaster General, Record Group 92; National Archives, Washington, DC.

This database contains records relating to Civil War Prisoners of War (POW). The database is comprised of four National Archives (NARA) microfilm series (M598 and M918).

Microfilm series **M598** contains records relating to Confederate POWs that were held by Federal authorities at various prisons and stations from 1861 to 1865 (with a few records from 1866). These records are arranged in three sections: (1) records of POWs and political prisoners with no specific prison or place of confinement, (2) records of individual prisons and stations, and (3) records of several prisons. Records contained in this series include:

- Registers of prisoners
- Registers of deaths of prisoners
- Registers of prisoners' applications for release and decisions
- Descriptive lists of prisoners and deserters
- Register of prisoners ordered to be released
- Register of applications made for release of prisoners
- Register of unclaimed money and valuables belonging to prisoners
- Register of the effects of deceased prisoners
- Permits granted by the Commissary General of Prisoners for clothing for the prisoners
- Lists of prison camp records received
- Letters sent and received
- Numeric report of prisoners received, transferred, paroled, released, and deceased
- Register of Confederate and Federal soldiers and civilians sentenced
- Register of prisoners discharged and released
- Register of prisoners transferred and escaped
- Morning reports of prisoners
- Ledgers of prisoners' accounts

Microfilm series **M918** contains a register of Confederate soldiers, sailors, and citizens who died in Federal prisons and military hospitals in the North between 1861 and 1865. The register is generally organized alphabetically by name of prison or hospital and then alphabetically by name of the deceased. (see 1912 Book)

CWSSY

The Civil War Soldiers and Sailors System is a computerized database containing very basic facts about servicemen who served on both sides during the Civil War. The initial focus of the CWSS is the *Names Index Project*, a project to enter names and other basic information from 6.3 million soldier records in the National Archives. The facts about the soldiers were entered from records that are indexed to many millions of other documents about Union and Confederate Civil War soldiers maintained by the National Archives and Records Administration. Other information includes: histories of regiments in both the Union and Confederate Armies, links to descriptions of 384 significant battles of the war and other historical information. Additional information about soldiers, sailors, regiments, and battles, as well as prisoner-of-war records and cemetery records, will be added over time. The Civil War Soldiers and Sailors System (CWSS) is a cooperative effort by the National Park Service (NPS) and several other public and private partners, to computerize information about the Civil War. The goal of the CWSS is to increase the American people's understanding of this decisive era in American history by making information about it widely accessible. The CWSS will enable the public to make a personal link between themselves and history. www.civilwar.nps.gov/cwss/info.htm

Dr Leach's register
Records of Dr. Leach's located with Dr. E. Burke Haywood papers at the Wilson Library at UNC in Chapel Hill, North Carolina. Dr. Leach was one of the main military doctors in the Raleigh, North Carolina, area during the war.

Edward Richter papers
A retired (now deceased) Long Island, New York, policeman who became an expert on North Carolinians at Gettysburg.

Family Tree Source Information:
Ancestry.com. *Public Member Trees* [database on-line]. Provo, UT, USA: The Generations Network, Inc., 2006. Original data: Family trees submitted by Ancestry members.

About *Public Member Trees*. This database contains family trees submitted to Ancestry by users who have indicated that their tree can be viewed by all Ancestry members. These trees can change over time as users edit, remove, or otherwise modify the data in their trees. Note: These trees are voluntarily submitted by Ancestry users. Ancestry.com cannot guarantee the completeness or accuracy of the information contained in this database.

FO, (date)
Fayetteville Observer newspaper during the war. Found on the NCGen Web Project, *North Carolina in the Civil War, Military Obituaries* by Diane Siniard.

Fort Delaware Society
Conducts research of Fort Delaware Confederate prisoners and members of the Union garrison. www.fordelaware.org

Gettysburg death Roster
The Confederate dead at Gettysburg, compiled by Robert K. Krick and Chris L. Ferguson, Morningside Bookshop/Press, Dayton, Ohio 2004.

Haywood papers
Dr. E. Burke Haywood, Military Commander of Raleigh area hospitals, papers located in the Wilson Library at UNC in Chapel Hill, North Carolina.

Hollywood Cem
Register of Confederate dead in Hollywood Cemetery in Richmond, Virginia.

Interment.net
A free online library of burial records from thousands of cemeteries across the the world, for historical and genealogy research.

LibVA
Library of Virginia, Manuscript Ledger of Woodland Cemetery in Ashland, Virginia, listing 250 soldiers that died between April 10 and May 27, 1862.

LMA
The Ladies Memorial Association of Raleigh, North Carolina – records of Confederate Soldiers buried in the Confederate section of Oakwood Cemetery, Raleigh, North Carolina.

NCS, (date)
North Carolina Standard newspaper printed in Raleigh during the war. Found on the NCGen Web Project, *North Carolina in the Civil War, Military Obituaries* by Diane Siniard.

Oakwood Cemetery Burial records
Buried records of Confederate soldiers buried in Oakwood Cemetery in Richmond located with the city of Richmond, Virginia and Sons of Confederate Veterans.

Oakwood Cemetery, Raleigh
Records located in the office of Oakwood Cemetery in Raleigh, North Carolina.

Petersburg
Ladies Memorial Association (LMA) Records, Petersburg, Virginia, 1866-1912, in the Virginia State Library. A total of 1,064 Civil War soldier burials were extracted for cemeteries in the vicinity of the Petersburg Fairground including the Poor House, South of Fairgrounds, and Southwest of Fairgrounds. Bethel Cemetery on Augusta Avenue is the only surviving cemetery except for a hundred or so unknown concrete markers with numbered brass plaques below the railroad tracks behind the Pecan Acres cul-de-sac. (Birdville.)

rost
North Carolina Troops 1861-1865, a Roster, volumes I to XVII, State Department of Archives and History. The first volume was printed in 1966 and the latest printed in 2009. An ongoing project started with the one hundredth anniversary of the Civil War. The purpose is to compile and publish information on every North Carolinian who served in the war.

Sons of Union Veterans
National Graves Registration Database on www.suvcwdb.org/home/index.php

State Troops
A Photographic Record of North Carolina's Civil War Soldiers, volume one, Greg Mast, North Carolina Department of Cultural Resources Division of Archives and History, 1995.

VA web site
Department of Veterans Affairs web site listings of 125 VA National Cemeteries and 14 Department of Interior's National Park Service Cemeteries. www.va.gov

Wasted Valor **by Gregory A. Coco**
The Confederate Dead at Gettysburg, printed 1990 by Thomas Publications, Gettysburg, PA.

www.37NC.org/11thphp3
Information of Watauga Co., North Carolina Confederate soldiers.

Additional Information
and
Amendments to the

NORTH CAROLINA TROOPS
1861 – 1865

Seventeen Volume Roster

Compiled by

Charles E. Purser Jr.
Garner, North Carolina

2010

The Scuppernong Press
Wake Forest, NC

Volume I – Artillery

1)-rost-Capt. **Robert G. Rankin**, co A, 1 Batt NC H Arty, mortally wounded at Bentonville 20 Mar 65.

FO, 29 Mar 65-Capt **Robert D. Rankin** of Wilmington died in Raleigh Sunday (26 Mar) of wounds received at Bentonville.

2)-rost- **David F. Croom**, co B, 1 Batt NC H Arty, died 27 Jan 1863 (place of death not given.)

FO, 16 Feb 1863- David F. Croom, Capt Taylor's Co. (co B, 1 Batt NC H Arty), age 21, died in Wilmington on 27 Jan 1863.

3)-rost- **William E. Smith**, co B, 1 Batt NC H Arty, detailed to work on Wilmington & Manchester Railroad, died 14 Jan 1864 of disease.

FO, 18 Jan 1864- William E. Smith, co B, 1 Batt NC H Arty, died Wilmington on 13 Jan 1864 of typhoid pneumonia.

4)-rost-QMSgt **Charles S. Ellis**, co B, 1 Batt NC H Arty, trans from co B, 25 SC Inf Jan 12, 1863 as Pvt. Detailed to QM Dept at Wilmington, NC on Feb 13, 1863, promoted to QMSgt Apr 12, 1864, absent detailed through Aug 1864, d Elmira on Mar 28, 1865 and bur Woodlawn Nat. Cem.

rost-Pvt **Charles T. Ellis** of co. K, 1 NC Arty, enlisted in New Hanover Mar 17, 1864, pre & acc through Oct 1864, capt Fort Fisher Jan 15, 1865, d Elmira Mar 28, 1865 of diarrhea

CWPOWrec- Charles S. Ellis, co B, 1 Batt NC H Arty, capt Ft Fisher on 15 Jan 65.

CWPOWrec- Pvt Charles S. Ellis, co K, 10 NC, capt Ft Fisher 15 Jan 65, d Elmira 28 Mar 65 of diarrhea, bur grave 2542, rec notated 'Chas. T.' in remarks.

1912 book- Pvt Charles S. Ellis, co B, 10 NC (1 Arty) d 28 Mar 1865 at Elmira and bur in grave 2502.

Family Tree on Ancestry.com-**Charles Stephen Ellis**, born Jan 10, 1835 in Wilmington, d May 23, 1921 in Savannah, Ga. He participated in bombardment of Fort Sumter as Pvt in Co A, Washington Light Inf., 25 SC Vol Regt. Surrendered with Gen. Bragg Mar 1865 at Durham Station as Capt and A2 M (should be QM Dept) of NC.

note: QMSgt Charles S. Ellis of 1 Batt NC H Arty surv the war and Pvt Charles T. Ellis of 1 NC Arty died at Elmira on Mar 28, 1865.

5)-rost-**James A. McKay**, co C, 1 Batt NC H Arty, res Columbus Co., detailed July 63-Aug 64 to Signal Corps.

LMA-James McKay, co C, 1 Batt SC Jr Res, d 9 Apr 65, grave 386 in Oakwood Cem, Raleigh, NC.

Dr Leach's register-Ernest Haywood papers, at Chapel Hill, p 39-James McKay of Columbus Co, Whiteville, NC admitted to Confederate hospital in Raleigh Apr 8, 1865.

6)-rost- **Elias Phillips**, co C, 1 Batt NC H Arty, died 11-25 July 1862 of disease.
  FO, 21 July 1862- **Lyas (Elias) Phillips**, McRae Arty (co C, 1 Batt NC H Arty), age 18 years and 3 days, died at Fort Fisher on 11 July 1862.

7)-rost- **William W. Williams**, co D, 1 Batt NC NC H Arty, wounded & capt 15 Jan 65 Fort Fisher, d 15 Jun 65 Morehead City of wounds.
  CWPOWrec- Wm W. Williams, 1 Batt NC, d 15 Jun 65 of secondary hemorrhage from gs wound of arm at Mansfield CH (Corps Hospital?), Beaufort, SC. Need more checking....

8)-rost- J. W. Flowers, co A, 1 NC Arty, capt Winchester 30 Jul 63.
  CWPOWrec- **James W. Flowers**, co A, 1 NC Arty, capt Winchester 30 Jul 63.
  note: add James as his first name.

9)-rost-**Joseph S. Fowler**, co B, 1 NC Arty, d 30 Mar 1865. no other info on death.
  LMA book-M.S. Fowler of co B, 1 NC Arty, d 30 Mar 1865 Raleigh, grave 33 in Oakwood Cem, Raleigh, NC.

10)-rost- **Jackson Towery**, co C, 1 NC Arty, enl 12 Aug 61, kia near Petersburg 22 Jul 64.
  CWPOWrec- Jackson Towery, co C, 1 NC Arty, capt Winchester 30 Jul 63, disposition unaccounted for.

11)-rost- James Williams, co D, 1 NC Arty, absent sick after 12 Nov 62, rep dead 7 Mar 64.
  Lynchburg, Old City Cemetery- **James W. Williams** of NC Artillery.

12)-rost- **W. C. C. Clamps**, co E, 1 NC Arty, died Elmira 20 Mar 65 and buried Woodlawn Nat Cem. (no other records).
  rost- **Wesley Clapp**, co E, 1 NC, res Alamance, capt Spotsylvania CH 12 May 64, conf at Point Lookout until trans to Elmira 6 Aug 64, died Elmira 20 Mar 65 of diarrhea.
  1912 Book- W. C. C. Clamps, co E, 1 NC Arty, died 20 Mar 65, Point Lookout
  CWPOWrec- W. C. Clamps, co E, 1 NC, capt Spottsylvania 12 May 64, trans to Elmira 6 Aug 64, died Elmira 20 Mar 65 of diarrhoea (in remarks column) 'on rolls Clapp, W.'
  note: W. C. C. Clamps of co E, 1 NC Arty should be deleted.

13)- rost-**Wesley Brafford**, co F, 1 NC Arty, conscripted New Hanover, capt Ft Fisher 15 Jan 65, died Elmira 10 Apr 65 of variola.
  rost-**Wesley Beofford**, co H, 1 NC Arty, died Elmira 10 Apr 65 and buried Woodlawn Nat Cem.
  CWPOWrec-Wesley Brafford, co F, 10 NC (which is the 1 NC Arty), capt Ft Fisher 15 Jan 65, died Elmira 10 Apr 65 of variola.
  note: Wesley Beofford of co H, 1 NC Arty should be deleted.

14)-rost-**Robert Overby**, co. G, 1 NC Arty, d 3 Mar 1864 of pneumonia, no info.

LMA- **R. W. Overby**, no unit, died 4 Mar 1864 and buried in Oakwood Cemetery, Raleigh, NC in grave 161.

15)-rost-**Wesley Beofford**, co H, 1 NC Arty, died Elmira 10 Apr 65 and buried Woodlawn Nat Cem.

rost-**Wesley Brafford**, co F, 1 NC Arty, conscripted New Hanover, capt Ft Fisher 15 Jan 65, died Elmira 10 Apr 65 of variola.

CWPOWrec-Wesley Brafford, co F, 10 NC (which is the 1 NC Arty), capt Ft Fisher 15 Jan 65, died Elmira 10 Apr 65 of variola.

note: Wesley Beofford of co H, 1 NC Arty should be deleted.

16)-rost-**O. Coughton**, co H, 1 NC Arty (of Carteret Co.), d Elmira 24 Feb 1865 & bur Woodlawn Nat Cem (only info noted).

rost-**Owen Congleton**, co K, 1 NC Arty (of Beaufort Co.), , enl New Hanover, capt Ft Fisher 15 Jan 65, died Elmira 24 Feb 65 of typh fever.

CWPOWrec- Owen Congleton, co H, 10 (1) NC Arty, capt Fort Fisher 15 Jan 1865, d 24 Feb 1865 of febris typhoid. ((note: **Abram, David, Henry Congleton** (all of Carteret Co.,) also in co H, 1 NC Arty.))

note: CWPOWrec has O. Coughton and Owen Congleton, but under one record of O. Coughton the notation "on rolls 'Owen Congleton' 10 NC A".

1850 Beaufort Co, NC census, Owen Congleton age 1

1860 Beaufort Co, NC census **Owin (or Orrin) Congleton**, age 13.

note: O. Coughton of co H, 1 NC Arty should be deleted.

17)-rost-**Battle Rhodes**, co I, 1 NC Arty, d 31 Jan 1864 pneumonia.

LMA- B. Rhoads of co I, 1 NC Arty, d 30 Jan 1864, buried Oakwood Cem, Raleigh, NC in grave 209.

18)- rost-**Owen Congleton**, co K, 1 NC Arty (of Beaufort Co.), enl New Hanover, capt Ft Fisher 15 Jan 65, died Elmira 24 Feb 65 of typh fever.

rost-**O. Coughton**, co H, 1 NC Arty (of Carteret Co.), d Elmira 24 Feb 1865 & bur Woodlawn Nat Cem (only info noted).

CWPOWrec- Owen Congleton, co H, 10 (1) NC Arty, capt Fort Fisher 15 Jan 1865, d 24 Feb 1865 of febris typhoid. ((note: **Abram, David, Henry Congleton** (all of Carteret Co.) also in co H, 1 NC Arty.))

note: CWPOWrec has O. Coughton and Owen Congleton, but under one record of O. Coughton the notation "on rolls 'Owen Congleton' 10 NC A".

1850 Beaufort Co, NC census, Owen Congleton age 1

1860 Beaufort Co, NC census **Owin (or Orrin) Congleton**, age 13. .

note: O. Coughton of co H, 1 NC Arty should be deleted.

19)- rost-Pvt **Charles T. Ellis** of co. K, 1 NC Arty, enlisted in New Hanover Mar 17, 1864, pre and acc through Oct 1864, capt Fort Fisher Jan 15, 1865, died Elmira Mar

28, 1865 of diarrhea

rost-QMSgt Charles S. Ellis, co B, 1 Batt NC H Arty, trans fm co B, 25 SC Inf Jan 12, 1863 as Pvt. Detailed to QM Dept at Wilmington, NC on Feb 13, 1863, promoted to QMSgt Apr 12, 1864, absent detailed through Aug 1864, died Elmira on Mar 28, 1865 and bur. Woodlawn Nat. Cem.

CWPOW rec- **Charles S. Ellis**, co B, 1 Batt NC H Arty, capt Ft Fisher on 15 Jan 65.

CWPOW rec- Pvt Charles S. Ellis, co K, 10 NC, capt Ft Fisher 15 Jan 65, died Elmira 28 Mar 65 of diarrhea, buried grave 2542, rec notated 'Chas. T.' in remarks.

1912 book- Pvt Charles S. Ellis, co B, 10 NC (1 Arty) died 28 Mar 1865 at Elmira and buried in grave 2502.

Family Tree on Ancestry.com-**Charles Stephen Ellis**, born Jan 10, 1835 in Wilmington, died May 23, 1921 in Savannah, Ga. He participated in bombardment of Fort Sumter as Pvt in Co A, Washington Light Inf., 25 SC Vol Regt. Surrendered with Gen. Bragg Mar 1865 at Durham Station as Capt and A2 M (should be QM Dept) of NC.

note: QMSgt Charles S. Ellis of 1 Batt NC H Arty surv the war and Pvt Charles T. Ellis of 1 NC Arty died at Elmira on Mar 28, 1865.

20)-rost-Pvt **J. R. Hewitt**, co B, 2 NC Arty, released from Elmira on 13 Jul 65 after oath.

1912 book- Pvt J. R. Hewitt, co B, 36 NC (2 Arty), died Elmira 15 Mar 65, buried in grave 1680.

CWPOWrec- J. R. Hewitt, co B, 36 NC, transferred 13 July 1865 from Elmira to Point Lookout 'and paroled for exchange…see Prison Records.'

note: not known why 1912 book has Hewitt buried at Elmira, but three CWPOWrec stated he was released.

21)-rost- **Neill McEachern**, 3rd co B, 2 NC Arty, age 40 in 1863, of Robeson Co, present and accounted for through August 1864.

FO, 13 Feb 1865- Neill McEachern, 42 years of age the 25th of August last, of Robeson Co, died in a hospital at Fort Fisher on 5 Dec 1864.

22)-rost-Corp **Levi H. Perry** of 3co B, 2 NC Arty, enl Bladen Co 26 Dec 61, capt Fort Fisher 15 Jan 65.

rost-Corp L. H. Perry, co B, 13 NC capt Fort Fisher 15 Jan 65, died Elmira on 6 Jul 65.

CWPOWrec- L. H. Perry, Corp, co B, 13 NC Batt, died Elmira 6 Jul 65 of chr diarr.

CWPOWrec- Elmira disposition of Prisoners' possessions- Levi H. Perry, one silver watch, transferred to him 2 July 1865.

note: 2n co B, 2 Arty was trans to co B, 13 Batt NC L Arty on 4 Nov 1863. Levi H. Perry had to be in the 2nd co B, 2 NC Arty which trans to the 13 Batt NC L Arty. His POW records recorded him as being in co B, 13 NC Batt. His military info should be changed from 3rd co B, 2 NC Arty to 2nd co B, 2 Arty with the statement that this unit transferred to the 13 Batt L.Arty, L. H. Perry of 13 NC should be deleted.

23)-rost- **William T. Jones**, 2nd co C, 2 NC Arty, died 30 Dec 1862 of wounds rec by bursting of a gun, place of death not listed.

FO, 19 Jan 1863- William T. Jones, Capt Braddy's Arty Co. (2nd co C, 2 Arty), age about 21, died at Fort Fisher on 30 Dec 1862 of lockjaw, consequent on cold being taken in a wound rec in the bursting of a gun.

24)-rost- W. Melvin, 2nd co C, 2 NC Arty, capt Ft Fisher 15 Jan 65, died Elmira 18 Mar 65 of variola.

rost- **William Snowden Melvin**, co H, 2 NC Arty, enl Bladen Co age 38 on 13 May 62, capt Ft Fisher 15 Jan 65, reported buried at Elmira 18 Mar 65 in Woodlawn Nat Cem and also as released after Oath on 11 July 65.

1912 book- William Melvin, co H, 36 NC, died Elmira 18 Mar 65, grave 1710.

CWPOWrec- W. Melvin, co C, 36 NC, capt Ft Fisher 15 Jan 65, died Elmira 18 Mar 65 of variola (in remarks col) 'Melvin, Co. L'.

CWPOWrec- William Melvin, co H, 36 NC, capt Ft Fisher 15 Jan 65, released 11 Jul 65 (note: on list of other members of the 36 NC.)

note: believe that William Snowden Melvin of co H, 2 NC Arty died at Elmira and was not released and that W. Melvin is the same person. If this is the case, W. Melvin of co C, 2 Arty should be deleted.

25)-rost-Pvt **Henry S. Gower**, 2nd co D, 2 NC Arty died 14 Mar 65 at Elmira.

1912 book-Pvt H. S. Gower, co D, 36 NC died 14 May 65 at Elmira, in grave 2800.

note: Spot checking others in graves 2797, 2801, 2806 and 2807 who died on 12, 4, 15 and 15 of May, resp. So, he died in May and not March.

26)-rost-**John Isom Bullard**, co E, 2 NC Arty, enl Columbus Co, p & a through Aug 64, capt Fort Fisher 15 Jan 65, died Elmira 27 Feb 1865 of pneumonia. (five Bullard in unit).

rost-John Isom Bullard, co K, 3 NC Arty, capt Fort Fisher 15 Jan 65, died 27 Feb 65 of pneumonia.

CWPOWrec- 3 POW records had him in co K, 40 NC.

note: John Isom Bullard of co K, 3 NC Arty should be deleted.

27)-rost-Pvt **Shipman B. Burney**, co E, 2 NC Arty, capt Ft Fisher 15 Jan 65, conf Point Lookout, released after oath on 14 May 65.

1912 book-Pvt Shipman Burney of Co E, 36 Regt. (2 NC Arty), died Point Lookout 15 Feb 1865.

CWPOWrec- S. B. Birney, co E, 36 NC, capt Ft Fisher 15 Jan 65, trans to Pt Lookout 31 Jan 65, trans to US Gen Hosp at Point Lookout 2 Feb 1865, died 15 Feb 1865, 'This man's name (on the death roll) is a mistake, the name on the Roll is S. Babances (or could be Balances)' see film 9099 on CWPOWrec, released Oath 17 May 1865.

note: the Roster is right, but all other sources (VA web site, Point Lookout Prisoner of War site and others) has Shipman Burney buried there. Need to notify those sources for correction.

28)-rost-**Jacob Strickland**, co E, 36 Regt (2 NC Arty), enl Columbus Co, capt Ft Fisher 15 Jan 65, d Elmira 16 May 65 of chr diarrhea.

rost- Jacob Strickland, co E, 30 NC, d Elmira 16 May 65 (no other info).

CWPOWrec- Jacob Strickland, co G, 36 NC, died Elmira 16 May 1865 of chr diarr.

note: the one in the 30 NC should be deleted.

29)-rost-**Nathaniel Strickland**, co E, 2 NC Arty. Trans fm CS Navy Feb 29, 1864, capt at Fort Fisher Jan 15, 1865, died Elmira Mar 12, 1865.

Ancestry.com-family trees- Nathaniel Strickland, born May 4, 1823, from Columbus Co., NC.

30)-rost- **Joseph J. N. Markes**, co F, 2 NC Arty, mortally wounded in action at Fort Fisher 15 Jan 65.

CWPOWrec- Jos. Marks, 14 NC Arty, capt Fort Fisher 15 Jan 65, arrived at Point Lookout from Fort Fisher 22 Jan 65, trans to U.S. Gen Hosp 2 Feb 65, died 5 Apr 1865 at Point Lookout of GS W of Head.

note: while unit is wrong in the CWPOWrec, this is the same soldier.

31)-rost- **Henry H. Goodman**, co G, 2 NC Arty, res Brunswick, mustered in 10 Feb 63, capt Ft Fisher 15 Jan 65, died Elmira 21 Feb 1865 of variola.

rost- Henry Goodman, co G, 26 NC, place and date of enlistment not reported, died Elmira 21 Feb 1865.

note: delete Henry Goodman of the 26 NC.

32)-rost-**James H. Joyner**, co G, 2 NC Arty, d 20 Mar 1865 Richmond, Va.

LMA book-James H. Joyner of co G, 2 NC Arty, d 20 Mar 1865, grave 310 in Oakwood Cem, Raleigh, NC..

33)-rost- **William Snowden Melvin**, co H, 2 NC Arty, enl Bladen Co age 38 on 13 May 62, capt Ft Fisher 15 Jan 65, reported buried at Elmira 18 Mar 65 in Woodlawn Nat Cem and also as released after Oath on 11 July 65.

rost- W. Melvin, 2ⁿᵈ co C, 2 NC Arty, capt Ft Fisher 15 Jan 65, died Elmira 18 Mar 65 of variola.

1912 book- William Melvin, co H, 36 NC, died Elmira 18 Mar 65, grave 1710.

CWPOWrec- W. Melvin, co C, 36 NC, capt Ft Fisher 15 Jan 65, died Elmira 18 Mar 65 of variola (in remarks col) 'Melvin, Co. L'.

CWPOWrec- William Melvin, co H, 36 NC, capt Ft Fisher 15 Jan 65, released 11 Jul 65 (note: on list of other members of the 36 NC.)

note: believe that William Snowden Melvin of co H, 2 NC Arty died at Elmira and was not released and that W. Melvin is the same person. If this is the case, W. Melvin of co C, 2 Arty should be deleted.

34)-rost- **William J. Howard**, co A, 3 NC Arty, died 11 April 1864.

FO, 16 May 1864- W. J. Howard, co A, 40 Regt (3 NC Arty), died at Fort Holmes on 11 April 1864.

35)-rost- **C. C. Partin**, co C, 3 Batt NC L Arty, Moore's Batt, d 24 Aug or Sep 24, 1864 of disease. (no further notes.)

LMA- C.C. ….., Moore's Batt., buried in Oakwood Cemetery, Raleigh, NC in grave 75.

36)-rost- W. T. Pittman, 1st co H, 3 NC Arty, died at Richmond 18 Jan 1863 of pneumonia and debilitas..

NCS, 12 Aug 1863- **William T. Pittman**, Capt. A. C. Latham's Artillery (1st co H, 3 NC Arty), died in Richmond on 20 June 1863 of pneumonia.

37)-rost-**John Isom Bullard**, co K, 3 NC Arty, capt Fort Fisher 15 Jan 65, died 27 Feb 65 of pneumonia.

rost-John Isom Bullard, co E, 2 NC Arty, enl Columbus Co, p & a through Aug 64, capt Fort Fisher 15 Jan 65, died Elmira 27 Feb 1865 of pneumonia. (five Bullard in unit).

CWPOWrec- 3 POW records had him in co K, 40 NC.

note: John Isom Bullard of co K, 3 NC Arty should be deleted.

38)-rost- Pvt **Elisha Brown**, co B, 10 NC Batt Hvy Arty, res Cumberland Co, present and accounted for to Oct 64.

VA web site-Pvt Elisha Brown died 31 Jan 65, buried Beaufort Nat Cem, SC, sec 53 – site 6415.

Interment.net-Pvt Elisha Brown of co B, 10 NC Bn, CSA died 31 Jan 65, bur Beaufort Nat Cem, grave 53-6415.

39)-rost- Pvt **Joseph M. Dunn**, co C, 10 NC Batt Hvy Arty, res Union Co, present and accounted for to Oct 64. Paroled Charlotte 3 May 65.

VA web site-J. M. Dunn, bur Beaufort Nat Cem, sec 53-6398.

CWSSY-Pvt Joseph M. Dunn of co C, 10 NC Batt Hvy Arty, POW at Jenkins Ferry, Ga 7 Dec 64, paroled 3 May 65 at Charlotte (at home at time of parole).

Interment.net/data/us/sc/Beaufort/Beaunat/index-Pvt J. M. Dunn, 10 CS Bty, Rebel plot 53-6398.

Sons of Union Veterans of the CW-Pvt Joseph M. Dunn of co C, 10 NC Batt Hvy Arty, died 24 Jan 65, buried Beaufort Nat Cem, grave 53-6398.

1860 Union Co., NC census- Joseph M. Dunn (34) Salina L. (32) Dellila A. E. (11) Cornelia (9) Joseph R. (8) James A. (4) Franklin (1)

1870 Union Co., NC census- Salina (42) Elizabeth (21) Joseph (17) John E. (8)

note: Theory: Dunn's unit logged him in the rec as being at home, but he was captured before he got home.

40)-Co. A, 13th Battalion NC Light Artillery – the following 38 soldiers were noted on the web site 'members.aol.com/jweaver300/grayson/harr-art.htm', but were not listed in the NC Roster (except for the two Officers, Horne and McNeill). The 'American Civil War Soldiers' site on 'Ancestry.com', these men were noted in Co. D, 12th Battalion Virginia Light Artillery. The Co. D, 12th Batt Va L Arty was trans to Co. A, 13th Batt NC L Arty on 4 Nov 1863. They should be added in a further volume on North Carolinians in other State's units.

BARRENTINE, CHARLES: Enl. 5/8/62 in Richmond Co., NC. Died on 7/16/62 of rubeola.

BARBER, BENJAMIN: Enl. on 4/28/62 in Richmond Co., NC. Pres. on 6/62 roll. Exchanged to Co. E, 38th NCT for Thomas H. Waters on 7/15/62.

BARRENTINE, SILAS L.: Enl. on 3/15/62 in Wilmington, NC. "Died in camp suddenly by visitation of God in the line of duty." per 6/62 roll.

BATTON, WILLIAM: Enl. on 3/15/62 in Richmond Co., NC. AWOL on 6/62 roll.

BRISTOW, JOHN: Enl. on 5/5/62 in Richmond Co., NC. Died of measles on 7/17/62.

BRISTOW, RICHARD: Enl. on 5/5/62 in Richmond Co., NC. Died of measles on 6/11/62.

BUTLER, JOHN E.: Enl. on 3/15/62 in Richmond Co., NC. Died on 7/30/62 of typhoid fever.

FREEMAN, JAMES L.: Enl. on 5/6/62 in Richmond Co., NC. AWOL on 7/1/62. Deserted on 8/20/63.

HALL, WILLIAM: Enl. on 5/23/62 in Rockingham Co., NC. Died on 5/27/62 with typhoid pneumonia.

HORNE, HENRY R.: 2nd Lt./1st Lt./Adjutant. Pres. on 6/62 and 2/63 rolls. Pres. on 2/64. Discharged from Gen. Hosp. #3, Goldsboro, NC on 9/12/64. Status not stated on 12/64 roll. Pres. on 2/65.

LIVINGSTON, JOHN: Enl. on 5/8/62 in Richmond Co., NC. AWOL on 6/62 roll.

McKETHAN, SANBORN: Enl. on 3/15/62 in Wilmington, NC. Died in hospital per 6/62 roll.

McKINNON, CHARLES E.: Enl. on 3/23/62 in Richmond Co., NC. Pres. on 6/62 and 2/63 rolls. NFR.

McNEILL, ARCHIBALD: 1st Sgt./2nd Lt., Enl. on 5/14/62 in Richmond Co., NC. Pres. on 6/62 and 2/63 rolls. Pres. 2/64. Status not stated on 12/64. Pres. on 2/65 roll.

McNEILL, DUNCAN: Corp., Enl. on 3/17/62 in Wilmington, NC. Promoted to Corp. on 5/16/62. Pres. on 6/62 roll. NFR.

McNEILL, MALCOLM D.: Sr. 1st Lt., Enl. on ?. Pres. on 6/62 rolls. Absent sick on 9/11/62. res. on 2/63 roll. Furloughed for 30 days on 7/23/63 from Gen. Hosp. #10, Richmond, VA, or remittent fever. Pres. on 2/64. Status not stated on 12/64 roll. Pres. on 2/65 roll. Res. of Springfield, NC.

MOODY, THOMAS W., Jr. 1st Lt., Pres. on 6/62, 9/62 and 2/63 rolls. Resigned on 5/28/63.

NORTON, ANDREW: Enl. on 4/28/62 in Richmond Co., NC. Never reported for duty, listed as AWOL on 6/62 roll.

NORTON, LODERICK: Enl. on 4/28/62 in Richmond Co., NC. Never reported for duty, listed as AWOL on 6/62 roll.

NORTON, WILLIAM: Enl. on 4/28/62 in Richmond Co., NC. Never reported for duty, listed as AWOL on 6/62 roll.

PATE, ALEXANDER: Enl. on 3/15/62 in Wilmington, NC. Discharged for disability due to phthisis on 7/7/62. Described as born in Richmond Co., NC, age 20, 5'11", light comp., blue eyes, red hair, occ. farmer.

PATE, ELDRIDGE: Enl. on 4/28/62 in Richmond Co., NC. Pres. 6/62. NFR.

PEELE, JOHN: Enl. on 4/28/62 in Richmond Co., NC. Never reported for duty, listed as AWOL on 6/62 roll.

PRICE, MOSES: Enl. in 5/63, conscript. Deserted on 6/15/63 on march from Franklin, VA to Petersburg, VA.

PRICE, ZACHARIAH: Enl. in 5/63, conscript. Deserted on 6/15/63 on march from Franklin, VA to Petersburg, VA.

SMITH, CAMERON: Enl. on 3/17/62 in Wilmington, NC. Pres. on 6/62 roll. NFR.

SMITH, CLEMENT: Enl. on 3/20/62 in Rockingham, NC. Discharged per 6/62 roll.

SNEAD, ISRAEL: Enl. on 9/8/62 in Richmond, VA. Died in hosp. at Jerusalem, VA on 2/23/63 of pneumonia.

SNEAD, JOSHUA JORDAN: Enl. on 5/3/62 in Richmond Co., NC. Pres. on 6/62 roll. Died on 9/16/62 of typhoid fever at Farmville, VA Gen. Hosp.

TAYLOR, JAMES P.: Enl. on 3/15/62 in Wilmington, NC. Pres. on 6/62. NFR.

TAYLOR, THOMAS H.: Enl. on 4/22/62 in Richmond Co., NC. Pres. on 6/62 roll. Discharged on 9/27/62 for disability. Born in Richmond Co., NC, age 21, 5'4", dark comp., light hair, blue eyes, occ. farmer.

WATERS, DAVID: Enl. on 4/28/62 in Richmond Co., NC. Never reported for duty, listed as AWOL on 6/62 roll.

WATERS, JOHN: Enl. on 4/28/62 in Richmond Co., NC. Never reported for duty, listed as AWOL on 6/62 roll.

WEBB, LEWIS (LOUIS) H.: Capt., Pres. on 6/62 roll. Pres. in arrest on 9/62 roll. Pres. on 2/63 roll. Pres. on all rolls thru 2/65. Res. of Richmond Co., NC. B. 1827. Living in Franklin, VA in 1901. D. 1902. Buried in the Poplar Springs Cem., Franklin, Isle of Wight Co., VA.

WRIGHT, CAMERON G.: Enl. on 4/28/62 in Richmond Co., NC. Pres. on 6/62 and 2/63 rolls. NFR.

WRIGHT, GEORGE P.: Enl. on 3/31/62 in RIchmond Co., NC. Pres. on 6/62 and 2/63 rolls. Admitted to Chimborazo Hosp. #1 6/28/63 with parotitis. Died on 7/2/63, "murdered at Rocketts."

WRIGHT, JAMES: Enl. on 3/17/62 in Wilmington, NC. Died on 6/18/62 or measles.

WRIGHT, THOMAS M.: Enl. on 5/14/62 in Richmond Co., NC. Pres. on 6/62 and 2/63 rolls.

Cause of deaths that were not listed in the NC Roster - Volume I

rank	name	co	unit	place of death	died	cause of death
Pvt	John Foust, Jr.	E	1 Arty	Washington	7/25/65	amp rt leg
Pvt	J. W. Lowry	E	1 Arty	Petersburg	4/5/65	gs lt thigh
QMSgt	Charles S. Ellis	B	1 Batt H Arty	Elmira	3/28/65	chronic diarrhoea
Pvt	William James McMillan	D	1 Batt H Arty	Point Lookout	6/7/65	acute dysentery
Pvt	Edward G. Terry	D	13 Batt L Arty	Point Lookout	1/3/64	smallpox
Pvt	Wiley Woolard	D	13 Batt L Arty	Point Lookout	7/14/64	lungs, inf of
Pvt	Archibald Brown	C	2 Arty	Point Lookout	3/21/65	lungs, inf of
Pvt	Hiram B. Cooper	D	2 Arty	Elmira	8/11/65	chronic diarrhoea
Pvt	William J. Willets	G	2 Arty	Elmira	3/4/65	pneumonia
Pvt	Albert Robeson	H	2 Arty	Baltimore	5/27/65	chronic diarrhoea
Pvt	Hiram Davis	I	2 Arty	Elmira	5/21/65	dibility
Pvt	Amos W. Smith	I	2 Arty	Fort Delaware	3/13/65	lungs, inf of/typh fever
Pvt	Thomas C. Guthrie	K	2 Arty	New Bern	4/19/65	chronic diarrhoea
Pvt	L.L. Lancaster	K	2 Arty	Point Lookout	6/5/65	lungs, inf of
Pvt	Christopher C. Barnes	B	3 Arty	Elmira	4/23/65	chronic diarrhoea
Pvt	David Emerson	D	3 Arty	Point Lookout	3/1/65	phthisis pulmonalis
Pvt	Isaac N. Lofton	G	3 Arty	Elmira	3/30/65	chronic diarrhoea
Pvt	Charles Perdue	G	3 Arty	Elmira	3/22/65	typhoid fever

Volume II – Cavalry

1)-rost-Pvt **Robert Evans**, co A, 1 NC Cav, res of Guilford Co and conscripted at age 29 on 15 Jul 62, c Gettysburg 3 Jul 63, d Point Lookout 30 Aug 64.

rost-Pvt Robert Evans, co A, 1 NC, enl Guilford Co 15 Jul 62, c Gettysburg 3 Jul 63, d Point Lookout 30 Aug 64.

note: co A, 1 NC is probably the correct unit as **W.W. Evans** of Guilford Co. enl 15 Jul 63 in that unit, plus co A, 1 NC Cav was formed in Ashe Co., NC while co A, 1 NC soldiers were from Chowan and Guilford Co., NC.

2)-rost- **Thomas Royal**, co A, 1 NC Cav, res Ashe Co, pre & acc through Dec 1864.

1912 War Book- Thos. A. Royal, co A, 1 NC Cav, died 1862, buried Mt. Moriah Cem, Phila. In grave 224.

CWPOWrec- **Thomas A. Rayl**, 1 NC Inf, died ?West_mittle?, Pa. on 23 Oct 1862 of febris typhoids.

3)-rost- **M. O'Brien**, co E, 1 NC Cav, enlisted in Lenoir Co 15 May 1862, died near Hanover CH 19 August 1862 of pneumonia. (note: A. and **Hugh O'Brien** in same company)

NCS, 15 Oct 1862- **Marcenas? O'Brien**, co E, 1 NC Cav, age 18 years 7 months, died near Hanover CH 19 Aug 62, son of Dr. John and Elizabeth O'Brien of Franklin Co, he vol with two other brothers in company.

1850 census Franklin Co., NC- Hugh, 14, and **MacEnas O'Brien**, 6, in John O'Brian's household

1860 census Franklin Co., NC- Hugh O'Brien, 24, and **MacCenas O'Brien**, 16, in John O'Brian's household

4)-rost- G. Coble, co H, 1 NC Cav, died Camp Chase or at Camp Dennison, near Cincinnati, Oh 5 June 65.

rost- **George Cobble**, co H, 1 NC, capt Salisbury 12 Apr 65, died Camp Chase, Oh 5 June 1865 of typhoid fever.

note: G. Coble of co H, 1 NC Cav should be deleted.

5)-rost- **William S. McCullen**, co H, 1 NC, died of diseas 21 Aug 1862

FO, 1 Sept 1862- **William S. McCullin**, co H, 1 NC, died Horn Quarter, King William Co., Va 21 Aug 1862 of typhoid pneumonia.

6)-rost- **William S. Boyett**, co I, 1 NC Cav, died of disease 5 Nov 1861.

note: W. S. Boyette, co I, 1 NC Inf, buried on Barton St., Fredericksburg, Va.

7)-rost-**Blaney W. Burton**, co I, 1 NC Cav, later served in co C, 59 Regt (5th Regt NC Cav).

note: should be 59 Regt (4th Regt NC Cav).

8)-rost-Pvt F. W. Sapp, co A, 2 NC Cav, capt Hanover CH 1 Jun 64, conf Point Lookout, trans to Elmira, killed or missing in RR accident at Shohola, Pa 15 Jul Jul 64.

rost-Pvt F. W. Sapt of co E, 22 NC, killed in RR accident near Shohola 15 Jul 64, no further rec.

CWPOWrec- F. W. Sapp, co E, 2 NC, capt Hanover CH 1 June 64, trans from Pt Lookout to Elmira 12 July 1864, 'supposed to have been killed en-route to Elmira July 15/64'.

CWPOWrec- F. W. Sapt, co E, 22 NC, capt Hanover CH 1 June 64, died in RR accident on Erie R.R., Pa 15 July 1864.

note: should be **Francis W. Sapp** born about 1831 according to the 1850 and 1860 census of Guilford Co., NC and the correct unit is the 2 NC Cav. F. W. Sapt of co E, 22 NC should be deleted.

9)-rost- does not have a H. O. Chapel in the Cav.

LMA-**H.O. Chapel** of co B, 2 NC Cav, d 6 Feb 1865, grave 298 in Oakwood Cem., Raleigh, NC.

10)-rost-**W. McHome**, co B, 2 NC Cav, died at Fort Delaware 14 Apr 1865 & bur Finn's Point. (only info entered. This info probably came from the 1912 book)

rost-**William Mahone**, co B, 2 Battalion NC Inf, res Surry Co., NC, trans fm co E, 53 NC 1 Sep 1862, capt at Gettysburg July 1863, and confined at Ft Delaware where he died 14 Apr 1865 of inflammation of lungs.

CWPOW rec- Pvt W. McHone, co B, 2 NC Batt, capt Waterloo 5 July 63, admitted 25 Feb 65, died 13 Apr 1865 at Ft Delaware.

note: McHome of 2 NC Cav should be deleted.

11)-rost-**Thomas J. Mims**, co D, 2 NC Cav, furloughed for 30 days 28 Sept 63 from Richmond hospital, wife filed claim for balance of pay 3 Feb 1865, date and place of death not given.

FO, 18 April 1864- Private Thomas J. Mims, co D, 2 NC Cav, age 45, died in this town (Fayetteville) 12 April 1864.

12)-rost- **William Lane**, co E, 2 NC Cav, capt Gettysburg 3 Jul 63, confined at Ft Delaware 15 Oct 63, died Ft Delaware "February 3, 1863" (prob should be 1864.)

rost- William Lane, co A, 3 NC, res in Greene Co, enl in Wayne Co age 30 on 13 May 62, wounded Gettysburg 2 Jul 63, capt Waterloo, Pa 5 Jul 63, trans from Ft Delaware to Pt Lookout 18 Oct 63, died Pt Lookout 3 Feb 1864.

note: William Lane of co E, 2 NC Cav should be deleted.

13)-rost-Capt. **James R. Nelson**, co F, 2 NC Cav, died 1 or 11 May 1863.

FO, 13 May 1863-Capt. Nelson, co G, 2 NC Cav, died on the Rappahannock 18 May 1863.

NCS, 3 June 1863- Capt. J. R. Nelson, co F, 2 NC Cav,

14)-rost- Captain **George Pettigrew Bryan**, co G, 2 NC Cav, killed in action 16 Aug 1864.

FO, 29 August 1864- Captain George Pettigrew Bryan, 2 NC Cav, age 22 Years, 10 months and 7 days, killed in the engagement near White's Tavern, Va., on the 16th inst.

15)-rost- **Richard Horton**, co K, 2 NC Cav, died of disease 24 Nov 1861.

FO, 9 Dec 1861- Richard Horton, Orange Cavalry, in a letter to the *Hillsborough Recorder* from Lt. J. P. L. (later Captain **John P. Lockhart**) he wrote: "Richard Horton, who was mentioned as very ill, died on Sunday night.…..… We thought of sending Horton's remains to Orange, but he was a poor friendless boy, all alone in this cold and selfish world; no father or mother or near relatives to receive the dust which will soon return to its native earth, would make a colder funeral at home than we could give him here. Some of our soldiers have been buried in the old field, on Mr. Thompson's plantation, where we are camped. The good people of Edenton allowed us to bury our comrade in arms in the grave yard of the Baptist Church. We buried him with military honors, close by the grave of a revolutionary soldier."

16)-rost- John Bostick, co B, 3 NC Cav, capt South Mountain or Gettysburg 4 July 63, died Fort Delaware 1 Aug 63.

rost- **John C. Bostick**, co B, 3 NC, res in Duplin Co, enlisted 15 July 62, wounded Gettysburg 2 July 63 and capt next day, died Fort Delaware 2 Aug 63 of chronic diarrhea.

note: delete John Bostick of co B, 3 NC Cav.

17)-rost- **James Harrelson**, co C, 3 NC Cav, capt at Hanover Court House, Va. 31 May 64 and confined at Point Lookout, no record of release.

CWPOWrec- **J. Haroldson**, co A, 3 NC Cav, died Point Lookout on 15 July 64 of febris typhoides.

note: believe these are the same soldier.

18)-rost- **Martin McPherson**, co D, 3 Cav, discharged near Petersburg 13 July 64 by ascites and double inguinal hernia.

FO, Dec 12, 1864- Martin McPherson, Murchison's Company (now Brooke's), 63 Cav, died Cumberland Co., NC 10 Nov 1864 of dropsy. (Note: Murchison and Brooke were the captains of co D, 3 NC Cav.)

19)-rost-**Shadrach Jackson** of co E, 3 NC Cav, p & a Oct 1864. No further record.

LMA-S. Jackson of co C, 27 NC, d 21 Mar 1865, grave 13 in Oakwood Cem., Raleigh, NC.

Haywood papers-Pvt S. Jackson of co G, 27 NC, Kirkland's Comm. from Ridgespring, NC.

1860 census Ridge Spring, Pitt Co., NC- Shadrack Jackson, age 25.

20)-rost-**Hugh Johnston Davis**, co G, 3 NC Cav, w & c near Petersburg 21 Jun 1864. d in Union hospital 7 Jul, 1864.

CWPOWrec- Hugh J. Davis, co G, 3 NC Cav, capt near Petersburg 21 Jun 1864, d Alexandria, Va 7 July 1864, effects one silver watch and two knives, turned over to Peter R. Davis, his nept? Takm?, also $107 Confederate money.

21)-rost- 2nd Lt **Alfred S. Wiggins**, co G, 3 NC Cav, killed 17 May 1863.

NCS, 10 June 1863- Lt Alfred S. Wiggins, Scotland Neck Cavalry (co G, 3 NC Cav), met his death in a brilliant skirmish which took place recently in the Isle of Wight, Virgina.

22)-rost- A. J. Melton, co H, 3 NC Cav, capt Swansboro 28 Apr 1864, died Point Lookout 19 Mar 65.

CWPOWrec- **Andew J. Melton**, co H, 41 NC-3NC Cav, capt Swansboro 30 Apr 1864, rec at Point Lookout from Fort Monroe 9 May 64, died Point Lookout on 19 Mar 65.

23)-rost- **F. F. Williams**, co H, 3 Cav, capt Greenville, NC 17 Dec 1863, confined Pt Lookout until exchanged 14 Nov 1864.

FO, 12 Dec 1864- T. F. Williams, co H, 3 Cav, exchanged (POW) soldiers from North Carolina that died in Savannah since the 20th ult. (20 Nov 1864.)

24)-rost-**B. F. Lowder** of co A, 4 NC Cav, d Raleigh 1 May 1864.

LMA-B. F. Lowder, no unit, d 25 May 64, grave 112 in Oakwood Cem., Raleigh, NC.

25)-rost- M. M. Sykes, co C, 4 NC Cav, died at home on detail 16 August 1864.

FO, 29 August 1864- **Murdock M. Sikes**, co C, 59 NC (4 Cav), died at his father's residence in New Hanover Co., NC at age 39 of typhoid diphtheria.

26)-rost- W. C. Stinson, co H, 4 NC Cav, capt Gettysburg 3 July 1863, rep wounded in Gen Lettleman hospital 10 Aug 1863.

CWPOWrec- W. C. Stinson, co H, 59 NC (4 Cav), capt Gettysburg 3 July 1863, transferred to Provost Marshall 14 Sept 1863.

CWPOWrec- Wm C. Stinson, co H, 49 Va, sent for exchange to City Point, Va from Baltimore on 25 Sep 1863.

note: Prob **William C. Stinson** of Co H, 4 NC Cav.

27)- rost-**William P. Barnes**, co I, 4 NC Cav, trans fm co B, 12 Batt NC Cav on 11 Jul 1864, capt in hospital at Petersburg 3 Apr 1865 where he had been adm with gs wound of left arm, died in Petersburg hospital on 21 May 1865.

rost-W. P. Barnes, co I, 4 NC, (only record noted as:) reported in Petersburg hospital with gs wound of left arm, no further records.

CWPOWrec-N. P. Barnes, co C, 4 NC, died Petersburg on 21 May 1865 of gs wound right arm.

Petersburg-W. P. Barnes, co B, 4 NC, died Petersburg on 21 May 1865, buried Petersburg Fair Ground vicinity.

note: William P. Barnes of co I, 4 NC Cav is the correct soldier. Delete W. P. Barnes of co I, 4 NC.

28)-rost- **Daniel S. Blue**, co A, 5 NC Cav, "died of pneumonia, November 11, 1864."
FO, 28 Mar 1864- Daniel S. Blue, of Capt. McKellar's Company (co A, 5 NC Cav), age 39, of Moore Co, died 11th inst. (11 March 1864.)

29)-rost- **Neill McLeod**, co A, 5 Cav, killed at Kennon's Landing, Va 24 May 1864.
FO, Nov 28, 1864- Died K. McIver, Co A, 5 Cav at Hampton Hospital 7 June 1864.
VA.Gov- **N. McCloud**, US Army, died 7 June 1864, buried sec E site 12, Hampton National Cemetery, Va. (all Confederate soldiers on this VA web site erroneously listed in 'US Army'.)

30)-rost-Pvt **Jonathan L. Duckworth**, co B, 5 NC Batt Cav, capt Big Hill, Ky 30 Jul 1863, while in confinement trans to co K, 6 Cav on 3 Aug 63, trans to Fort Delaware on 29 Feb 64. Paroled and exchanged 21 Feb 65.
CWPOWrec- J. L. Duckworth, co B, 5 NC, sent to hospital 23 Mar 64, d 3 April 1864 of smallpox, buried on Jersey Shore.
1912 Book and the 'Fort Delaware' book-Pvt J. L. Duckworth, co B, 5 NC, capt Big Hill, Ky, d Fort Delaware on 3 Apr 1864 of smallpox.
note: there were 17 prison records noted on J. L. Duckworth with five noted his death on 3 April 1864 at Fort Delaware. No release record were noted.

31)-rost-Pvt **Manassas S. Hennessey** of co B, 5 Batt NC Cav, capt Irvine, Ky on 17 Jul 1863, absent in conf when trans to co K, 65 NC (6 NC Cav) on 3 Aug 1863 and promoted to 3Lt. "died in prison. Time not yet known." No Federal records were found to his capt and imprisonment.
CWPOWrec- M. S. Hennessey, co B, 5 NC Cav, capt Irvne, Ky 31 July 1863, trans to Fort Delaware 29 Feb 1864, rec at Ft Delaware from Camp Chase, Ohio on 4 March 64, died 8 April 1864.
1912 book-Pvt M. Hennesey of co B, 5 NC Cav died 8 Apr 1864 at Fort Delaware, buried at Finn's Point, NJ.

32)-rost-Pvt **Ingram A. Holland**, co C, 5 NC Batt Cav, capt Big Hill, Ky 30 July 1863, conf Camp Chase, trans to co H, 6 NC Cav while in POW, trans to Fort Delaware on 29 Feb 1864. No further record.
1912 book-Pvt J. A. Holland of co C, 5 Ala died 12 Jul 1864 at Fort Delaware.
Fort Delaware Society-Pvt J. A. Holland of either co C or D, 5 NC or Ala., died 12 Jul 1864.
CWPOWrec- Ingram A. Holland, co K, 2 Tenn Cav, capt Big Hill, Ky 30 July 1863, trans to Ft Delaware 29 Feb 1864.

CWPOWrec- J. A. Holland, co C, 5 NC Batt., d Ft. Delaware 12 July 1864.

33)-rost-Pvt **Peyton Rash** of co C, 5 NC Batt Cav, capt Hawkins Co, Ky 30 Jun 1863, conf Camp Chase, Ohio, trans to co H, 6 Cav 3 Aug 1863 (trans along with Joseph Rash of Wilkes Co., NC) while Peyton was a POW, died 10 Sep 1863 at Fort Delaware.

rost-Pvt **Payton Rash** of co M, 58 NC, enl Watauga Co, NC 26 Sep 1862, dest Jackson, Tn 29 Dec 1862, rtd 20 Mar, 1863, trans to co G, 58 NC May 1863, dest Clinton, TN, prior 1 Jul 1863, conf Fort Delaware, died 10 Sep 1863 of measles.

1912 book-Pvt Peyton Rash of co M, 58 NC died 10 Sep 1863 at Fort Delaware, buried Finn's Point, NJ.

CWPOWrec- Peyton Rash, co N, 65 NC, capt Hawkins Co., Tenn 20 June 1863, trasn to Ft Delaware 14 July 1863, died 10 Sept 1863.

note: eleven POW records found on P., Payton or Peyton Rash and all stated 58th or 65th NC. None were found for the 5th Batt or 6th NC Cav. Rash of the Cav should be deleted.

34)-rost-**Henry Ray**, co D, 5 Batt NC Cav, enl 8 Jul 1862, trans to co B, 65 NC 3 Aug 1863, reported on a register of soldiers killed in battle or who died of wounds or disease, but date or place of death not given.

CWPOWrec- Henry Ray, co D, 5 NC Cav, died at Camp Chase 9 Oct 1863, also he was stated as being in co C, 2 Conf. Cav in most records.

1912 book- Henry Ray, co C, 2 Conf. Cav, died Camp Chase 9 Oct 1863.

note: since there was a person by Henry Ray of Ashe Co., NC in co D, 5 Batt NC Cav and that he was stated in POW records proves that he was prob the one who died in prison.

35)-rost- **Kenneth McIver**, co A, 5 NC Cav, killed at Kennon's Landing, Va 24 May 1864.

FO, Nov 28, 1864-J. McLeod, co A, 5 NC Cav, died at Hampton Hospital 7 June 1864.

VA.Gov- Kenneth McIver, US Army, died 6 June 1864, buried sec D site 2075, Hampton National Cemetery, Va.

36)-rost- **W. H. Speas**, co I, 5 NC Cav, wounded near Hagerstown 10-12 July 1863 and died of wounds at Williamsport, Md.

FO, 15 Feb 1864- W. H. Spece, co H, 5 NC Cav, died at Martinsburg on 15 July 1863 of gangrene.

37)-rost- J. W. Wilson, co I, 5 NC Cav, died in Hagerstown 29 July 1863.

FO, 21 Dec 1863- **John W. Wilson**, Guilford Co., 63 regt (co I, 5 NC Cav), died near Hagerstown 19 July 1863.

38)-rost- **Benjamin Clark**, co K, 5 NC Cav, capt Ashland Station 1 June 1864, conf at Point Lookout, tran to Elmira where he died 8 Oct 1864 of typhoid fever.

rost- Benjamin Clark, co F, 31 NC, res Martin Co., capt Roanoke Island and paroled, capt Cold Harbor 1 June 1864, died Elmira 8 Oct 1864 of typhoid fever.

note: Benjamin Clark of the 5 Cav should be deleted.

39)-rost- James Smith, co A, 6 NC Cav, rep as "captured at Philadelphia, Tenn., Oct 20, 1863" on Conf. rec, no Fed Provost Marshal rec relative to his capt and imprisonment were found.

rost- **James B. Smith**, co A, 6 NC Cav, died Camp Chase, Ohio 9 Feb 1864 of consumption (only notation).

CWPOWrec- James B. Smith, co F, 66 NC, capt Monroe Co., Tenn 20 Oct 1863, died Camp Chase 9 Feb 1864.

CWPOWrec- James B. Smith, co A, 65 NC, died Camp Chase 9 Feb 1864 of consumption.

note: James Smith and James B. Smith of co A, 6 NC Cav in the Roster are the same person and records should be combined.

40)-rost- **Drew D. Burnett**, co C, 6 NC Cav, capt New Hope, NC 17 Mar 1865, released from Point Lookout 23 Jun 1865 after taking Oath.

CWPOWrec- Drew D. Burnett, co C, 6 NC Cav, capt Kinston, NC 17 mar 1865, released from Point Lookout 23 Jun 65 after taking oath, died Richmond, Va. 1 July 1865 of chr diarr.

41)-rost- **John Fouts**, co E, 6 NC Cav, rec at Rock Island 24 Jan 64, no record of release.

CWPOWrec- John Fouts, co A, 65 NC, capt Jacksboro, Tn 27 Aug, rec Rock Island 24 Jan 64, sent for exchange to Point Lookout 21 Mar 65 rel on Oath 16 June 65.

42)-rost- **Ingram A. Holland**, co H, 6 NC Cav, trans fm co C, 5 Batt NC Cav, conf Camp Chase, trans to Fort Delaware 29 Feb 1864, no further records.

CWPOWrec- J. A. Holland, co C, 5 Batt, died Fort Delaware 17 May 1864.

43)-rost- **Peyton Rash**, co I, 6 NC Cav, while in the 5 Batt he was capt at Hawkins Co., Ky 20 June 1863 and conf at Camp Chase, Oh, trans fm co C, 5 Batt NC Cav 8 Aug 1863 while POW at Ft Delaware, died Ft Delaware 10 Sep 1863.

rost- **Payton Rash**, co M, 58 NC, enlisted Watauga Co. 26 Sept 1862, deserted fm camp at Jacksboro, Tn 29 Dec 1862, ret to duty 20 Mar 1863, tran to co G of this regiment in May 1863, deserted at Clinton, TN, prior to 1 July 1863, died at Ft Delaware 10 Sep 1863 of measles.

note: on CWPOWrec there are 11 rec for P. or Peyton Rash, 7 listed him in the 65 NC (6 Cav) while 2 had the 58 NC, and one rec had '65' written above '58' under unit, capt Hickory Co., Tn 20 June 1863, tran fm Lexington, Ky to Camp Chase 29 June 1863, tran fm Camp Chase to Ft Delaware 14 July 1863, died Ft Delaware 10 Sept 1863, he was 24 at time of death, 6 ft, blue eyes and sandy hair. While confused as to the correct unit this is the same man listed in both cases.

44)-rost- **Jonathan L. Duckworth**, co K, 6 NC Cav, tran fm co B, 5 Batt NC Cav 3 Aug 1863 while a POW, tran fm Camp Chase to Ft Delaware 29 Feb 1864, paroled and exchanged 21 Feb 1865.

CWPOWrec- J. L. Duckworth, co B, 5 NC, died Ft Delaware 3 Apr 1864 of smallpox and buried on Jersey Shore.

note: several POW rec notes his death and no paroled rec were noted.

45)-rost- 3rd Lt. **Manassas S. Hennessey**, co K, 6 NC Cav, tran fm co B, 5 Batt NC Cav 3 Aug 1863 with rank of Private, app 3rd Lt Sept-Dec 1863, muster roll had remarks 'Absent Prisoner of war' 'captured in Kentucky in 1863' 'died in prison. Time not yet known'. No Fed Provost Marshal rec were found.

CWPOWrec- Pvt M. S. Hennessy, co B, 5 NC Cav, capt Irvine Co., Ky 31 July 1863, rec at Fort Delaware from Camp Chase 14 Mar 1864, sent to hospital 22 Mar 1864, died Fort Delaware 8 April 1864.

note: evidently Hennessey as a Prisoner of War never knew that he was transferred to the 6 Cav and promoted to 3rd Lt.

46)-rost-Pvt **Gideon Lowe**, co K, 6 NC Cav, capt Knox Co, Ky 9 Aug 1863, conf Camp Chase, Ohio, trans to Rock Island, Ill 22 Jan 1864, no further rec as of 24 Jan 1864.

rost-Pvt Gideon Low, co K, 62 NC, res Jackson Co, farmer, enl Transylvania at age 29 on 14 Jul 1862, capt Knox Co., Ky 9 Aug 1863, conf Rock Island, Ill 24 Jan 1864, died Rock Island on 2 Feb 1864.

CWPOWrec- Gideon Lowe, co K, 62 NC, capt Knox Co., Ky 9 Aug 1863, rec Louisville, Ky 25 Aug 1863, sent to Camp Chase 1 Sep 1863, died Rock Island 29 Feb 1864 of variola.

note: Gideon Lowe of 6 NC Cav should be deleted.

47)-rost-Pvt **Leonard J. Glimpse**, co A, 7 NC Batt Cav, enl at 36 on 7 Jul 1862, 'captured 5 July 1863', while absent captured trans 3 Aug 1863 to co E, 6 NC Cav, no further record.

rost-Pvt James L. Glimps of co C, 6 NC, p & d enl not reported, capt 13 Jul 1864 in Washington, DC, trans 23 Jul 1864 to Elmira, died 29 Mar 1865 at Elmira.

1912 book-Pvt J. L. Glimpse of co C, 6 NC Cav died 29 Mar 1865 at Elmira.

CWPOWrec- J. L. Glimps, co C, 6 NC (noted in different sources as Infantry and Cav), capt near Washington 13 July 1864, and died 29 Mar 1865 at Elmira.

note: James L. Glimps of 6 NC should be deleted and enter 'James Leonard Glimpse, co C, 6 NC Cav'.

48)-rost- G. W. Kirkendoff, co F, 7 Batt NC Cav, died in hosp at Raleigh 21 Nov 1862.

rost- **William G, Kuykendall**, co G, 56 NC, born Henderson Co, res farmer, enl age 20 on 12 Apr 1862, died in Raleigh on 21 Nov 1862 of disease.

note: G. W. Kirkendoff of 7 Batt NC Cav should be deleted.

49)-rost-**Clements Bridgers**, co B, 15 Batt Cav, present and accounted for until he 'died

1 July 1864'.

LMA-Clement Bridgers of Holliday's Comm, d 26 Jun 1864, grave 256 in Oakwood Cemetery, Raleigh, NC. Note: Maj. Holliday was commander of 15 Batt NC Cav.

50)-rost- **John Sasser**, co C, 16 NC Batt Cav, trans fm co F, 7 Conf Cav 11 Jul 1864, present and accounted for through 1 Oct 1864.

Fort Delaware Society book-Pvt John Sasser of co F, 16 NC Batt Cav dead, note: found on various other tapes.

note: no CWPOWrec were found on John Sasser.

51)-rost-Philip A. Hauser, co D, 16 Batt NC, trans from co G, 7 Conf Cav, reported capt Petersburg 27 Oct 1864, on roll as prisoner of war at Point Lookout, no further record.

CWPOWrec- Philip Hauser, co G, 7 Conf Cav, capt near Petersburg 27 Oct 1864, (in remarks col had a star for some reason, while others on list either died or exchanged.)

CWPOWrec- P. A. Hoosier, co G, 7 SC Cav, had 10 dollars.

Ancestry.com family info-**Philip Alexander Hauser**, b 19 Apr 1843 in Forsyth Co, NC, died 8 Dec 1929 in Lewisville Twp, Forsyth Co, NC. Buried Union Hill Bapt, Clemmons, NC. Surv the war.

52)-rost- J. A. Turner, co E, 16 Batt NC Cav, trans fm co M, 7 Conf Cav 11 Jul 1864 while absent in confinement at Point Lookout, Md as a POW, died Pt Lookout 13 Feb 1865 of phthisis.

'Confederate Service Records' on Ancestry.com- **John A. Turner**, co M, 7 Conf Cav, enlisted 20 Jun 1863 at Mocksville, horse valued at $437, wounded and taken prisoner 5 Mar 1864 at Suffolk, Va, no horse since 5 Mar 1864, confined Guard House, Fort Monroe, Va until trans to Pt Lookout on 13 May 1864, d of phthisis on 13 Feb 1865 at Pt Lookout.

53)-rost-**Frederick Grady**, co C, 8 Batt NC Part. Rangers, w in leg & capt Sandy Ridge, NC 13 Feb 1863, died of wound 15 Feb 1863.

CWPOWrec- Frederick Grady, co D, 8 Batt, died 15 Feb 1863 at New Bern, NC.

54)-rost- Corp. **Curtis A. Webb**, co E, McRae's Batt NC Cav, rep as absent on detached service on muster roll dated 5 Dec 1863.

Shenandoah County (Virginia) Tombstone Inscriptions- Massanutten Cemetery, C. Webb, Pvt, co E, McRae's Battery, NC Cav, CSA. (no date)

55)—rost-2nd Lt W. H. Montague, miscellaneous of McRay's Batt Cav, receipt roll for clothing 29 Feb 64, no other info.

Oakwood Cemetery-**Walter H. Montague**, 8 Aug 1840-16 Aug 64, killed near Richmond.

On web site-Henry Walter Montague, born 3 Aug 1840, killed in Richmond, Va 16 Aug 1864, grad of UNC in 1862.

56)-rost-**R. H. Heffler** in Miscellaneous section of McRae's Batt NC Cav, d hosp at Raleigh 5 Apr 1864.

LMA-**R. H. Heflin** of McRae's Batt d 5 Apr 1864. Grave 224 in Oakwood Cem., Raleigh, NC.

57)—rost-Captain Spencer's Ind. Comp. NC Cav.-Capt. Spencer, Lt. S. P. Sparrow, and twenty-six men of this company were captured on 20 Feb 1864 at Fairfield, NC. (note: this roster lists eighteen of them.)

rost- Company A, 66 NC Inf.—list members of Spencer's Rangers that were transferred to this company on an unspecified date (probably in February-September, 1864) while Prisoners of War. (note: this list has nineteen men that were captured at Fairfield, NC on 20 Feb 1864.)

CWPOWrec- all the follow prisoner of war records on the above men and those not listed in the two volumes of *NC Troops*, were recorded as being in the 66 NC, with a few noted as being in company A of that unit. This indicates that Spencer's Rangers were transferred to Co. A, 66 NC before 20 Feb 1864.

1) Those listed in Spencer's Company, but not in co. A, 66 NC: Capt. William H. Spencer and Pvt. David R. O'Neal.

2) Those listed in Co. A, 66 NC, but not in Spencer's Company. Pvt. **James T.(or J.) Midgett**, Pvt. **William J. Brooks** and Pvt. **William P. Bryan.**

3) Leroy Smith, no rank, listed in Spencer's on bounty roll dated 4 Apr 1863 to 29 Aug 1863 and listed in Co. A, 66 NC with a pension record of being wounded in the arm and hand. CWPOWrec has Corp. **Leroy Smith**, 66 NC, capt Fairfield, NC on 20 Feb 1864 and exchanged 14 Mar 1865.

4) The following soldiers were not listed in either Spencer's Company or co. A of the 66 NC. They were all captured at Fairfield, NC on 20 Feb 1864:

a. Pvt **David Calhoun** died at Point Lookout on 8 May 1864,

b. Pvt **Elaser Curtrell** (see miscellaneous section of 66 NC) died at Point Lookout on 3 Sep 1864,

c. Pvt **Tillman Dunbar** was released on Oath 25 Apr 1864,

d. Pvt **William G. Murray** was exchanged at Aikens Laning on 30 Oct 1864

e. Pvt **William Sawyer** was released on 14 May 1865.

5) The six names in items 3 and 4 should be added to Co. A, 66 NC.

Cause of deaths that were not listed in the NC Roster - Volume II

rank	name	Co.	unit	place of death	died	cause of death
Pvt	Jesse A. Colvard	A	1 Cav	Pt Lookout	9/12/64	epilepsy
Pvt	T. M. R. McEwen	A	1 Cav	Pt Lookout	6/25/64	consumption
Sgt	George F. Adams	D	1 Cav	Washington	4/22/65	pyemia
Pvt	E. M. Lunsford	G	1 Cav	Pt Lookout	1/24/64	chronic diarrhoea
Sgt	E. S. Patterson	G	1 Cav	Pt Lookout	3/6/64	pneumonia
Pvt	Losson L. Teague	G	1 Cav	Pt Lookout	12/26/63	pneumonia

Pvt	James Baisden	I	1 Cav	Ft Delaware	10/18/63	diptheria
Pvt	Gabriel Cox	K	1 Cav	Alexandria	6/23/63	of wounds
QMSgt	William Rose	-	16 Batt Cav	Pt Lookout	1/24/65	lungs, inf of
Pvt	Wiley Jones Ellis	E	16 Batt Cav	Elmira	12/30/64	pneumonia
Pvt	Charles Hofler	C	2 Cav	Pt Lookout	10/15/64	acute diarrhoea
Pvt	John W. Rogers	C	2 Cav	Pt Lookout	6/2/64	dysenteria, chronic
Pvt	Henry E. Taylor	H	2 Cav	Pt Lookout	6/22/64	chronic diarrhoea
Pvt	John Hootman	H	2 Cav	Ft Delaware	8/24/65	dysentery
Pvt	William H. Sumner	H	2 Cav	Ft Delaware	10/14/63	smallpox
Pvt	Uriah R. Parrish	I	2 Cav	Gettysburg	8/30/63	fract thigh
Pvt	M. D. Tomkins	A	3 Cav	Pt Lookout	3/3/65	brain, congestion of
Pvt	Elisha Puett	F	3 Cav	Pt Lookout	7/27/64	acute dysentery
Pvt	Hugh Johnston Davis	G	3 Cav	Alexandria	7/7/64	gs amp lt arm
Pvt	Jere H. Southerland	H	3 Cav	Richmond	6/11/65	pyaemia
Pvt	Jesse D. Smith	H	3 Cav	Pt Lookout	9/5/64	febris remit
Pvt	James Gurkin	K	3 Cav	Pt Lookout	9/15/64	chronic diarrhoea
Corp	William R. Teal	A	4 Cav	Farmville	5/24/65	gs wound
Pvt	James C. Brandon	B	4 Cav	Ft Delaware	10/3/63	chronic diarrhoea
Pvt	John O. Stanfield	B	4 Cav	Ft Delaware	9/20/63	ac. bronchitis/ typh fever
Pvt	Joseph B. Austin	B	4 Cav	Pt Lookout	12/15/63	chronic diarrhoea
Pvt	Lorenzo D. Rudd	B	4 Cav	Ft Delaware	10/3/63	chronic diarrhoea
Pvt	William J. Hensley	B	4 Cav	Ft Delaware	10/6/63	lungs, inf of
1Lt	Thomas Ruffin	D	4 Cav	Johnson's Island	9/24/64	chronic diarrhoea
Pvt	Nimrod Hartsell	E	4 Cav	Ft Delaware	10/3/63	chronic diarrhoea
Pvt	William E. Peele	F	4 Cav	Pt Lookout	8/7/64	bowels, inf of
Pvt	Zachob J. Burden	F	4 Cav	Pt Lookout	12/4/63	diarrhoea
Pvt	Charles E. West	G	4 Cav	Ft Delaware	10/11/63	lungs, inf of
Corp	Samuel A. Etheridge	G	4 Cav	Pt Lookout	10/15/63	febris typhoid
Pvt	James G. Whitehead	H	4 Cav	Pt Lookout	11/22/63	smallpox
Pvt	Hardy Rackley	C	5 Cav	Pt Lookout	1/20/64	chronic diarrhoea
3Lt	Levi Branson Williams	E	5 Cav	Johnson's Island	9/29/63	consumption
Pvt	William Randolph Erwin	F	5 Cav	Pt Lookout	8/21/64	febris remit
Pvt	Robert A. Close	I	5 Cav	Pt Lookout	10/15/63	pneumonia
Capt	Carter W. Gillespie	C	6 Cav	Johnson's Island	9/9/63	febris typhoides
Sgt	James R. Gillespie	C	6 Cav	Pt Lookout	5/3/64	typh malarial fever
Pvt	John C. Martin	F	6 Cav	Columbus	11/22/63	acute dypenteria
Pvt	Peter F. Davis	I	6 Cav	Columbus	9/13/63	dysenteria, acute
3Lt	Manassas S. Hennessey	K	6 Cav	Ft Delaware	4/8/64	febris typhoides
Pvt	David A. Givens	A	McRae's Batt Cav	Rock Island	3/22/64	In Barracks
Pvt	David R. O'Neal	-	Spencer's Cav	Pt Lookout	6/22/64	acute diarrhoea

Additional Information and Amendments to the North Carolina Troops 1861-1865

Volume III - 1st to 3rd Infantry, 1st Battalion Local Defense, 1st Battalion Sharpshooters, 2nd Battalion

1)-rost- **Duncan Moore**, co D, 1 NC (6 months), mustered out 12-13 November 1861.
FO, 30 Sept 1861- Duncan Moore, Capt. Ashe's Chapel Hill Co. (co D), 1 NC, died at Yorktown (no date.)

2)-rost- **Jeptha Hall**, co H, 1 NC (6 months), enlisted in Cumberland Co at age 26 in 1861, mustered out 12-13 Nov 1864.
FO, 6 June 1864- Mr. Jeptha Hall, soldier of the Confederate Army, died in Cedar Creek Dist. In Cumberland Co. at age 29.

3)-rost- Sgt. G. M. Cole, co A, 1 NC, capt Winchester 19 Sep 1864, sent to Pt Lookout 23 Sep 1864 (only info).
rost- 1st Sgt **Goodson M. Cole**, co A. Walker's Battalion, Thomas Legion, capt Winchester 19 Sep 1864, conf at Point Lookout on or about 26 Sep 1864, paroled on or about 1 Nov 1864.
CWPOWrec- Sgt. Goodson M. Cole, co A, Thomas Legion, capt Winchester 19 Sep 1864, trans fm Harpers Ferry to Pt Lookout 26 Sept 1864, trans to Aikens Landing for exchange 1 Nov 1864.
note: G. M. Cole of 1 NC should be deleted.

4)-rost- Sgt. R. L. Cooper, co A, 1 NC, capt Winchester 19 Sep 1864, sent to Pt Lookout 23 Sep 1864 (only info).
rost- Sgt **Rufus L. Cooper**, co A, Walker's Battalion, Thomas Legion, capt Winchester 19 Sep 1864, conf Point Lookout 26 Sep 1864, paroled 15 Mar 1865.
CWPOWrec- Sgt. R. L. Cooper, co A, Thomas Legion, capt Winchester 19 Sep 1864, trans fm Harpers Ferry to Pt Lookout 26 Sept 64, exchange 13 Mar 65, rec at Aiken Landing 15 Mar 65.
note: R. L. Cooper of 1 NC should be deleted.

5)-rost-**Michael C. Davis**, co A, 1 NC, capt Spotsylvania CH 12 May 64, trans from Pt Lookout to Elmira 6 Aug 64, died Elmira 20 Dec 64 of pneumonia.
rost-**Merideth C. Davis**, co A, 1 Batt NC Jr Res, rep on detached service on 11 June 64, capt by enemy on unspecified date and conf at Elmira, died Elmira on 20 Dec 64, cause not reported.
CWPOWrec-M. C. Davis, co A, 1 NC, capt Spotsylvania (or some reports 'Wilderness') on 12 May 64, trans from Pt Lookout to Elmira 3 Aug 64, died Elmira on 20 Dec 64 of pneumonia.
Note- 'no further records' should be entered for Merideth C. Davis of 1 Batt NC Jr Res and that he died at Elmira should be deleted.

6)-rost-Pvt **Robert Evans**, co A, 1 NC, enl Guilford Co 15 Jul 62, c Gettysburg 3 Jul 63, d Point Lookout 30 Aug 64.

rost-Pvt Robert Evans, Co A, 1 NC Cav, res of Guilford Co and conscripted at age 29 on 15 Jul 62, c Gettysburg 3 Jul 63, d Point Lookout 30 Aug 64.

hint: as to correct person-**W.W. Evans** of Guilford Co. enl 15 Jul 63 into Co A. 1 NC.

note: co A, 1 NC is the correct unit as W.W. Evans of Guilford Co. enl 15 Jul 63 in that unit, plus co A, 1 NC Cav was formed in Ashe Co., NC while co A, 1 NC soldiers were from Chowan and Guilford Co., NC.

7)-rost-Pvt **Thomas Loyd**, Co A, 1 NC, res Guilford Co, NC, w & c Gettysburg 3 Jul 1863, conf at Fort Delaware, died 20 Sept 1863 of chr diarr..

rost-Pvt Thomas Loyd, co B, 1 NC, deserted 1 Nov 1862, under sentence of court-martial from 29 Feb through Dec 1864, Fed cem register states that he died at Fort Delaware 20 Sep 1863.

CWPOWrec- Thomas Loyd, co A, 1 NC, died Ft Delaware 20 Sept 1864 of febris intermit.

note: Loyd of co A is the one who died at Fort Delaware.

8)-rost-Pvt **Thomas Loyd**, co B, 1 NC, deserted 1 Nov 1862, under sentence of court-martial from 29 Feb through Dec 1864, Fed cem register states that he died at Fort Delaware 20 Sep 1863.

rost-Pvt Thomas Loyd, Co A, 1 NC, res Guilford Co, NC, w & c Gettysburg 3 Jul 1863, conf at Fort Delaware, died 20 Sept 1863 of chr diarr..

CWPOWrec- Thomas Loyd, co A, 1 NC, died Ft Delaware 20 Sept 1864 of febris intermit.

note: Loyd of co A is the one who died at Fort Delaware.

9)-rost-**Nelson Paris**, co B, 1 NC, capt Spotsylvania CH, conf Point Lookout, trans to Elmira 3 Aug 1864.

CWPOWrec-Nelson Paris, Pvt, co B, 1 NC, capt Spotsylvania 12 May 1864, released May 29, 1865.

note: name Nelson was crossed out and J. added; this J. Paris is prob John L. Parrish of co. A, 1 NC.

10)-rost-**Samuel Wilkerson**, co B, 1 NC, res Wilkes Co & enl Wake age 20 on May 31, 1861, capt Spotsylvania May 12, 1864. conf Point Lookout until trans to Elmira Aug 6, 1864, d Elmira Jun 30, 1865 of chronic diarrhea.

rost-Samuel Wilkinson, co B, 18 NC, p & d enlistment not reported. Rec of Fed Provost Marshal indicate he d at Elmira Jan 30, 1865.

VA web site-Samuel Wilkinson, Pvt CSA, d 30 Jan 65, grave 1813 in Elmira.

note: deaths at Elmira of Jan to Mar 65 in grave series 17..-18.. range, while deaths of Apr-Jun 65 are in 28.. grave range. So, delete Samuel Wilkinson of B, 18 NC and change death date to Jan 30, 1865 for him in co B, 1 NC.

Additional Information and Amendments to the North Carolina Troops 1861-1865

11)-rost- **David P. Herring**, co C, 1 NC, killed in action at Sharpsburg 17 Sept 62.

CWPOWrec- D. P. Harring, co C, 1 NC, died of wounds after 17 Sept 62 at D. Smith's farm at Sharpsburg.

12)-rost- **P. Hinnard**, co C, 1 NC, c Gettysburg 3 July 63, conf Ft Delaware until trans to Pt Lookout 18 Oct 63 (only info).

rost- **Ransom J. Hinnant**, co C, 1 NC, c Gettysburg 3 July 63, conf Ft Delaware until trans to Pt Lookout 15 Oct 63, rel 26 Jan 64 after Oath.

CWPOWrec- P. Hinnart, co C, 1 NC, capt Gettysburg, released after Oath 26 Jan 64 (only rec with P. Hinnart).

CWPOWrec-Ransom Hinnant, co C, 1 NC, capt Gettysburg 3/5 July 63, of Johnson Co., NC, joined the U.S. Army 26 Jan 64. (3 records on Ransom).

note: believe the one item with P. Hinnart should be for Ransom J. Hinnant and that P. Hinnard of co C, 1 NC should be deleted.

13)-rost- **Ransom J. Hinnant**, co C, 1 NC, c Gettysburg 3 July 63, conft Ft Delaware until trans to Pt Lookout 15 Oct 63, rel 26 Jan 64 after Oath.

rost- P. Hinnard, co C, 1 NC, c Gettysburg 3 July 63, conf Ft Delaware until trans to Pt Lookout 18 Oct 63 (only info).

CWPOWrec- P. Hinnart, co C, 1 NC, capt Gettysburg, released after Oath 26 Jan 64 (only rec with P. Hinnart).

CWPOWrec-Ransom Hinnant, co C, 1 NC, capt Gettysburg 3/5 July 63, of Johnson Co., NC, joined the U.S. Army 26 Jan 64. (3 records on Ransom).

note: believe the one item with P. Hinnart should be for Ransom J. Hinnant and that P. Hinnard of co C, 1 NC should be deleted.

14)— rost- **Wesley Clapp**, co E, 1 NC, res Alamance, capt Spotsylvania CH 12 May 64, conf at Point Lookout until trans to Elmira 6 Aug 64, died Elmira 20 Mar 65 of diarrhea.

rost- **W. C. C. Clamps**, co E, 1 NC Arty, died Elmira 20 Mar 65 and buried Woodlawn Nat Cem. (no other records).

1912 Book- W. C. C. Clamps, co E, 1 NC Arty, died 20 Mar 65, Point Lookout

CWPOWrec- W. C. Clamps, co E, 1 NC, capt Spottsylvania 12 May 64, trans to Elmira 6 Aug 64, died Elmira 20 Mar 65 of diarrhoea (in remarks column) 'on rolls Clapp, W.'.

note: W. C. C. Clamps of co E, 1 NC Arty should be deleted.

15)-rost- W. Bumgartner, co G, 1 NC, capt Winchester 19 Sep 64, 'sent to Point Lookout' 23 Sep 64, no other rec relative to his service were found.

rost- **William Bungarner**, co G, Thomas Legion, prev in 16 NC, capt Winchester 19 Sep 64, conf Point Lookout 26 Sep 64, paroled 15 Mar 65, rec for exchange Boulware's Wharf 18 Mar 65.

CWPOWrec- W. Bumgarner, co G, 1 NC Thomas Legion, capt Winchester 19 Sep 64, trans to Point Lookout 26 Sep 64, exchanged 15 Mar 1865.

note: W. Bumgartner of 1 NC should be deleted.

16)-rost- **J. W. Collins**, co G, 1 NC, died Lynchburg 24 Feb 64.
Lynchburg, Old City Cemetery- James W. Collins, co G, 1 NC.

17)-rost- **James M. Frazier**, co G, 1 NC, …discharged on 20 Apr 64 by reason of
chronic diarrhea of 18 months standing.
Lynchburg, Old City Cemetery- J. M. Frazier, co G, 1 NC.

18)-rost- **Reuben Messer**, co G, 1 NC, list of POW at Staunton, Va 8 Jun 64 'capt by
Gen Hunter's forces and sent to Wheeling July 1864.
rost- Reuben Messer, co G, Thomas Legion, trans from co F, capt Piedmont, Va 5 Jun
64, conf Camp Morton until paroled 15 Mar 65, rec Boulware's Wharves 23 Mar 65
for exchange.
CWPOWrec- Reubon Messer, co G, Thomas (Legion) NC Troop, capt Piedmont, Va,
rec at Camp Morton 21 Jun 64, trans for exchange 15 Mar 65.
note: Reuben Messer of 1 NC should be deleted.

19)-rost- **George Cobble**, co H, 1 NC, capt Salisbury 12 Apr 65, died Camp Chase, Oh
5 June 1865 of typhoid fever.
rost- **G. Coble**, co H, 1 NC Cav, died Camp Chase or at Camp Dennison, near
Cincinnati, Oh 5 June 65.
note: G. Coble of co H, 1 NC Cav should be deleted.

20)-rost-**Albert Richards**, co H, 1 NC, died in April 1862.
LibVa-Albert Richards, co H, 1 NC, died at Ashland, Va 21 April 1862, buried
Woodland Cem. In Ashland.

21)-rost- Pvt **Noah P. Robertson**, co H, 1 NC, res Martin Co., NC, born ca 1827,
released from Elmira on 27 Jun 65 after oath.
rost-**William Riley Diggs**, co B, 31 NC, res Anson Co., born ca 1828, died Elmira on
26 Nov 1864 of chr diarrhoea.
1912 book-Pvt N. Robertson, co H, 1 NC, in grave 980, died 26 Nov 64.
VA site- N. P. Robertson, died 26 Nov 1864, buried site 980 Woodlawn Cem, Elmira.
CWPOWrec-Pvt N. P. Robertson, co H, 1 NC, died Elmira 26 Nov 1864 of chr
diarrhea, roll 629, (note: written above the death statement 'Diggs, William R. Pvt
31 N.C. Co B. came in Robertson's place and'.
CWPOWrec- 'Robertson N.P. Pri 1st NC H (capt and when) not given (died) Elmira)
(when) Nov 26, 64, chr diarrhoea (number) 954 (locality) sec 2 Woodlawn Cem
(letter mar) 629 (letter mark) 629.T (effects) EntD on folio 80 as Wm R Diggs'.
(note: seems this line on Robertson was penciled in at the top of the page later after
the others on page were entered).
CWPOWrec- William R. Diggs, co B, 31 NC, died Elmira 26 Nov 64 of chr diarrhea,
in grave 954 Woodlawn Cem, 'on rolls as W. P. Robintson 1 N.C. R. see R folio 210'.

1860 Anson Co., NC census-Riley Diggs, 48, Mary, 47, Wm, 23, Thomas, 15.

1870 Richmond Co., NC census- Wm Diggs, 43 (living along); in next household on page: Thomas E. Diggs, 30, Mary, 25.

1880 Richmond Co., NC census- William Diggs, 53 (living along).

1860 Martin Co., NC census-Noah Robason, 23, Mary, 20, wife, Leah, 65, widower.

note: did Robertson (Robason) died at Elmira and Diggs came home?

22)-rost-**J. D. Weathers**, co I, 1 NC, res Wake Co, muster roll of 31 Aug 64 stated 'absent prisoner of war since May 12, 1864', Roll of honor states he 'died in prison at Elmira, New York', no Federal rec found.

rost- **A. Withers**, co I, 1 NC, capt Spotsylvania 12 May 64, trans from Pt Lookout to Elmira 3 Aug 64.

rost-**James D. Withers**, co I, 1 NC, capt Spotsylvania Ch, Va May 12, 1864, died Elmira 26 Sept 1864 of typhoid fever.

1860 Wake Co., NC census-no Withers near Wake Co

1850 Wake Co., NC census- **James D. Weathers** age 22

1860 Wake Co., NC census- J. D. Weathers age 32, marry with 3 children

CWPOWrec- A. Withers, co I, 1 NC, (3 Point Lookout records noted as) capt Spotsylvania 12 May 64, arr from Bell Plains 18 May 64, trans to Elmira 3 Aug 64.

CWPOWrec- James D. Withers, co I, 1 NC, capt Spotsylvania 12 May 64, died Elmira 26 Sep 64 of typh fever.

1912 book- James D. Withers, co I, 1 NC, died Elmira 26 Sept 64, buried Woodlawn National Cemetery in grave 371.

note: the three above soldiers are the same soldier and correct name is James D. Weathers. Delete A. and James D. Withers after compiling all three data.

23)-rost- **Wiley A. Rowe**, co B, 1 Batt Local Defense, reported as 'taken prisoner June, 1863' and 'not paroled.'

CWPOWrec- Wiley Rowe, co B, 11 NC, capt New Bern 20 June 63, exchanged Aikens Landing 29 Oct 64.

note: during the June-July 1863 period the 1st Batt Loc Def was around New Bern while the 11th NC was in the Gettysburg campaign. The POW rec stated the unit wrong, but this is the same soldier.

24)-rost- **S. J. Caudle**, co A, 1 Batt Sharpshooters, capt Farmville 6 Apr 65, conf Newport News 15 Apr 65, date of release not reported.

CWPOWrec- **S. J. Caddell**, co A, 1 NC, died Newport News 19 June 65 of measles.

25)-rost- **J. W. Vestal**, co A, 1 Batt Sharpshooters, res Yadkin Co., NC, took Oath Hart's Island, NY Harbor 17 June 65, date and place of capture not reported.

CWPOWrec- J. W. Vestall, co A, 1 NC, res Yadkin Co., NC, capt Petersburg 3 Apr 65, released after oath 17 June 65.

26)-rost-**William Mahone**, co B, 2 Battalion NC Inf, res Surry Co., NC, trans fm co E, 53 NC 1 Sep 1862, capt at Gettysburg July 1863, and confined at Ft Delaware where he died 14 Apr 1865 of inflammation of lungs.

rost-**W. McHome**, co B, 2 NC Cav, died at Fort Delaware 14 Apr 1865 & bur Finn's Point. (only info entered. This info prob came from the 1912 book)

CWPOW rec- Pvt W. McHone, co B, 2 NC Batt, capt Waterloo 5 July 63, admitted 25 Feb 65, died 13 Apr 1865 at Ft Delaware.

note: McHome of 2 NC Cav should be deleted.

27)-rost-**John Robinson**, co B, 2 NC, w in knee & permanently disabled at Malvern Hill 1 July 62, retired to the Invalid Corps on 29 April 64.

CWPOWrec-John Robinson, co B, 2 NC, died at Roanoake Island, NC on 8 May 64 of phthisis pulmis.

note: a little over a week after he was retired to the Invalid Corps, Robinson died as a Prisoner of War in North Carolina.

28)-rost-Pvt A. M. Hager of 2nd co C, 2 NC, capt Gettys 3 Jul 63, died Fort Delaware 26 Oct 63 (only info entered).

rost-Pvt **Adam Miller Hager**, co G, 52 NC, res Lincoln Co., NC, enl 62, capt Gettys 3 Jul 63, conf on or about 10 Jul 63 at Fort Delaware, no further rec.

1912 book-Pvt A. M. Hager of co C, 2 NC died Fort Delaware 26 Oct 63, bur Finn's Point, NJ.

note: Hager of 2 NC should be deleted after combining info to Adam Miller Hager.

29)-rost- no **C. C. Southerland** listed in co 2nd co C, 2 NC. (note: many Duplin County soldiers in unit.)

FO, 14 Oct 1861- Pvt. C. C. Southerland, co C, 2 NC, of Duplin Co., died in Camp Carolina near Norfolk.

30)-rost-Pvt **J. D. May**, 2Co E, 2 NC, w & c Gettysburg, died 21 Jul 63 at Davids Island of gs wound..

rost-Pvt J. D. May of Co E, 22 NC, enl at age 25 on 22 Feb 1862, w & c Gettysburg, died Davids Island 31 July 1863 of wounds (nine May's in this unit).

CWPOWrec-J. D. May, co E, 22 NC, died 31 July 63 at Davids Island, NY of vulnus sclopit.

CWPOWrec- J. D. May, co E, 2 NC, capt Gettysburg July 63, died Davis Island, NY Harbor, 31 July 63 of g shot wound, buried 735 Cypress Hill Cem.

1912 book-**John D. May**, co F, 2 NC, died 31 July 63, buried Cypress Hills Nat. Cem. In Brooklyn, NY.

note: based on the enlistment info in the 22 NC, J. D. May of 2 NC should be deleted.

31)-rost- **William Lane**, co A, 3 NC, res in Greene Co, enl in Wayne Co age 30 on 13 May 62, wounded Gettysburg 2 Jul 63, capt Waterloo, Pa 5 Jul 63, trans from Ft Delaware to Pt Lookout 18 Oct 63, died Pt Lookout 3 Feb 1864.

rost- William Lane, co E, 2 NC Cav, capt Gettysburg 7/3/63, confined at Ft Delaware 15 Oct 63, died Ft Delaware "February 3, 1863" (prob should be 1864.)
note: William Lane of co E, 2 NC Cav should be deleted.

32)-rost-Pvt **J. A. Smith**, co A, 3 NC, capt at Fort Fisher on 25 Dec 64, conf at Fort Monroe, Va 29 Dec 64. (only info noted in roster).
CWPOWrec- J. A. Smith, co A, 3 NC Res, capt Ft Fisher 25 Dec 1864, trans fm ft Monroe to Pt Lookout 2 Jan 1865, released 30 Jun 1865.
note: there was no 3 NC at Fort Fisher on 25 Dec 64, but the 3 NC Jr Res was capt on 25 Dec at Fort Fisher.

33)-rost-Pvt **William Weason**, co A, 3 NC, capt Winchester 19 Sept 64, conf Point Lookout 23 Sept 64 (only info noted).
CWPOWrec-'Roll of Prisoners at Point Lookout', William Weason, co A, 3 NC, capt Winchester 19 Sept 64, trans from Harpers Ferry to Point Lookout 26 Sept 64, exchange 15 Mar 65.

34)-rost- **John C. Bostick**, co B, 3 NC, res in Duplin Co, enlisted 15 July 62, wounded Gettysburg 2 July 63 and capt next day, died Fort Delaware 2 Aug 63 of chronic diarrhea.
rost- John Bostick, co B, 3 NC Cav, capt South Mountain or Gettysburg 4 July 63, died Fort Delaware 1 Aug 63.
note: delete John Bostick of co B, 3 NC Cav.

35)-rost- **W. A. James**, co B, 3 NC, capt Gettysburg and confined DeCamp Gen Hosp Davids Island, NY Harbor 17-24 Jul 63 (only info noted).
CWPOWrec- W. A. James, co B, 3 NC, trans to City Point, Va 23 Sept 63.

36)-rost-J. F. Cameron, co C, 3 NC, absent sick July 14-Nov 1, 1862, appeared on muster roll May 15-Aug 11, 1863 "Dead but no official report received."
FO, 29 Sept 1862- **John F. Cameron**, co C, 3 NC, age 23, died in the College Hospital, Lynchburg, Va on 25 Aug 1862, native of Moore Co. where his remains were interred.

37)-rost- D. C. McDonald, co C, 3 NC, age not given, died at Danville 5 Jan 1863.
FO, 16 Feb 1863- **Daniel C. McDonald**, co C, 3 NC, age 20, died at Danville 14 Feb 1863.

38)-rost-Pvt E. Frederick, co D, 3 NC.
1912 book-Pvt Elisha Frederick of co D, 3 NC.
CWPOWrec- **Elisha Frederick**, co D, 3 NC, capt Spottsylvania 12 May 64, died Elmira 22 Jan 65.
note: first name Elisha.

39)-rost- **Benjamin B. Jackson**, co E, 3 NC, killed 17 Sep 62 at Sharpsburg.

CWPOW REC- Benjamin B. Jackson, co E, 3 NC, died 20 Sept 62 at Sharpsburg of vulous sclopet.

note: Jackson was not killed but wounded, captured and died of wounds three days later.

40)-rost-Pvt **James M. Piner**, co E, 3 NC, res Onslow, enl age 23 on 13 May 61, prom Corp Jun 62, reduced to Pvt Oct 62, capt Spots 20 May 64, conf Point Lookout, trans to Elmira 3 Jul 64, died Elmira 4 Mar 65.

rost-Pvt **James J. Piner** of co E, 30 NC, res New Hanover, enl age 27 on 21 Aug 63, capt Spots 20 May 64, conf Point Lookout, trans Elmira 3 Jul 64, died Elmira 4 Mar 65.

1912 book-Pvt J. Pyner of co E, 3 NC died Elmira 4 Mar 65, grave 1964.

CWPOWrec- J. M. Piner, co E, 3 NC, paroled 20 Feb 65, morning report 5 Mar 65 Elmira, ward 27, died 4 Mar 65 of variola.

CWPOWrec- J. Pyner, co E, 30 NC, died Elmira 4 Mar 65.

1860 Onslow census- J. M. Piner, 22 (no other census found on him).

1860 New Hanover census- John J. Piner, 25, wife Matilda, 20.

1870 New Hanover census- James Piner, 40, wife Matilda

1880 New Hanover census- James Piner, 46, wife Matilda 39

Note: James M. Piner of 3 NC died on 4 Mar 65 at Elmira.

John James/James John Piner of 30 NC came home after the war.

Delete death date of 4 Mar 65 for James J. Piner of 30 NC.

41)-rost- **William L. Rowe**, co F, 3 NC, Mortally wounded at Sharpsburg 17 Sept 1862.

CWPOWrec- W. L. Rowe, co F, 3 NC, wounded in Battle, died at Antietam.

note: add that William L. Rowe was wounded and captured at Sharpsburg.

42)-rost- **Samuel Bell**, **Thomas Cross** and **Joseph J. Hinton**, all of co I, 3 NC, wounded Sharpsburg 17 Sep 62 and died at Frederick 1 Oct, 15 Oct and 23 Oct 62, respectfully.

CWPOWrec- they were all wounded and captured on 17 Sep 62 and died in Federal hands.

43)-rost- **Anderton Brown**, co I, 3 NC, enl Wake Co on 27 Oct 63, wounded and capt Mine Run 27 Nov 63, conf at 1st Div hosp in Alexander, Va, died in Alexander 14 Dec 63 of wound.

Rost- A. Brown, co I, 5 NC, res Forsyth Co, capt Mine Run 27 Nov 63, died Alexander 14 Dec 63 of gun shot wound.

note: these two soldiers are the same person and believe that Anderton Brown of 3 NC is the correct info and A. Brown of the 5 NC should be deleted.

NC soldiers buried on Barton Street in Fredericksburg, Virginia – their graves were unmarked until April 18, 2009

Pvt **William Gooding**, co G, 2 NC Inf – died 26 Oct 1861 Pratt's Point, Prince George Co

Pvt **Asa Howlett**, co E, 2 NC Inf – died Dec 1861, place of death not listed

Pvt **Sylvester Hunt**, co E, 1 NC Inf – date and place of death not given

Pvt **Jordan Modlin**, co F, 1 NC Inf – died 26 Oct 1861 Fredericksburg

Pvt **Joseph Pickett**, co E, 1 NC Inf – died 5 Dec 1861 Fredericksburg

Pvt **Albert B. Pleasants**, co D, 1 NC Inf – died 27 Nov 1861 Fredericksburg

Pvt **Samm**, co B, 2 NC Inf (not listed in the Roster)

Pvt **Linsey Vickers**, co B, 1 NC Inf - died 7 Jan 1862 Fredericksburg

Pvt **Elias Williams**, co D, 3 NC Inf – died 8 Nov 1861 Fredericksburg

Cause of deaths that were not listed in the NC Roster - Volume III

rank	name	co	unit	place of death	died	cause of death
Pvt	Robert Evans	A	1	Point Lookout	8/30/64	chronic diarrhoea
Sgt	Francis A. Harris	A	1	Point Lookout	12/21/63	chronic diarrhoea
Pvt	Thomas Loyd	A	1	Fort Delaware	9/20/63	Febris Inter./chronic diarrhoea
Pvt	Robert J. Phibbs	A	1	Elmira	2/3/65	chronic diarrhoea
Pvt	Benjamin Thomas	A	1	Point Lookout	7/31/64	acute dysenteria
Pvt	John W. Brown	C	1	Point Lookout	6/2/64	lungs, inf of
Pvt	George W. Moore, Jr.	C	1	Point Lookout	8/18/64	chronic diarrhoea
Pvt	Henry L. Hines	D	1	Point Lookout	8/5/64	chronic diarrhoea
Pvt	William Cornelius Paul	D	1	Gettysburg	7/12/63	flesh wnd abdoman
Pvt	George W. Williams	D	1	Point Lookout	12/21/63	pneumonia
Pvt	Henry E. Ross	E	1	Point Lookout	9/16/64	acute diarrhoea
Corp	Benjamin S. Davenport	G	1	Point Lookout	2/19/64	febris typhoides
Pvt	J.O. Dennis	H	1	Columbus	1/5/64	typhoid fever
Pvt	John M. Gladson	H	1	Camp Chase	6/21/65	dropsy
Pvt	Joseph R. Hardison	H	1	Point Lookout	1/20/65	lungs, inf of
Pvt	William R. May	H	1	Fort Delaware	10/7/63	scurvy
Pvt	Elias Neese	H	1	Fort Delaware	10/14/63	chronic diarrhoea
Pvt	Oscar D. Sharp	H	1	Frederick	11/21/62	amp lt thigh
Pvt	McGilbert Taylor	H	1	Point Lookout	8/10/64	febris remit
Pvt	Clinton White	H	1	Gettysburg	7/26/63	amp rt thigh
Pvt	Augustus Hicks	I	1	Point Lookout	8/21/64	acute dysenteria
Pvt	Samuel G. Hunt	I	1	Point Lookout	9/9/64	chronic diarrhoea
Pvt	John C. Mitchell	I	1	Point Lookout	6/24/64	dysenteria, chronic
Pvt	F.M. Young	I	1	Fort Delaware	10/6/63	smallpox
Pvt	Edmond Cobler	A	2	Point Lookout	7/31/64	chronic diarrhoea
Pvt	Greenville Cobler	A	2	Point Lookout	1/30/64	dysenteria, chronic
Pvt	David Hall	A	2	Point Lookout	1/31/64	chronic diarrhoea
Pvt	Allen Martin	A	2	Point Lookout	2/9/64	chronic diarrhoea
Pvt	Eli Whitesell	A	2	Point Lookout	12/28/63	acute dysenteria
Pvt	Willis F. Wright	A	2	Point Lookout	8/18/64	chronic diarrhoea
Pvt	George T. Boyette	B	2	Baltimore	1/1/65	gs wound
Pvt	J. Osborne	B	2	Point Lookout	2/18/64	smallpox
1Lt	George W. Britt	C	2	Winchester	10/17/64	gs side
Pvt	R. E. Bruce	C	2	Winchester	9/30/64	gs lungs
Pvt	Council B. Jones	C	2	Point Lookout	7/20/64	febris remit
Pvt	Alfred P. McCan	C	2	Point Lookout	12/27/63	pneumonia
Pvt	Charles H. Summerlin	C	2	Fort Delaware	9/8/63	chr. Diarr./typhoid fever
Pvt	H.W. Spurle	D	2	Fort Delaware	10/9/63	acute diarrhoea

Pvt	Alexander T. Maxwell	E	2	Point Lookout	1/5/64	variola
Pvt	David W. Baldwin	G	2	Winchester	10/20/64	gs knee
Pvt	William Jackson Stone	I	2	Point Lookout	7/18/64	febris remit
Corp	Anson B Fulford	K	2	Point Lookout	2/11/64	bronchitis chronic
Pvt	J.C. Blackburn	A	3	Point Lookout	7/28/64	acute diarrhoea
Pvt	Robert Hall	A	3	Point Lookout	7/13/64	measles
Sgt	Matthew F. Randolph	A	3	Point Lookout	7/11/64	febris remittent
1Lt	Thomas Cowan, Jr.	B	3	Washington	10/4/62	dysentery
Pvt	Matthew Jones	B	3	Point Lookout	1/4/64	chronic diarrhoea
Pvt	Daniel M. Kelly	B	3	Frederick	6/19/63	fract thigh
Pvt	Laomi Reevs	B	3	Frederick	11/6/62	vulnus sclopst
Pvt	Elias Sutton	B	3	Antietim	10/1/62	of wounds
Pvt	Amos Thigpen	B	3	Frederick	11/19/62	vulnus sclopst
Pvt	J.A. Fisher	C	3	Point Lookout	6/17/64	acute diarrhoea
Pvt	J.B. Horne	C	3	Frederick	9/26/62	vulnus sclopst
Sgt	David D. King	C	3	Point Lookout	12/4/63	smallpox
Pvt	Angus Smith	C	3	Fort Delaware	10/8/63	lungs, inf of
Pvt	Lewis S. Phillips	E	3	Frederick	10/30/62	of wounds
Pvt	James M. Piner	E	3	Elmira	3/4/65	variola
Pvt	Calvin Davis	F	3	Point Lookout	7/17/64	chronic diarrhoea
Pvt	Nelson Parrish	F	3	Richmond	6/14/65	consumption
Sgt	James W. Simpson	F	3	Point Lookout	11/22/63	chronic diarrhoea
Pvt	Jackson L. Shepard	G	3	Point Lookout	9/11/64	acute diarrhoea
Pvt	Travis L. Porter	H	3	Point Lookout	12/23/63	smallpox
Pvt	Alexander A. Britt	K	3	Newport News	6/26/65	pneumonia
Pvt	James H. Carter	K	3	Point Lookout	10/20/63	acute diarrhoea
Pvt	George H. Cowan	K	3	Frederick	10/24/62	vulnus sclopst
Pvt	Alfred A. Taylor	K	3	Point Lookout	8/8/64	chronic diarrhoea
Pvt	Ephriam B. Simmons	A	2 Batt	Point Lookout	8/8/64	acute dysenteria
Pvt	Henry N. Brakefield	E	2 Batt	Point Lookout	3/15/64	diarrhoea
Pvt	Dawson Lewallen	F	2 Batt	Point Lookout	7/12/64	apoplexy
Corp	Wisdom P. Welborn	G	2 Batt	Fort Delaware	10/12/63	chronic diarrhoea
Pvt	William Willard	G	2 Batt	Point Lookout	5/11/65	acute diarrhoea
1Sgt	James M. Carver	H	2 Batt	Richmond	6/9/65	gs wound
2Lt	Joseph N. Duckett	H	2 Batt	Gettysburg	7/7/63	of wounds

Additional Information and Amendments to the North Carolina Troops 1861-1865

Volume IV – 4th to 8th Infantry

1)-rost- **William M. McKenzie**, Field and Staff, 4 NC, hospital steward, died at Raleigh, date and cause of death not reported.

FO, 13 Oct 1862- Dr. W. W. McKenzie, 4 NC, assistant surgeon, age 25, died in Raleigh 4 Aug 1862.

2)-rost- **John N. Barnes**, co A, 4 NC, hospital rec indicate that he died at Richmond on or about June 27, 1862; however, Roll of Honor states that he was killed at Seven Pines May 31, 1862.

Oakwood Cemetery Burial records, Richmond, Va-J. N. Barnes, co A, 4 NC, buried June 28, 1862 in Oakwood Cem.,

3)-rost- W. J. Roberts, co B, 4 NC, place and date enl not reported, wounded in leg and capt Winchester 19 Sept 64, leg ampt, adm to Wincester hosp 24 Sept 64, died 12 Oct 64.

rost- **William J. Roberts**, co D, 4 NC, res Wayne Co., enl age 19 in 61, w Chancellorsville 3 May 63, p & a until he died at Winchester, Va 13 Oct 1864, cause of death not reported.

CW POW REC- W. A. Roberts, co D, 4 NC, died at Winchester, Va 13 Oct 1864 with g s thigh.

note: W. J. Roberts of co B, 4 NC should be deleted after merging his data into the record of William J. Roberts of co D, 4 NC.

4)-rost-**E. Harris**, co E, 4 NC, died in Nov 1862, place, exact date and cause of death not reported.

note: List noted on the internet of Confederates burial at Mount Jackson Cemetery in Virginia states that E. E. Harris of co E, 4 NC died at Mount Jackson in Nov 1862.

5)-rost-**Alvin Atkinson**, co F, 4 NC, died May 24, 1862, p & c of death not reported.

Oakwood Cemetery Burial records, Richmond, Va- **A. H. Atkerson**, co F, 4 NC, burial date May 24, 1862.

6)-rost- **George W. Winstead**, co F, 4 NC, res Wilson Co and enl at age 19 on 2 Aug 63, no further rec.

Shenandoah County (Virginia) Tombstone Inscriptions- Massanutten Cemetery, George W. Winstead, co F, 4 NC, no dates.

7)-rost- **J. H. Cranfield**, co G, 4 NC, capt Burkeville 6 Apr 65, conf Newport News until rel 14 Jun 65 after Oath.

CWPOWrec- J. H. Cranfield, co G, 4 NC, died Fort Monroe 15 Jun 65 of chr diarr.

8)-rost- **William H. Owen**, co G, 4 NC, muster roll indicate he was killed Gaines' Mill 26 Jun 62, however, Fed Medical rec indicate that he died at Point Lookout 18 Apr 65 of pneumonia.

CWPOWrec- W. Owens, co G, 4 NC, capt Currituck Co., NC 19 Dec 64, died Point Lokout 18 Apr 65 of inf. of lungs.

9)-rost- **Albert Madison**, co H, 4 NC, wounded Spotsylvaina CH 19 May 64, died 6-7 June 64 of wounds.

Lynchburg, Old City Cemetery- A. Madison, co H, 4 NC.

10)-rost-W. P. Barnes, co I, 4 NC, (only record noted as:) reported in Petersburg hospital with gs wound of left arm, no further records.

rost-**William P. Barnes**, co I, 4 NC Cav, trans fm co B, 12 Batt NC Cav on 11 Jul 1864, capt in hospital at Petersburg 3 Apr 1865 where he had been adm with gs wound of left arm, died in Petersburg hospital on 21 May 1865.

CWPOWrec-N. P. Barnes, co C, 4 NC, died Petersburg on 21 May 1865 of gs wound right arm.

Petersburg-W. P. Barnes, co B, 4 NC, died Petersburg on 21 May 1865, buried Petersburg Fair Ground vicinity.

note: William P. Barnes of co I, 4 NC Cav is the correct soldier. Delete W. P. Barnes of co I, 4 NC.

11)-rost- **James Campbell**, co I, 4 NC, p & a until rep as a deserter on company muster roll dated 31 Aug-31Oct 63, rec of Fed Provost Marshall indicate he was captured at Williamsport 14 Jul 63 or 26 Aug 63, adm to hosp at Chester, Pa 17 Sep 63.

CWPOWrec- James Campbell, co I, 4 NC, capt Winchester 30 Jul 63, disposition unaccounted for.

12)-rost- Thomas Gill, co A, 5 NC, died in Virginia on 3 Sept 1861.

FO, 16 Sept 1861- **Thomas H. Gill**, Capt Sinclair's Co., 5 NC, died at Manassas on 6 inst. (6 Sept 1861.)

13)-Rost-Pvt **Thomas Henry** of co A, 5 NC, res Chatham Co., NC, was capt Gettysburg, conf at Fort McHenry, trans to Fort Delaware in July 63. No further record.

1912 book-Pvt Thomas Henry of co A, 5 MO Inf (should be NC Inf) died 4 Sep 63 at Fort Delaware, buried at Finn's Point, NJ.

CWPOWrec- Thomas Henry, co A, 5 NC, capt Gettysburg 2 July 63, died 5 Sept 63 (written in heavy print over 'NC', 'Gettysburg' & '2 July 63' were 'Mo', 'Big Black' & 'May 17').

CWPOWrec- Thomas Henry, co A, 5 Mo, died Ft Delaware 4 Sept 63 of anaemie/ typhoid.

note: seems that the Union records first record Henry of 5 NC death, but than changed the data to state that Henry of 5 Mo. Instead died.

14)-rost- **J. G. Anton**, co D, 5 NC, Place and date enl not rep, died Elmira 19 May 65, cause of death not rep.

rost-**J. E. Austin**, co D, 5 NC, born Johnston Co., enl age 18 on 16 Jul 62, capt Spotsylvania 12 May 64, conf Point Lookout, trans to Elmira 7/3/64, died Elmira 19 May 65 of variola.

CWPOWrec- J. G. Anton, co D, 5 NC, (four rec) capt Spotsylvania 17 May 64, trans to Elmira 6 Jul 64, died Elmira 19 Mar 65 of variola, (remarks on record) 'on rolls Austin, J. J.'

CWPOWrec- J. J. Austin, co D, 5 NC, capt Spotsylvania 17/18 May 64, tran to Elmira 3 Jul 64, died Elmira 19 Mar 65 of variola.

note: J. G. Anton is the same soldier as J. E. (or J. J.) Austin and J. G. Anton of the 5 NC should be deleted.

15)-rost- **James N. Caps**, co F, 5 NC, p & d enl not reported, capt Spotsylvania 12 May 64, conf Pt Lookout, trans to Elmira 3 July 64, died Elmira 27 Feb 65.

rost- Monroe Crepps, co F, 5 NC, b Stanly Co, enl Northampton Co 8 Aug 62, capt Spotsylvania 12 May 64, died Elmira 27 Feb 65.

Va site- J. Crepps, died 27 Feb 65, buried in 2128.

CWPOWrec- J. Crepps, co E, 5 NC, capt Spotsylvania 12 May 64, joined station (Elmira) 6 Feb 64, died 27 Feb 65 of variola, grave 2189, date of alternation 28 Feb 65 – "Caps, J.M." Co. "F".

CWPOWrec- list had J.M. Caps, but ' see Crepps' was written over the name J. M. Caps.

note: no Monroe Crepps in CWPOW records. Believe these are the same person and his record should show **James Monroe Crepps** of co F, 5 NC. James N. Caps of co F, 5 NC should be deleted.

16)-rost- **Monroe Crepps**, co F, 5 NC, b Stanly Co, enl Northampton Co 8 Aug 62, capt Spotsylvania 12 May 64, died Elmira 27 Feb 65.

rost- James M. Caps, co F, 5 NC, p&d enl not reported, capt Spotsylvania 12 May 64, conf Pt Lookout, trans to Elmira 3 July 64, died Elmira 27 Feb 65.

Va site- J. Crepps, died 27 Feb 65, buried in 2128.

CWPOWrec- J. Crepps, co E, 5 NC, capt Spotsylvania 12 May 64, joined station (Elmira) 6 Feb 64, died 27 Feb 65, grave 2189, date of alternation 28 Feb 65 – "Caps, J.M." Co. "F".

CWPOWrec- list had J.M. Caps, but 'Crepps' was written over the name Caps.

note: no Monroe Crepps in CWPOW records. Believe these are the same person and his record should show 'James Monroe Crepps of co F, 5 NC". James N. Caps of co F, 5 NC should be deleted.

17)-rost- **T. H. Harman**, co F, 5 NC, died at Lynchburg 19 Mar 62.

Lynchburg, Old City Cemetery- **Thomas Hartman**, co F, 5 NC.

18)-rost-Pvt **Calvin C. Taber**, co G, 5 NC, place and date enl not rep, w in head and capt Petersburg 27 Mar 65, held City Point, trans to Washington, DC 9 Apr 65, died hosp in Washington 16 Apr 65 of wounds.

rost-Pvt Calvin C. Tabor, co G, 56 NC, pre in co F-14 NC, trans 4 Jan 65, w in head and capt Petersburg 27 Mar 65, died hosp Washington 16 Apr 65 (note Alexander Taber of Henderson Co. in unit.)

note: Calvin C. Taber of 5 NC should be deleted.

19)-rost-Pvt **John B. Ralph**, co. H, 5 NC, wounded and captured at Williamsburg on May 5th, 1862. He died of wounds. Place and date of death not reported.

CWPOWrec- John B. Ralph, co H, 5 NC, died Cliffburn Gen Mil Hosp (Washington, DC) on 14 Jun 1862 of gun shot wounds.

VA web site- J. B. Ralph of Co. H, 5 NC Inf. died June 14th, 1862 and buried in Confederate Section site 125 at Arlington Cemetery.

20)-rost-Pvt B.F. Bean of co I, 5 NC died Elmira on 7 Dec 64.

CWPOWrec-Pvt **Benjamin F. Bean** of co I, 5 NC died Elmira on 7 Dec 64.

note: name Benjamin F. noted in four records.

21)-rost- A. Brown, co I, 5 NC, res Forsyth Co, capt Mine Run 27 Nov 63, died Alexander 14 Dec 63 of gun shot wound.

rost- **Anderton Brown**, co I, 3 NC, enl Wake Co on 27 Oct 63, wounded and capt Mine Run 27 Nov 63, conf at 1st Div hosp in Alexander, Va, died in Alexander 14 Dec 63 of wound.

note: these two soldiers are the same person and believe that Anderton Brown of 3 NC is the correct info and A. Brown of the 5 NC should be deleted.

22)-rost- J. B. Whitman, co K, 5 NC, place and date of enlistment not rep, died in Newport News hosp 29 Apr 186..

rost- **John A. Whitman**, co K, 57 NC, res Rowan Co, capt Farmville 6 Apr 65, died Newport News on or about 6 May 1865 of chr dysentery.

CWPOWrec- John A. Whitman, co K, 57 NC, capt Farmville 6 Apr 65, died Newport News 6 May 1865.

note: Suspect both are the same soldier and J. B. Whitman should be deleted.

23)-rost- **William Cash**, co B, 6 NC, died Williamsburg on 1 May 1862

BDL- William Cash, co B, 6 NC, died at College hospital, 29 Apr 1862 $10 for making coffin, $2 for digging grave, $1 to convenyance to the ground, buried in grave 8 of the North Carolina row at (Cedar Grove Cemetery) Williamsburg, Virginia.

note: William Cash probably died on 28 Apr vice 1 May 1862 since the burial records were on 29 Apr 1862.

24)-rost-1st Lt **William E. McManning**, co B, 6 NC, resigned 30 Oct 1861, reason he resigned not reported.

NCS, 26 Nov 1862-Col. **William E. McMannen**, was first 2ⁿᵈ Lt of the 'Flat River Guards' from Orange Co, attached to the 6ᵗʰ NC (as company B), but the last of October 1862 he bid adieu to his comrades on the banks of the Potomac because of his health, having improved some he was made colonel of the 45ᵗʰ Regiment Militia with directions to superintend the draft, he contracted a fresh cold and from that time sank rapidly, giving way to comsumption, In July (1862) he repaired to the Rockbridge Alum Springs, he died 14 August 1862, age 22

NC Conf Militia Officers Roster, page 120-Colonel William E. McMannen, Field and Staff, 11ᵗʰ Brigade, 45ᵗʰ Hillsboro Regiment, Orange County, date 20 Nov 1861, South Lowell, dead.

25)-rost- **John Moore Brown**, co C, 6 NC, died Richmond in May 1862.

Hollywood Cem, Richmond, Va rec- J. M. Brown, co A, 6 NC, died 11 May 62, grave G96.

26)-rost-Pvt **John Dawson** of co C, 6 NC, place and date of enlistment not reported, died Point Lookout 22 Feb 65.

rost-Pvt John Dawson of co C, 61 NC, born Craven, res in Lenoir Co, enl in Craven 62, capt Globe Taven, Va 19Aug 64, conf Point Lookout 24 Aug 64, died at Point Lookout 22 Feb 65.

note: John Dawson of co C, 6 NC should be deleted.

27)-rost-Pvt **James L. Glimps** of co C, 6 NC, p & d enl not reported, capt 13 Jul 64 in Washington, DC, trans 23 Jul 64 to Elmira, died 29 Mar 65 at Elmira.

rost-Pvt **Leonard J. Glimpse**, co A, 7 NC Batt Cav, enl at 36 on 7 Jul 62, 'captured 5 July 63', while absent captured trans 3 Aug 63 to co E, 6 NC Cav, no further record.

1912 book-Pvt J. L. Glimpse of co C, 6 NC Cav died 29 Mar 65 at Elmira.

CWPOWrec- J. L. Glimps, co C, 6 NC (noted in different sources as Infantry and Cav), capt near Washington 13 July 64, and died 29 Mar 65 at Elmira.

note: James L. Glimps of 6 NC should be deleted and enter '**James Leonard Glimpse**, co C, 6 NC Cav'.

28)-rost- **Rayman Gibson**, co D, 6 NC, capt Charles Town, WVa 22 Aug 64 and conf at Fort Delaware. No further records.

rost- **Raymond Gibson**, co D, 57 NC, res Stokes Co, enl Forsyth Co 4 July 62 at age 31. Capt Gettysburg, paroled, capt Rappahanock Station, paroled, prior to 22-23 Aug 64 capt near Charlestown, WVa, conf Elmira, released 16 Jun 65.

CWPOWrec- Raymond Gibson, 57 NC, co D , capt Charlestown, WVa 22 Aug 64 and released 19 Jun 65.

note: delete Rayman Gibson of co C, 6 NC.)

29)-not in rost- **Claudius P. Griffin**, co D, 6 NC, note: his records are mixed in the Compiled Service Records of **Charles P. Griffin** of co E, 33 NC.

CWPOWrec- Claudius P. Griffin, co D, 6 NC, capt Mechanisville, Va 30 Jun 1864, d

Lincolin Gen Hosp, Washington, DC 10 July 1864 at 13:30 pm of gs r thigh, age 19, admin is **Thomas B. Griffin** of Beaver Dam, Union Co., NC.

LMA-Claudius P. Griffin, co D, 6 NC, buried in Arlington mass grave in Oakwood Cem, Raleigh, NC.

1860 Union Co., NC census- Claudius P. Griffin, age 15, son of Thomas and **Jane Griffin**.

30)-rost- **Samuel Martin**, co D, 6 NC, died Williamsburg on 1 May 1862.

BDL- Samuel Martin, Co D, 6 NC, died at Methodist Church hospital, 25 Apr 1862 $10 for making coffin, $2 for digging grave, $1 to convenyance to the ground, buried in grave 7 of the North Carolina row at (Cedar Grove Cemetery) Williamsburg, Virginia.

note: Samuel Martin probably died on 24 Apr vice 1 May 1862 since the burial records were on 25 Apr 1862.

31)-rost- **William Chatham**, co H, 6 NC, mort wounded & capt Sharpsburg 17 Sep 62, date of death not reported.

CWPOWrec- William Chatham, 6 NC, died of wounds 17 Sep 62 at Antitam.

32)-rost- **H. Drake**, co H, 6 NC, place and date of enlistment not rep, died Elmira 15 Feb 65, cause of death not rep.

CWPOWrec- H. Drake, co B, 6 NC, captured Washington, DC 12 Jul 64, trans to Elmira 23 Jul 64, rec Elmira 25 Jul 64, "on rolls H. J. of 57 NC", died Elmira 15 Feb 65 of variola. (there were at least 4 rec on H. Drake of Co B, 6 NC)

CWPOWrec- H. J. Drake, co B, 57 NC, capt Washington, DC 12 Jul 64, rec Elmira 25 Jul 64, died Elmira 15 Feb 65 of variola. (there were at least 3 rec on H. J. Drake of Co B, 57 NC; on one rec "see 6" was written above the unit 57 NC.)

note: The Federal authorities were confused if this soldier was H. Drake of the 6 NC or H. J. Drake of the 57 NC. At this time no Confederate rec have been noted as to the correct soldier. Will identity him as H. Drake of Co B, 6 NC Inf until further info are found.

33)-rost- S. J. Holeman, co I, 6 NC, enl Chatham Co at age 17 on 25 Feb 62, died Ashland, Va 16 Apr 62 of disease.

Newspaper-*Raleigh Spirit of the Age*- 5 May 62- Pvt **Silas J. Holleman**, age 17, Capt York's Co, 6 NC, died at Ashland, Va 14 Apr 62.

34)-rost-Pvt C. Tanner, co I, 6 NC, p & d enl unknown, capt Spots 12 May 64, died Fort Delaware 10 Jul 64.

rost-Pvt **Calton Tanner**, co I, 20 NC, res Sampson Co., enl Fort Johnston 61, capt Getts 1-3- Jul, died Fort Delaware 10 Jul 64.

CWPOWrec- C. Tanner, co I, 6 NC, capt Spotsylvania 12 May 64, died Fort Delaware 10 July 64 of chronic diarrhea.

CWPOWrec- C. Tanner, co I, 20 NC, capt Gettysburg 4 July 1863, Ft Delaware rec from Fort Wood, NY, died 10 July 1864 of chr diarrhea, buried Jersey Shore.

note: in CWPOW records only one item of Tanner in the 6th and seven of Tanner in the 20th. The item with the 6th NC had an 'x' beside 'Spottsylavia, Va' in the captured column. All items stated that Tanner died 10 July 1864 of chronic diarrhea at Fort Delaware.

note: based on the above notes C. Tanner of co I, 6 NC should be deleted.

35)-rost- K. Shields, co K, 6 NC, p & d of enl not reported, w in left thigh at Gettysburg & capt 4 Jul 63, left leg amp, died 29 Jul 63 at Chester, Pa hosp.

rost- **Allen R. Shields**, co E, 26 NC, res Chatham Co & enl age 25 on 15 May 62, p & a until w right leg & capt Gettysburg 1-3 Jul 63, trans to Chester about 25 Jul 63, died 29 July 63 at Chester of exh. Following ampt of right leg.

CWPOWrec- K. Shields, co K, 6 NC, capt Gettysburg 4 July 63, died July 29 1863 (only info on K. Shields, casue of death not noted).

1912 book- Allen Shields, co E, 26 NC, died 29 July 63, buried Philadelphia Nat. Cem.

CWPOWrec- Allen Shields, co E, 26 NC, died 29 July 63 at Chester, Pa from exh. Following ampt of rt leg (four reconds on Allen).

note: K. Shields of 6 NC should be deleted.

36)-rost- Assistant Surgeon **William Ed. White**, Field and Staff, 7 NC, died 7 Nov 1861, place and cause of death not reported.

FO, 18 Nov 1861- Dr. **W. Edward White**, Assistant Surgeon, 7 NC, age 25, died Charlotte, NC Saturday last (note: prob 9 Nov 1861) of fever he took about six weeks ago at Carolina City.

37)-rost- Quartermaster Sergeant **John Willis**, Field and Staff, 7 NC, died at Orange CH prior to 15 Dec 1862, cause and exact date of death not reported.

FO, 20 Oct 1862- Quartermaster Sergeant John Willis, 7 NC, age 22 of Rockingham Co, died near Orange CH on 25 Aug 1862 of typhoid fever.

38)-rost-**George W. Millsaps**, co A, 7 NC, died 1 Sep 1864, place not reported.

Petersburg-**G. W. Milsaks**, co A, 7 NC, died Petersburg on 1 Sep 1864, burial Petersburg Fair Ground vicinity.

39)-rost- **William A. McClellan**, co B, 7 NC, rep in conf 4 Jun 62 at Fort Columbus, NY, died prior to 8 Dec 62, p & cause of death not rep.

CWPOWrec- William McClellan, co B, 7 NC, died 19 Jun 1862 at Fort Columbus, NY Harbor of typhoid fever.

40)-rost- **William T. Dula**, co C, 7 NC, capt Camp Vance 28 Jun 64 & reported in confinement at Camp Douglas Jan 65.

CWPOWrec- William T. Dula, conscript unassigned, capt Burk Co., NC 28 Jun 64, rec Camp Douglas 15 Jul 64, discharged 5 Jun 65.

41)-rost- **Bucharon Hussey**, co C, 7 NC, capt Salisbury 12 Apr 65 & conf Camp Chase 4 May 65, no further rec.

CWPOWrec- **Buchanan Hussey**, co C, 7 NC, capt Salisbury 12 Apr 65, released 13 Jun 65 by order 6 Jun 65 A.G.O.

42)-rost-Pvt **Benjamin T. Register**, co C, 7 NC, capt Hanover Court House, VA, reported in Federal hospital on 30 May, 1862 company records indicate he was killed at Hanover, no further rec.

interment.net-Yorktown Nat Cem-Pvt B. T. Register of 7 NC died 27 May 62, grave 1198.

note: shows photo of grave.

43)-rost-Pvt **P.L. Cogleman**, co. D, 7 NC, capt Gettysburg, confined Fort McHenry, trans to Fort Delaware in July 1863, no fur record.

rost-Pvt **P.L. Fogleman** of same unit, dest South Mountain in Jul 1863 and capt near Gettysburg around 3-5 July, 1863, confined Fort Delaware, trans to Point Lookout on Oct 15-18, 1863, took oath Jan 26, 1864 and joined US Services; however, adm to US hospital at Point Lookout on Jan 29, 1864 with 'remitten fever' and died Feb 24, 1864.

1860 Guilford County census has **Peter L. Fogleman**, born 1842.

note: P.L. Cogleman is the same person as Peter L. Fogleman and P. L. Cogleman of 7 NC should be deleted.

44)-rost- **Daniel Hedgecock**, co G, 7 NC, resided in Montgomery Co. and enlisted at age 28 on 17 May 1863, wounded in left leg at Gettysburg 3 July 63, company muster rolls indicate that he was captured at Gettysburg, however records of the Federal Provost Marshal do not substantiate that report. Present through Oct 64, however he was reported absent without leave during much of that period, paroled at Greensboro on 13 May 1865.

rost- D. Hitchcock, co G, 7 NC, captured at Gettysburg 3-5 July 63, conf at Ft Delaware until paroled and transferred to City Point where he was received 1 Aug 63, admitted to Richmond hospital 27 May 64, no further report.

CWPOWrec- Dan'l Hitchcock, co G, 7 NC, captured Gettysburg 3 July 63, received Ft Delaware 7 July 63, trans to City Point 30 July 63.

CWPOWrec- D. Hitchcock, co G, 7 NC, exchanged from Ft Delaware 31 July 1863.

note: Daniel Hedgecock and D./**Daniel Hitchcock** are the same soldier and D. Hitchcock of co. G, 7 NC should be deleted.

45)-rost-Sgt **William S. Jinkins**, co. G, 7 NC, born Chatham Co and res in Wake Co. Wounded and captured at Gettysburg — however, records of Federal Provost Marshall do not substantiate the report of his capt.

Wasted Valor by Gregory A. Coco, p 117. '..Lt. Abner R. Small of Union Forces came upon Sgt William Jinkins the day after Pickett's assault….I remember stopping by one poor fellow…his wants were few. 'Only a drink of water, I'm cold, so cold, won't you cover me up?. Could he write to his home? His father's name is **Robert Jenkins** and my name is Will'. Lt Small though he heard him say he belonged to the 7 NC and came from Chatham Co. His words falted into silence. I covered his face. The source for the book was *Road to Richmond*, by Abner R. Small, 1939, p 107

46)-rost-E. A. McGee, co G, 7 NC, capt at Gettysburg 3 July 63, conf at Ft Delaware until trans to Point Lookout 18 Oct 63, no further record.

rost- **Paschal A. McGeehee**, co G, 7 NC, born in Wake Co., enlisted in Wake at age 30 on 26 June 61, captured Gettysburg 3 July 63, conf Ft Delaware until trans to Point Lookout 15 Oct 63, died at Point Lookout 4 Jan 1864.

CWPOWrec- W. H. and E. A. McGee, co G, 7 NC, captured Gettysburg 5 July 63, W. H. McGee was exchanged 31 July 63.

CWPOWrec-P. A. McGee, co G, 7 NC, was trans to Point Lookout in Oct 63 and died there 4 Jan 1864.

1860 census Wake Co.- Paschell McGee age 29 and brother Obediah age 20; also William H. McGee age 28. No McGeehee in Wake County census.

note: E. A. McGee and Paschal A. McGeehee are the same soldier but E. A. McGee of co G, 7 NC should be deleted and Paschal A. McGeehee's name should be changed to **Paschal A. McGee.**

47)-rost- **Merrit D. Yates**, Corporal, co G, 7 NC, ….conf at Point Lookout until paroled and trans to Venus Point, Savannah River, Ga. Where he was rec 15 Nov 1864, for exchange.

CWPOWrec- M. D. Yates, 1st Sgt, co G, 7 NC, died of gs wound head on 6 May 1865 at 1 Div Hosp, 1 Army Corps, Register 4 AC.

note: Yates evidently rejoined his unit after his Nov 1864 released.

48)-rost- **David R. Winecoff**, co H, 7 NC, res in Cabarrus Co., enlisted age 28 on 17 Aug 61, capt Gettysburg 2 July 63, conf at Ft Delaware until trans to Point Lookout 15 Oct 63, died at Point Lookout 11 Jan 1864.

Rost- D. R. Winker, co H, 7 NC, captured Gettysburg 2 July 63, conf at Ft Delaware until trans to Point Lookout on 18 Oct 1863, no further records.

CWPOWrec- D. R. Winnekoffer, co H, 7 NC, capt Gettysburg 2 July 63, received at Ft Delaware on 6 July 1863.

note: believe David R. Winecoff and D. R. Winker, both of co H, 7 NC are the same soldier and D. R. Winker should be deleted.

49)-rost-miscellaneous section-**Giles H. Cooper**, 2nd Lt, 7 NC, capt n Richmond 28 Jun 1862, conf Fort Columbus, until trans to Fort Warren 8 Jul 1862. no further records.

CWPOWrec-Giles H. Cooper, 2nd Lt, 24 Va Vol, sent to Fort Monroe from Fort Warren, Boston 31 July 1862 to be exchange. Note: only one record stated 7 NC with at least three others stated 24 Va,

1850 Franklin Co., Va-Giles H. Cooper, age 17

1860 Franklin Co., Va-Giles H. Cooper, age 24

Amer. CW Soldiers- Giles Cooper, enl as Pvt on 11 June 1861 into co D, 24 Va, pro to full Corp, pro to full 2nd Lt 10 May 62, died of wounds as POW at Gettysburg 28 Sep 1863.

note: Giles H. Cooper of the 7 NC should be deleted as he was in the 24 Va. Vol.

50)-rost-**Elijah H. Holterson**, misc, 7 NC, name appears on an undated list of Confederate prisoners which states he was wounded in the left leg, no further records.

CWPOWrec- **E. H. Holterton**, 7 NC, died 20 Sept 62 at Sharpsburg of vulnis sclopst?

51)-rost-**John C. Dough**, co B, 8 NC, died Elmira on 22 Nov 64 or 2 Apr 65.

1912 book-Jno. C. Dough of co B, 8 NC died Elmira 22 Nov 64, grave 928

CWPOWrec-Jno. Dough died Elmira 22 Nov 1864.

note: see Thomas T. Dough next item.

52)-rost-**Thomas T. Dough**, co B, 8 NC died Elmira on 22 Nov 64 or 2 Apr 65.

1912 book-Thos. T. Dough of co B, 8 NC died Elmira 2 Apr 65, grave 2572

CWPOWrec- T. T. Dough, died Elmira 2 Apr 1865

note: see John C. Dough item above.

53)-rost-**Gabriel Barfield**, co E, 8 NC, enlisted 7 Aug 1861, present and accounted for until he died at home on 12 Mar 1862, cause of death not reported.

FO, 17 Mar 1862- Pvt **Gabriel Barefield**, co E, 8 NC, age 42 years and 6 months, in the fight at Roanoke Island, taken prisoner and released on parole with his fellow soldiers when he returned home, after one day at home he was confined to his bed and suffered severe pain for twelve days, died at his residence in Bladen Co. of Pleurisy on 12 Mar 1862.

note: with the newspaper account above he had to have been captured at Roanoke Island on 8 Feb 1862 and released from Elizabeth City on 21 Feb 1862.

54)-rost- **John B. Clark**, co E, 8 NC, died 10 Feb 1862, cause of death not reported.

FO, 24 Mar 1862- John B. Clark, Capt. Murchison's Co. (co E), 8 NC, died at Camp Raleigh on Roanoke Island on 10 Feb 1862 of typhoid fever.

55)-rost-**J. T. Furguson**, co E, 8 NC, trans fm hosp steamer 'Hero of Jersey' 2 Oct 64 to Gen Hosp, no further record.

VA web site-J. T. Furgerson, co E, 8 NC, d 1 Oct 64 in grave 4126 at City Point National Cemetery.

56)-rost-**John Patterson**, co E, 8 NC, paroled Elmira 11 Oct 64, trans to Venus Point, Savannah River, Ga and received for exchange 15 Nov 1864.

FO, 12 Ded 1864- John Patterson, 8 NC, the Richmond Ambulance Committee furnishes a list of soldiers who died in going to Savannah for exchange.

57)-rost-1ˢᵗ Lt. **Wellington D. Smith**, co G, 8 NC, prev in co G, 6 NC Sen Res, p & d enl in this co not reported, died Camp Chase 16 May 65, p & d captured and cause of death not reported.

CWPOWrec-1ˢᵗ Lt Wellington D. Smith, co G, 8 NC, capt Salisbury, NC 12 Apr 65, forward to Louisville, Ky 24 Mar 1865, trans to Camp Chase 2 May 1865, died Camp Chase 16 May 65 of typhoid Fever.

VA web site-W. D. Smith, CSA, died 16 May 65, buried Camp Chase Confederate Cemetery, sec O site 1968.

note: There was no Company (G) in the 8th NC Senior Reserves, should be Co G, 6th NC Senior Reserves.

58)-rost-Pvt **John A. Barrier**, co H, 8 NC, rep absent wounded or sick through 20 Jan 65.

1912 book-Pvt Jno. A. Barrier of co H, 8 NC died Elmira 14 Jan 65, grave 1462.

59)-rost- **Levi C. Barrier**, co H, 8 NC, capt Cold Harbor 1 Jun 64, trans to Elmira 12 Jul 64, Fed cemetery rec indicate he died at Elmira 23 Mar 65, however, Fed Provost Marshal state he was paroled at Elmira 11 Oct 64, trans to Venus Point, Savannah, Ga where he was rec 15 Nov 64 for exchange, no further rec.

rost- **Tobias A. Barrier**, co H, 8 NC, capt Cold Harbor 31 May 64, conf Pt Lookout until trans to Elmira 8 Jul 64, died Elmira 23 Mar 65 of pneumonia.

CWPOWrec- Levi C. Barrier, co H, 8 NC, capt Coal Harbor 31 May 64, rec at Elmira 11 July 64, died Elmira 23 Mar 65 of pneumonia, grave 1677, "on rolls T. A. Briner."

CWPOWrec- T. A. Barriere, co H, 8 NC, capt Gaines Mills 1 Jun 64, trans from Elmira to Point Lookout 14 Oct 64, trans to Aikins Landing 29 Oct 64 for exchanged.

note: Levi C. Barrier died at Elmira and Tobias A. Barrier was released.

60)-rost- **William A. Brown**, co H, 8 NC, died 9 Jan 1863 of typhoid fever, place of death not reported.

FO, 23 Feb 1863- William A. Brown, 8 NC, age 26, died at Camp Whiting near Wilmington of bronchitis. (no date given)

Cause of deaths that were not listed in the NC Roster - Volume IV

rank	name	co	unit	place of death	died	cause of death
Pvt	Ransom H. Duke	B	4	Point Lookout	8/8/64	scurvy
Pvt	James A. Lewis	C	4	Point Lookout	3/10/64	dropsy
Pvt	Thomas M. Lewis	C	4	Point Lookout	3/3/64	sconbutus/chr diarrhoea
Pvt	Peter Daniel Jones	D	4	Point Lookout	7/28/64	hospital gangrene
Pvt	William R. Rousley	E	4	Newport News	6/11/65	chronic diarrhoea
Pvt	Harrison Waters	E	4	Point Lookout	1/26/64	chronic diarrhoea
Pvt	J. H. Cranfield	G	4	Fort Monroe	6/15/65	chronic diarrhoea
2Lt	James E.M. Howard	I	4	Winchester	10/16/64	vulnus sclopst
Sgt	Foster Jarvis	I	4	Point Lookout	2/21/64	chronic diarrhoea
Pvt	Abner Prevett	I	4	Elmira	7/5/64	on passage fm Ft. Delaware
Pvt	Leroy C. Colley	K	4	Antietim	9/18/62	of wounds
Pvt	Nathan M. Brady	A	5	Washington	7/8/64	gs left thigh
Pvt	Simon W. Fowler	A	5	Fort Monroe	5/19/62	vulnus sclopst
Pvt	Nevil Gee	A	5	Fort Delaware	10/11/63	dysentery, chronic
Pvt	Josiah Johnson	A	5	Point Lookout	6/4/64	febris typhoides
Pvt	Jonathan H. Nickens	A	5	Washington	5/20/62	vulnus sclopst
Pvt	Jeremiah Tillman	A	5	Point Lookout	6/17/64	febris remit
Pvt	William H. Hare	B	5	Fort Monroe	5/24/62	vulnus sclopst
Sgt	Calvin Hays	B	5	Point Lookout	12/22/63	smallpox
Pvt	Richard A. Saunders	B	5	Gettysburg	7/21/63	gs thigh
Pvt	J.J. Jernigan	D	5	Point Lookout	1/4/64	smallpox
Pvt	Young J. Westbrook	D	5	Point Lookout	10/20/64	chronic diarrhoea
Pvt	Edmond F. Dick	F	5	Fort Delaware	10/4/63	lungs, inf of
Sgt	James F. Garrett	F	5	Fort Monroe	5/12/62	vulnus sclopst
Pvt	Aaron Hughes	F	5	Point Lookout	6/28/64	acute dysenteria
Pvt	Johnathan J. Leicester	F	5	Baltimore	5/27/62	vulnus sclopst
Pvt	Pleasant Ritchey	F	5	Point Lookout	7/8/64	chronic diarrhoea
Pvt	William Turner Stone	F	5	Fort Monroe	6/10/62	vulnus sclopst
Corp	Aquilla Todd	F	5	Frederick	12/11/62	vulnus sclopst
Pvt	Henry Dardin	G	5	Fort Monroe	5/17/62	vulnus sclopst
Pvt	William Dixon	G	5	Gettysburg	7/19/63	vertebrae, fract
Pvt	Joseph L. Petway	G	5	Fort Monroe	5/25/62	of wounds
Pvt	William Fanney	H	5	Fort Monroe	6/11/62	vulnus sclopst
Pvt	Thomas J. Jones	H	5	Baltimore	5/22/62	vulnus sclopst
Pvt	John Herbert	I	5	Baltimore	5/13/62	vulnus sclopst
Pvt	Thomas J. Johnson	I	5	Fort Monroe	5/18/62	vulnus sclopst
Pvt	Thomas B. Travis	I	5	Fort Monroe	5/12/62	gs wound/pneumonia
Pvt	J.M. Garver	K	5	Point Lookout	5/26/64	chronic diarrhoea
Pvt	J.C. Turner	K	5	Point Lookout	7/4/65	ascetis/dropsy

Pvt	Jesse Chambers	A	6	Fort Delaware	10/7/63	febris typhoid
Pvt	Nash Duke	B	6	Point Lookout	6/24/64	dysentery, acute
Pvt	Jacob W. Shamel	B	6	Columbus	11/27/64	smallpox/gangrene
Pvt	James Wright	B	6	Point Lookout	12/7/64	inf of liver, acute
Pvt	George W. Berry	D	6	Washington	11/10/63	variola
Pvt	Robert P. Howell	E	6	Point Lookout	11/5/63	chronic diarrhoea
Pvt	Jacob H. Smallwood	E	6	Gettysburg	7/29/63	gs arm & breast
Pvt	M.H. Carswell	F	6	Point Lookout	10/6/64	chronic diarrhoea
Pvt	John A. Gibson	F	6	Point Lookout	2/24/64	chronic diarrhoea
Pvt	George W. Moore	F	6	Gettysburg	7/5/63	of wounds
Pvt	Thomas R. Smart	G	6	Point Lookout	8/31/64	vulnus sclopst
Pvt	Wlilliam Chatham	H	6	Antietim	9/17/62	of wounds
Pvt	William B. Miles	H	6	Antietim	9/17/62	of wounds
Corp	Charles W. Rial	H	6	Washington	11/14/63	gs wound chest
Pvt	Wyatt Heart	K	6	Point Lookout	4/4/64	pneumonia
Pvt	Leonard Allman	B	7	Point Lookout	3/8/64	chronic diarrhoea
Pvt	Allison Furr	B	7	Point Lookout	1/6/64	chronic diarrhoea
Pvt	W.A. McPhetres	C	7	Antietim	-	vulnus sclopst
Corp	Henderson Bains	E	7	Gettysburg	7/26/63	gs r hip
Corp	James E. Batchelor	E	7	Point Lookout	7/31/64	acute diarrhoea
Pvt	Kinchen Liles	E	7	Point Lookout	8/25/64	acute dysenteria
Pvt	Eliphalet Worley	F	7	Fort Delaware	10/10/63	bronchitis, chronic
Sgt	Paschal A. McGee	G	7	Point Lookout	1/4/64	chronic diarrhoea
Pvt	Thomas Upchurch	G	7	Fort Delaware	10/1/63	smallpox
Pvt	Andrew J. Myers	H	7	Point Lookout	3/10/64	diarrhoea
Pvt	David A. Williams	I	7	Point Lookout	1/8/64	chronic diarrhoea
Pvt	Daniel J. McIntosh	K	7	Point Lookout	8/15/64	acute diarrhoea
Pvt	John C. Dough	B	8	Elmira	11/22/64	pneumonia
Pvt	John V. Doxy	B	8	Elmira	11/13/64	pneumonia
Pvt	G.M. Owens	B	8	Point Lookout	8/5/64	measles
Pvt	John Dorman	E	8	Elmira	9/9/64	typh fever/chronic diarr.
Pvt	Hyman Flake	G	8	Point Lookout	7/2/64	dephtheria
1Lt	Wellington D. Smith	G	8	Columbus	5/16/65	febris typhoides
Pvt	Furnifold Tripp	G	8	Point Lookout	7/6/64	measles
Pvt	Tobias A. Dry	H	8	Elmira	3/14/65	chronic diarrhoea
Pvt	Henry Penninger	H	8	Elmira	9/2/64	chr diarrhoea & rubiola
Pvt	Benjamin F. Canup	K	8	Baltimore	10/14/64	chronic diarrhoea
Pvt	Thomas W. Hess	K	8	Fort Monroe	10/7/64	of wounds
Pvt	Abraham Shaver	K	8	Fort Monroe	10/22/64	gs rt side

Additional Information and Amendments to the North Carolina Troops 1861-1865

Volume V - 11th to 15th Infantry and 13th Batt Infantry

1)-rost- **Patrick Johnson Lowrie**, F&S, 11 NC, died Wilmington 12 July 1862 of disease.

FO, 21 July 1862- P. J. Lowrie, died of bilious cholic, body sent to Ansonville.

2)-rost-Pvt R. P. Farthing of co A, 11 NC, died Camp Chase or Camp Dennison, Ohio 24 Apr 65, date and place of capt not reported.

CWPOWrec- R. P. Farthing, co A, 11 NC Batt, capt Watauga Co., NC 2 Feb 65, sent to Chattanooga than to Louisville, Ky by 19 Feb 65, trans to Camp Chase 3 Mar 65, died Camp Chase, Ohio 24 Apr 65 of pneumonia.

www.37nc.org/11th.php3-"Watauga Co, NC", 11 NC Battalion Home Guard had 2 companys (A and B), poss 200 to 250 men served in this unit. Only about 120 names have surfaced. "**Paul Farthing** and his nephew, **Reuben P. Farthing**, were captured 5 Feb 1865 at Camp Mast and died at Camp Chase, Ohio."

note: R. P. Farthing of 11 NC should be deleted and info added to future volume on 11 NC Battalion Home Guard.

3)-rost-Sgt Paul Farthing, co A, 11 NC, died Camp Chase, Ohio or Camp Dennison, Ohio 11 Apr 65, place and date capt not reported.

CWPOWrec- 1st Sgt Paul Farthing, co A, 11 Batt, capt Watauga Co., NC 2 Feb 65, sent to Chattanooga than to Louisville, Ky by 19 Feb 65, trans to Camp Chase 3 Mar 65, died Camp Chase 11 Apr 1865 of erysipelas.

www.37nc.org/11th.php3- "Watauga Co, NC", 11 NC Battalion Home Guard had 2 companys (A and B), poss 200 to 250 men served in this unit. Only about 120 names have surfaced. "Paul Farthing and his nephew, Reuben P. Farthing, were captured 5 Feb 1865 at Camp Mast and died at Camp Chase, Ohio."

note: Paul Farthing of 11 NC should be deleted and info added to future volume on 11 NC Battalion Home Guard

4)-rost- **M. Kinston**, co B, 11 NC, died 23 Apr 65 at Point Lookout, place & date capt. And cause of death not rep.

CW POW REC- M. Kinston, co B, 11 NC, capt Petersburg 27 Oct 64 and died of chronic dysentery.

5)-rost- J. A. Bowers, co C, 11 NC, died 5 May 65 Point Lookout, p & d capt not rep.

CWPOWrec- **John A. Bowers**, co C, 11 NC, capt 2 Apr 65 at Petersburg.

6)-rost-**Levi Carpenter**, co C, 11 NC, p & d enl not rep, d Camp Douglas 12 Dec 1864, p & d capt not rep.

CWPOWrec- Levi Carpenter, co C, 111 NC Batt, capt Bakersville, NC 28 July or 11 Sep 64, sent to Chattanooga 22 Sep 64, tran to Nashville, Louisville, rec at Camp Douglas 26 Nov 64, died 12 Dec 64 of debility.

note: Carpenter of 11 NC should be deleted.

7)-rost- **Seaborn McQuay**, co E, 11 NC, died at Wilmington in June 1862 of disease.
 FO, 28 July 1862- Solomon? McQuay, Capt. Nichols' co (co E), 11 NC, died at
    Wilmington on 1 July 1862 of typhoid fever.

8)-rost-Pvt **John R. Abernathy** tran fm co. A, 12 NC to co. B, 2 NC Cav and became
    Lt. in that unit. Also, Pvt F. D. Abernathy was in co B, 2 NC Cav.
 1860 Catawba Co. shows that John R. and Franklin D. Abernathy were brothers.

9)-rost-1Sgt **Robert B. Carr**, 1st co C, 12 NC, born Duplin Co, enl age 33 on 15 Apr
    61, company disbanded 18 Nov 61.
 rost-1st Lt Robert B. Carr, co A, 43 appointed 2nd Lt 6 Mar, 62, promoted 1st Lt 20 Mar
    62, w in left foot 3 Jul 63 at Gettys, capt in ambulance train 4 Jul 63.
 note: same soldier and data should be combined, add that Sgt Carr was the longest held
    Prisoner of War.

10)-rost-Elvis Green Adcock, co 2nd C, 12 NC.
 LMA-from Arlington, Elvis A. Adcock of 12 NC.
 CWPOWrec- **Elvis A. Adcock**, co C, 12 NC, died US C. H. Judiciary Sq. Washington,
    DC 30 May 64 of gs wound right lung and arm.

11)-rost- R. Evans, co F, 12 NC, died Petersburg on 11 Feb 1865.
 Petersburg- **Joseph Evans**, co F, 12 NC, died Petersburg on 6 Feb 1865, burial
    Petersburg Fair Ground Vicinity.

12)-rost- A. N. Boone, co G, 12 NC, enlisted Norfolk, Va 22 August 1862, present
    through February 1862.
 FO, 21 July 1862- **Augustus N. Boon**, co C, 12 NC, age 21 of Northampton Co., died
    of wounds received in battle of Malvern Hill on 1 July 1862.

13)-rost-D. W. Jones, co H (1st), 12 NC, died at Elmira on Dec 2, 1864.
 VA web site-Pvt **David W. Jones** died Elmira on Dec 2, 1864. grave 1009 in Woodlawn
    Nat Cem.

14)-rost- **James Fletcher**, co I, 12 NC, died on or about 10 Mar 1862 of measles. Place
    of death not reported.
 Haywood papers- James Fletcher of 11 NC, died 11 Apr 1862 in Raleigh hospital of
    Rubola and Bronchites. (had unit nr wrong, but feel that this is the same person.)

15)-rost- **George W. Harper**, co I, 12 NC, died 12 July 1862, place of death not
    reported.
 FO, 8 Sept 1862- George W. Harper, co I, 12 NC, died at Bird Island Hospital,
    Richmond on 12 July 1862.

16)-rost- Lt. **Simpson Latta**, co A, 13 Battalion NC, trans to co A, 66 NC October 1863. (note: Capt. **Joseph W. Latta** and 2ⁿᵈ Lt **James G. Latta** were trans to co A, 66 NC on same date.)

NCS, 26 August 1863- Lt. Sampson Latta, Capt. J. W. Latta's company (co A, 13 Batt NC), died at home in Persons Co. on 2 August 1863 of typhoid fever.

1860 census Orange Co., NC- Simpson Latta age 40.

note: Joseph W. and James G. Latta are noted in co A, 66 NC roster.

17)-rost-Corp L. H. Perry, co B, 13 NC capt Fort Fisher 15 Jan 65, died Elimra on 6 Jul 65.

rost-Corp **Levi H. Perry** of 3co B, 2 Arty, enl Bladen Co 26 Dec 61, capt Fort Fisher 15 Jan 65.

CWPOWrec- L. H. Perry, Corp, co B, 13 NC Batt, died Elmira 6 Jul 65 of chr diarr.

CWPOWrec- Elmira disposition of Prisoners' possessions- Levi H. Perry, one silver watch, transferred to him 2 July 1865.

note: 2n co B, 2 Arty was trans to co B, 13 Batt NC L. Arty on 4 Nov 1863. Levi H. Perry was first assigned to 2ⁿᵈ co B, 2 Arty and trans to the 13 Batt L. Arty. His POW records recorded him as being in co B, 13 NC Batt. His military info should be changed from 3ʳᵈ co B, 2 Arty to 2ⁿᵈ co B, 2 Arty with the statement that this unit transferred to the 13 Batt L.Arty. L. H. Perry of 13 NC should be deleted

18)-rost-Pvt **William W. Gordon**, co C, 13 NC, left sick at Yorktown on 3 May 62, company rec indicate that he was believed to have died in the hands of the enemy, no further records.

Interment.net-Yorktown Nat Cem-Pvt William W. Gordon of 13 NC died Mar 62, grave 1570.

note: Yorktown rec has March as death month, but believe they should have wrote down May vice March.

19)-rost- **Clarence D. Martin**, co C, 13 NC, died or was discharged in June 1862, no further records.

FO, 28 July 1862- **C. Dudley Martin**, co C, 13 NC, died at Kenansville, NC 27 June 1862 of typhoid fever.

20)-rost- N. R. Bell, co F, 13 NC, died at Gordonsville 15 Apr 1864, cause of death not reported.

NCS, 8 June 1864- N. R. Bell, 13 NC, died at Gordonsville 12 April 1864 of typhoid fever, from Yadkin County.

21)-rost- **William Barnes**, co H, 13 NC, died in Richmond Sept 11 or Oct 10, 1862.

Oakwood Cemetery Burial records- William Barnes, co H, 13 NC, buried Sep 11, 1862.

22)-rost- Colonel **Philetus W. Roberts**, F&S, 14 NC, died 5 July 1862, place and cause of death not reported.

FO, 14 July 1862- Col. P. W. Roberts, 14 NC, died 5 July 1862 at the residence of Mr. H. W. Tyler in Richmond of typhoid fever.

23)-rost- Lt Col. **George S. Lovejoy**, F&S, 14 NC, defeated for reelection when the regiment was reorganized on 26 April 1862, NC Adj Gen indicate he died 20 July 1862, no further records.

NCS, 23 July 1862- Col. George S. Lovejoy, 14 NC, had been in feeble health for some time and on this account compelled to retire, died at his father's residence in this city (Raleigh) on Sunday night last (20 July 1862.)

24)-rost-Pvt **Felix Scarlett**, co A, 14 NC, enl Wake Co age 20 on 16 Jun 62, capt Sharpsburg 17 Sep 62, died 12 Nov 62 of disease, place of death not reported.

Fort Delaware Society book-Pvt Felix Scarlet of co A, 14 NC died 12 Nov 62, also on Nat Archives tape 47.

25)-rost- **George L. Stanback**, co C, 14 NC, age 20 in 1861, killed at Bethesda Church in May 1864.

FO, 12 Sept 1864- George L. Stanback, born 25 March 1842, fell in battle of Bethesda Church on 30 May 1864.

26)-rost-**W. O. Dixon** of co D, 14 NC.

LMA-from Arlington, **William Dyon** of 14 NC, buried Oakwood Cem., Raleigh, NC.

27)-rost- **William Cooley**, co E, 14 NC, res Wake Co, enl 24 May 61, died Elmira 10 Jun 65.

rost- **Wesley Cooley**, co I, 43 NC, res Anson Co., NC, enl 9 May 62, capt Bethesda Ch, Va 30 May 1864, conf Pt Lookout 8 June 1864, trans to Elmira 9 July 1864, died Elmira 10 Jun 1865 of chr diarr.

VA site- Wesley Coley, died Elmira 10 June 65, buried grave 2888.

CWPOWrec- **Wm. C. Coley**, co E, 14 NC, capt Waterloo, Pa. 5 July 63, sent for exchange City Point 30 July 63.

CWPOWrec- C. Coolie, co I, 14 NC, capt Old Church 30 May 1864, died 10 June 1865 of chr diarr, (notation on end had): 'Collie Wesley real name'(on the next line down)

W. Coley, co I, 43 NC, capt Mechanisville 30 May 1864, rel 29 May 1865.

note: both were received at Elmira from Point Lookout 15 July 1864

CWPOWrec- Wesley Coley, co I, 43 NC, capt Old Church 30 May 64, joined Elmira 12 Jul 64, died Elmira 10 June 65 of chr diarrhoea, date of alteration 11 Jun 65,(in remarks) 'Coolie, C. 14 NC'.

1912 book- Wesley Coley, co I, 43 NC, died Elmira 10 June 1865, grave 2888

1860 Anson Co., census- **Wesley Coley** (20)

1850 Wake Co., census- Wesley Cooly (20)

1860 Wake Co., census- Wesley Cooley (30)

1860 Wake Co., census- William Cooley (20)

note: seems the Federal record keepers were confused about which Cooley died or released. In most of the records, they were on the same page, one line above the other. Too many variables to say which is which at this writing. The above data is for future researchers.

28)-rost- **J. M. Cranford**, co G, 14 NC, wounded right arm at Chancellorsville 1-3 May 1863, died in Montgomery Co., NC on 12 June 1863, Fayettevill Observer of 14 May 1863 stated one of his legs was amputated.

FO, 1 Feb 1864- **John Milton Crawford**, co G, 14 NC, age 23, wounded right arm at Chancellorsville, right arm amputated, conveyed to Richmond and took typhoid fever, his father took him home where he survived only a few days, died in Montgomery Co., NC on 12 June 1863.

1860 census Montgomery Co., NC- John Crawford, age 19.

note: change name from J. M. Cranford to John Milton Crawford.

29)-rost-W. H. Fort, co H, 14 NC, place & date of enl not reported, died at Elmira 18 Dec 1864, cause of death not reported.

Rost- **William H. Fort**, co H, 43 NC, res Anson Co., age 21 in 1862, capt Washington, DC 14 Jul 1864, 54ans to Elmira 23 Jul 64, died Elmira 18 Dec 1864 of pneumonia.

CWPOWrec-Pvt Wm H. Fort, Co H, 14 ('43' written above the '14') NC, capt Washington, DC on 14 Jul 1864, died of pnuenonia on 18 Dec 1864 at Elmira.

note: W. H. Fort of 14 NC should be deleted.

30)-rost- **James Harling**, co K, 14 NC, capt prior to 10 Jan 1864 when he was hosp at Pt Lookout with gunshot wound of left thigh, however, place and date wounded not rep, exh 27 Apr 1864, died Richmond hosp, Va 4 May 1864 of bronchitis.

CWPOWrec – James Harling, co K, 14 SC, capt Gettysburg 5 July 1863, trans to Bedloe's Island 24 Oct 1863, sent for exchange to City Point 27 Apr 1864.

CWSSY- F. L., James, Joseph, Lemuel, Rufus, T. Harling all in co K, 14 SC Inf.

1860 census Edgefield Co., SC- James Harling, age 21.

note: delete James Harling of co K, 14 NC.

31)-rost- **Jacob M. Rogers**, co K, 14 NC, died in Richmond 14-15 July 1862 of disease.

NCS, 23 July 1862- Jacob M. Rogers, co K, 14 NC, died Winder Hosp in Richmond of brain fever, remains brought to Raleigh.

32)-rost- **John Bowers**, co A, 15 NC, died on Sep 1, 1862. Place of death not reported.

Oakwood Cemetery Burial records- John Bowers, co A, 15 NC, buried Sep 1, 1862.

note- add died in Richmond, Va.

33)-rost- John T. Brown, co A, 15 NC.

Oakwood Cemetery Burial records- **John Thomas Brown**, co A, 15 NC.

note: add died in Richmond, Va.

34)-rost- Captain **Samuel T. Stancell**, co A, 15 NC, wounded at Lee's Mill on 16 April 1862, defeated for reelection when the regt was reorganized on 2 May 1862.

NCS, 23 April 1862- Capt. Stancil, co A, 15 NC, "we regret to learn from the Petersburg Express that Capt. Stancil has died of wounds he received in the Battle of Lee's Mills." (no death date given)

35)-rost- **J. J. Speck**, co D, 15 NC, died at Williamsburg on 15 Nov 1861.

BDL-**John Speck**, co D, 5 NC, died at African Church, 4 Nov 1861 $10 for making coffin, $2 for digging grave, $1 to convenyance to the ground, buried in grave 1 of the North Carolina row at (Cedar Grove Cemetery) Williamsburg, Virginia.

note: John Speck probably died on 3 Nov 1861 vice 15 Nov 1861 since his burial records were on 4 Nov 1861.

36)-rost- **Willie Perry, Jr.**, co E, 15 NC, died 19 July 1862, place of death not reported.

NCS, 13 Aug 1862- Capt. Willie Perry, 15 NC, died in Richmond on 19 July 1862.

37)-rost- **Henry B. Holland**, co F, 15 NC, died 5 October 1861, place of death not reported.

FO, 18 Nov 1861- Henry B. Holland, died in Wake Co., NC on 5 October 1861, he was taken sick at Yorktown, lingered there four months, when he was brought back home and died after about 10 days.

38)-rost-**Thomas B. Wiggins**, co F, 15 NC, died 15 Nov 1861, place of death not reported.

BDL- T. B. Wiggins, co F, 5 NC, died at the African Church, 16 Nov 1861 $10 for making coffin, $2 for digging grave, $1 to convenyance to the ground, buried in grave 4 of the North Carolina row at (Cedar Grove Cemetery) Williamsburg, Virginia.

39)-rost-**John Medley**, co K, 15 NC, died 15 Nov 1861, place of death not reported.

BDL- John Medley, co F, 5 NC, died at the hospital, 5 Nov 1861 $10 for making coffin, $2 for digging grave, $1 to convenyance to the ground, buried in grave 2 of the North Carolina row at (Cedar Grove Cemetery) Williamsburg, Virginia.

40)-rost- J. T. McClenahan, co M, 15 NC, died 2 July 1862

NCS, 27 Aug 1862- James T. McClenahan, Chatham Rifles (co M), 15 NC, died 2 July 1862.

Family Tree- **James Taylor McClenahan**, died 2 Jul 1862, burial St. Bartholomew's Episcopal Church Cem., Pittsboro, NC (see 'Gravesites of Chatham County".)

Cause of deaths that were not listed in the NC Roster - Volume V

rank	name	co	unit	place of death	died	cause of death
Pvt	John R. Bigham	A	11	Point Lookout	8/30/64	vulnus sclopst
Pvt	Thomas M. Hendersoon	A	11	Point Lookout	2/9/64	chronic diarrhoea
Pvt	Robert F. McGinn	A	11	Point Lookout	2/2/64	chronic diarrhoea
Pvt	Sidney A. McGinnis	A	11	Point Lookout	2/15/64	dysenteria, chronic
Pvt	N.C.H. Orr	A	11	Point Lookout	9/30/64	chronic diarrhoea
Pvt	John S. Smith	A	11	Gettysburg	7/15/63	of wounds
Pvt	John J. Keller	B	11	Point Lookout	12/21/63	smallpox
Pvt	David E. Moody	B	11	Columbus	5/31/65	pneumonia
Pvt	Alexander Stone	E	11	Point Lookout	1/28/64	syncope/acute diarrhoea
Sgt	Robert Leroy Wilson	E	11	Point Lookout	4/10/65	chronic diarrhoea
Corp	James E. Creecy	F	11	Point Lookout	2/15/64	febris congestion
Pvt	Henry Floyd	F	11	Fort Delaware	10/6/63	chronic diarrhoea
Pvt	B.F. Goodwin	F	11	Point Lookout	1/6/64	chronic diarrhoea
Pvt	Sidney Bolick	I	11	Point Lookout	10/30/63	pneumonia
Pvt	David Carpenter	I	11	Point Lookout	3/19/64	chronic diarrhoea
Pvt	B. Monroe Hovis	I	11	Point Lookout	5/3/64	chronic diarrhoea
Pvt	Elijah Sigman	I	11	Point Lookout	11/26/63	chronic diarrhoea
Pvt	Perry Wood	I	11	Point Lookout	5/19/65	chronic diarrhoea
Pvt	Monroe Morris	K	11	Point Lookout	2/2/64	pneumonia
Pvt	Rufus P. Weathers	E	12	Baltimore	10/27/64	chronic diarrhoea
Pvt	William E. Darnell	F	12	Point Lookout	8/7/64	dysenteria, acute
Pvt	Abraham Gossett	H	12	Point Lookout	4/19/65	fever, cong. Int.
Pvt	R.B. Fooshee	E	13	Fort Delaware	9/7/63	chr. Dysent/bronchitis, acute
Pvt	William Stier	I	13	Point Lookout	6/22/64	acute diarrhoea
Pvt	George Coghill	K	13	Point Lookout	6/21/64	febris typhoid
Sgt	Curtis Hardy	A	14	Antietim	10/16/62	of wounds
Pvt	Charles E. Harriss	A	14	Point Lookout	2/6/64	bronchitis
Corp	Walter J. Moore	B	14	Point Lookout	6/13/64	chronic diarrhoea
Pvt	W.S. Adderton	D	14	Point Lookout	10/30/64	chronic diarrhoea
Pvt	William R. Beasley	K	14	Point Lookout	1/12/64	chronic diarrhoea
Pvt	Joespeh E. Moore	K	14	Winchester	12/4/64	gs w lungs
Pvt	Elisha Phelps	A	15	Elmira	9/4/64	chr diarrhoea & scorbuitis
Pvt	William Conder	B	15	Point Lookout	2/19/64	chronic diarrhoea
Pvt	Amos Miller	F	15	Point Lookout	3/13/64	diarrhoea
Pvt	Samuel A. Stewart	H	15	Point Lookout	2/23/64	chronic diarrhoea
Pvt	William Wagoner	H	15	Point Lookout	12/24/63	chronic diarrhoea
Pvt	W.W. Black	I	15	Point Lookout	7/21/64	acute dysenteria
Pvt	Willie Johnson	I	15	Point Lookout	11/31/63	pneumonia
Pvt	Ambrose Huneycut	K	15	Burkittsville	11/21/62	of wounds
Pvt	Bryant Jarvis	K	15	Point Lookout	3/17/64	diarrhoea

Additional Information and Amendments to the North Carolina Troops 1861-1865

Volume VI - 16th - 18th and 20th - 21st Infantry

1)-rost- 1Sgt **George W. Koone**, co D, 16 NC, wounded & captured Seven Pines 31 May 62, hosp at Ft Monroe & rt leg ampt, died of wounds, place and date of death not reported.

CWPOWrec- Sgt. G. W. Koon, co D, 16 NC, died Mill Creek, Va 12 Sept 1862 of Vulnis Sclopt?

2)-rost- **L. Dowe Alexander**, co F, 16 NC, died on or about 10 Feb 1864, place of death not reported. **Erasmus B. Alexander** noted in same unit.

FO, 21 March 1864- L. D. Alexander, co F, 16 NC, died in Buncombe Co., NC on 16 Feb 1864, age 29 years, 9 months and 15 days

1850 census Buncombe Co., NC- Erasmus and **Lorenzo D. Alexander** (brothers.)

3)-rost-**William Johnson**, co F, 16 NC, born Va, res Mabinsville, Place and date enl not reported, capt unk date and d unk 3 Jan 63 of variola confluent, age 23.

rost-**William G. Johnston**, of co F, 6, enl Alamance age 18, Jun 25, 63, w l thigh & capt Rappahannock Station, Va 7 Nov 63. Adm hosp Washington 12 Nov 63 & trans Kalorama Hosp, Washington 23 Dec 63. No fur rec.

CWPOWrec- Wm A. Johnston, co F, 16 NC, died Kalorama Gen hosp, Washington, DC on 3 Jan 1864 of variola confluent.

note: the correct unit prob co F, 6 NC.

4)-rost-Pvt **J. C. Ryan**, co L, 16 NC, no place and date of enl, capt Falling Waters, Md 14 Jul 63, conf Old Capitol Prison, Washington, DC, trans 9 Aug 63 to Point Lookout, trans 16 Aug 63 to Elmira, died 17 Spe 64 at Elmira.

rost-Pvt **John C. Rhyne**, co M, 16 NC, res Gaston Co, enl age 22 in 1861 capt Falling Waters 14 Jul 63, no Federal Provost Marshall records, never rejoined company, no further records.

1912 book-Pvt J. C. Ryan, co M, 16 NC died 17 Sep 64 Elmira, grave 317.

1860 Gaston Co., NC census- two John Rhyne at age 20.

note: has to be company M, as co L was trans 5 Oct 62 to co E, Thomas Legion.

note: data from both records should be combined as John C. Rhyne of co M, 16 NC and J. C. Ryan of co L, 16 NC should be deleted.

5)-rost-**Ben F. Abernathy**, co M, 16 NC, died in April 1862, place of death not reported.

LibVa-Alberthanetty, no unit listed, died at Ashland, Va 22 Apr 1862, buried in Woodland Cem., Ashland, Va.

6)-rost-Pvt **James Kiser**, co M, 16 NC, capt prior to 1 Sep 63, died either at Fort Delawara 23 Aug 63 or Penn. On 1 Oct 63.

1912 book-Pvt **Jas. Keyser** of co C, 16 NC died 23 Aug 63 at Fort Delaware, bur Finn's Point, NJ.

CWPOWrec- Jas. Keyser, co C, 16 NC, capt Gettysburg 4 July 63, died Ft Delaware 23 Aug 63 of general debilty.

7)-rost-Pvt **John C. Rhyne**, co M, 16 NC, res Gaston Co, enl age 22 in 1861 capt Falling Waters 14 Jul 63, no Federal Provost Marshall records, never rejoined company, no further records.

rost-Pvt **J. C. Ryan**, co L, 16 NC, no place and date of enl, capt Falling Waters, Md 14 Jul 63, conf Old Capitol Prison, Washington, DC, trans 9 Aug 63 to Point Lookout, trans 16 Aug 63 to Elmira, died 17 Spe 64 at Elmira.

1912 book-Pvt J. C. Ryan, co M, 16 NC died 17 Sep 64 Elmira, grave 317.

1860 Gaston Co., NC census- two John Rhyne at age 20.

note: has to be company M, as co L was trans 5 Oct 62 to co E, Thomas Legion.

note: data from both records should be combined as John C. Rhyne of co M, 16 NC and J. C. Ryan of co L, 16 NC should be deleted.

8)-rost-Pvt **William Taylor**, co A, 17, capt in hosp at Raleigh on 13 Apr 65, no further records.

LMA-William Taylor of 17 NC died 22 Apr 65, buried grave 238 in Oakwood Cem., Raleigh, NC.

9)-rost-Pvt **McG. Roberson**, 1st co F, 17 NC, Martin Co. labor, enl 1 May 61, died 10 Oct 61, place and cause of death not reported.

1912 book-Pvt McG. Roberson of co F, 7 NC died 11 Oct 61 (New York Harbor) and buried in grave 4446 in Cypress Hills Nat Cem in Brooklyn, NY.

note: name is **McG Robason** in 1850 and 1860 Martin Co., NC census.

10)-rost-Pvt **David L. Rogerson**, 1st co F, 17 NC, Martin Co, labor, enl 1 May 61, died 8 Oct 61, place and cause of death not reported.

1912 book-David L. Rogerson, co F, 7 NC, died 8 Oct 1861 (New York Harbor) and buried in grave 4445 in Cypress Hills Nat Cem in Brooklyn, NY.

11)-rost-Pvt **Hosea G. Blount**, 1st Co H, 17 NC.
State Troops by Mast- Hosea Grey Blount.

12)-rost-**Joseph R. Rawls**, co H, 17 NC, rep in hosp in Greensboro 1 Mar 65.
LMA-J. Rawls of co A, 17, grave 96, reburied from Mordecai's land.

13)-rost-**W. H. Johnson**, co L, 17 NC, court mar & sent to death; however sent commuted, rep in confinement at Castle Thunder Prison, Richmond 15 Mar 1865.
LMA-W. H. Johnson of co L, 17 NC, no date, grave 236. reburied from Mordecai's land.

14)-rost-Pvt **Gerhard D. Hackeman**, co A, 18 NC w and capt Hanover Court House, Va, died 1 Jun 62 at Yorktown of wounds.

interment.net-Yorktown Nat Cem-Pvt Gerhard D. Hackeman of 18 NC died 1 Jun 62, grave 1361 in Yorktown National Cemetery.

15)-rost-1st Lt **George A. Johnston**, co A, 18 NC w and c Hanover Court House, Va on 27 May 1862, died in hands of the enemy of wounds, place and date of death not reported.
Interment.net-Yorktown Nat Cem-1st Lt George A. Johnston of 18 NC died 9 Jun 62, grave 1048 in Yorktown National Cemetery.

16)-rost- **J. M. Thomas**, co A, 18 NC, capt by enemy in April 1865, died Hart's Island 21 May 1865.
CWPOWrec- J. M. Thomas, co A, 18 NC, capt Marlboro on 28 March 1865, died 21 May 1865.

17)-rost-**Samuel Wilkinson**, co B, 18 NC, p & d enlistment not reported. Rec of Fed Provost Marshal indicate he d at Elmira Jan 30, 1865.
rost-Samuel Wilkerson, co B, 1 NC, res Wilkes Co & enl Wake age 20 on May 31, 1861, capt Spotsylvania May 12, 1864. conf Point Lookout until trans to Elmira Aug 6, 1864, d Elmira Jun 30, 1865 of chronic diarrhea.
VA web site-Samuel Wilkinson, Pvt CSA, d 30 Jan 65, grave 1813 in Elmira.
note: deaths at Elmira of Jan to Mar 65 in grave series 17..-18.. range, while deaths of Apr-Jun 65 are in 28.. grave range. Delete Samuel Wilkinson of D, 18 NC and change death date to Jan 30, 1865 for him in co B, 1 NC.

18)-rost-**William K. Gore**, co C, 18 NC, died 1 Sept 1862 of wounds, place of death not reported.
FO, 15 Sept 1862-Captain William K. Gore, Co C, 19 NC (note:should be 18 NC), died at his residence in Columbus Co. on 1 Sept 1862 of putrid sore throat, he was wounded in the battle of Slush? Church, Mechanicsville, Gaines Mills, and Frazier's Farm, in which last he was severely wounded in the thigh.

19)-rost-Pvt **Wallace W. Long**, co C, 18 NC w and c Hanover Court House, Va, died in the hands of the enemy of wounds, place and date of death not reported.
Interment.net-Yorktown Nat Cem-Pvt W. W. Long of 18 NC died 25 Jun 62, grave 1080 in Yorktown National Cemetery.

20)-rost-Pvt E. J. Britt, co D, 18 NC wounded and capt 27 May 62 Hanover Court House, Va, died of wounds, place and date of death not reported.
Interment.net, Yorktown Nat Cem-Pvt **Everett J. Brett** of 18 NC died 27 May 62, grave 1212 in Yorktown National Cemetery.

21)-rost-Pvt **James A. Evans**, co D, 18 NC, enl 9 Oct 61, w Fredericksburg, capt Spotts, conf Point Lookout, trans to Elmira 3 Aug 64, died Elmira 28 Dec 64.
rost-Pvt J. A. Evans, co I, 18 NC died 28 Dec 64 at Elmira.

note: J. A. Evans of co I, 18 NC should be deleted.

22)-rost- **Miles Fox**, co D, 18 NC, died in Va prior to 6 Feb 64.
note: buried in Emory, Virginia with listed death date 8 Feb 1863.

23)-rost-Pvt **George F. De Bouse**, co E, 18 NC wounded and capt 27 May 62 Hanover
Court House, Va, died of wounds, place and date of death not reported.
Interment.net-Yorktown Nat Cem-Pvt George F. DeBouse of 18 NC died 15 Jun 62,
grave 1359 in Yorktown National Cemetery.

24)-rost-Pvt **Thomas Waters**, co F, 18 NC, capt Spotsylvania CH 12 May 64, pension
rec indicated he dead at Point Lookout, date and cause of death not reported.
CWPOWrec- no Thomas Waters of the 18 was found in the Prisoners of War records,
the only one close is Pvt Thos Waters of co C, 61 NC, capt Petersburg 22 July 64,
died Point Lookout 14 Aug 64 of inf. of lungs (but no Thomas Waters was found in
the NC Roster for the 61st NC.)

25)-rost-Pvt **William H. McNeill**, co F, 18 NC, w and c Hanover Court House, Va, died
8 Jun 62 at Yorktown of wounds.
Interment.net-Yorktown Nat Cem-Pvt William H. McNeil of 18 NC died 14 Jun 62,
grave 1057 in Yorktown National Cemetery.

26)-rost-Corp **Gabriel R. Lilly**, co H, 18 NC w and c Hanover Court House, Va, died
of wounds, place and date of death not reported.
Interment.net-Yorktown Nat Cem-Cpl Gabriel R. Lilly of 18 NC died 27 May 62, grave
1489 in Yorktown National Cemetery.

27)-rost-Pvt **John Sibbit**, co H, 18 NC, w and c Hanover Court House, Va, died in hosp
at Yorktown 11 Jun 62 of wounds.
Interment.net-Yorktown Nat Cem-Pvt John Sibbet of 18 NC died 11 Jun 62, grave
1233 in Yorktown National Cemetery.

28)-rost- Sgt. **Thomas P. Bryan**, co I, 18 NC, killed at Chancellorsville 3 May 1863.
FO, 13 May 1863- Sgt. Thomas Bryan, co I, 18 NC, died near Fredericksburg 9 May
1863 of wounds.

29)-rost-Pvt J. A. Evans, co I, 18 NC died 28 Dec 64 at Elmira.
rost-Pvt **James A. Evans** of co D, 18 NC, enl 9 Oct 61, w Fredericksburg, capt Spotts,
conf Point Lookout, trans to Elmira 3 Aug 64, died Elmira 28 Dec 64.
note: J. A. Evans of co I, 18 NC should be deleted.

30)-rost- **J. M. Wagoner**, co K, 18 NC, p & a until sent to hosp 1 Oct 1862, never rtn
to duty.
CWPOWrec- **John Wagoner**, co K, 18 NC, died 23 Oct 1862 at Winchester, Va.

31)-rost- **George W. Barrier**, co B, 20 NC, res Cabarrus Co, enl 29 Mar 62, w in thigh & capt at Gettysburg 1-3 Jul 63, conf at various Federal hosp until paroled and trans to City Point 20 Mar 64 for exchange.

rost- **S. W. Barrier**, co B, 23 NC, place, enlistment, promotion rec not reported, w & c Gettysburg 1 July 63, rep in hosp at Gettysburg 10 Aug 63, no further records.

CWPOWrec- S. W. Barrier, co B, 23 NC, capt Gettysburg 1 July 63, trans to West Bldg Baltimore on 15 Nov 63.

CWPOWrec- G. W. Barrier, co B, 20 NC, capt Gettysburg 4 Jul 63, rel fm US hospital West's Bldg Baltimore to City Point 10 Jan 64, sent for exchange to City Point 17 Mar 64.

note: believe this is the same person and George W. Barrier of co B, 20 NC is the correct soldier.

32)-rost- **J. Neel**, co B, 20 NC, place and date of enlistment not report, capt Mine Run, Va 3 Dec 63, died Old Capital Prison, Washington, DC, 9 Apr 64, cause of death not reported.

rost- **Isaiah Neally**, co D, 20 NC, born in Brunswick Co, enl at age 40 in 61, capt Mine Run, Va 3 Dec 63, died Washington, DC 24 Dec 63 of pneumonia.

1912 book- Isaiah Neally, co D, 20, died 9 Apr 64 and buried in the Congressional Cemetery in Washington, DC, grave 209 r 95.

note: J. Neel of co B, 20 NC should be deleted and the death date for Isaiah Neally of Co D, 20 NC should be change to 9 Apr 64.

33)-rost-**John Henry May**, co C, 20 NC, capt Ft Stedman, d 26 Mar 65, place of death not reported.

City Point National Cemetery- C. May, co C, 20 NC, died 26 Mar 65 in grave 3656.

34)-rost- **Isaiah Neally**, co D, 20 NC, born in Brunswick Co, enl at age 40 in 61, capt Mine Run, Va 3 Dec 63, died Washington, DC 24 Dec 63 of pneumonia.

rost- **J. Neel**, co B, 20 NC, place and date of enlistment not report, capt Mine Run, Va 3 Dec 63, died Old Capital Prison, Washington, DC 9 Apr 64, cause of death not reported.

1912 book- Isaiah Neally, co D, 20, died 9 Apr 64 and buried in the Congressional Cemetery in Washington, DC, grave 209 r 95.

note: J. Neel of co B, 20 NC should be deleted and the death date for Isaiah Neally of Co D, 20 NC should be change to 9 Apr 64.

35)-rost-Pvt **Amos Bassnight**, co E, 20 NC capt at Gettysburg, conf at Fort Delaware, apparently released at Ft. Delaware after taken oath.

1912 book-Pvt Amos Bassnight, co F, 11 NC, died 6 Oct 63 at Fort Delaware, bur Finn's Point, NJ.

CWPOWrec- Amos Basnight, co E, 20 NC, capt Gettysburg 1 July 63, died Elmira 6 Oct 63 of chronic diarrhoea, 'recruit in Cavalry not mustered' (while the 1912 book stated 'co F, 11 NC', one prisoner of war record had Amos Basnight with his unit blank and the line above him had Henry Floyd of co F, 11 NC, plus they both died on 6 Oct 63. Floyd is also listed in the 1912 book.)

36)-rost- **William Sadler**, co E, 20 NC, p & enl not rep, conf Elmira, died 19 Jan 65 (only records noted.)

CWPOW rec-William Sadler, co E, 20 SC, several records in POW file, capt Petersburg 31 Jul 64 died 19 Jan 65.

note- delete William Sadler of co E, 20 NC.

37)-rost- **Isaac Stricklin**, co H, 20 NC, wounded and captured at Hagerstown, Md on or about 7 Jul 63, died at Hagerstown or at Winchester, Va on or about 31 July 63 of wounds.

CWPOWrec- **Isaac Strickland**, co A, 20 NC, captured Winchester Hospital on 30 July 1863 and died 31 July 1863.

note: delete capt Hagerstown on 7 Jul 63 and died at Hagerstown on 31 July 63.

38)-rost-Pvt **Calton Tanner**, co I, 20 NC, res Sampson Co., enl Fort Johnston 61, capt Getts 1-3- Jul, died Fort Delaware 10 Jul 64.

rost-Pvt C. Tanner, co I, 6 NC, p & d enl unknown, capt Spots 12 May 64, died Fort Delaware 10 Jul 64.

CWPOWrec- C. Tanner, co I, 6 NC, capt Spotsylvania 12 May 64, died Fort Delaware 10 July 64 of chronic diarrhea.

CWPOWrec- C. Tanner, co I, 20 NC, capt Gettysburg 4 July 1863, Ft Delaware rec from Fort Wood, NY, died 10 July 1864 of chr diarrhea, buried Jersey Shore.

note: in CWPOW records only one item of Tanner in the 6th and seven of Tanner in the 20th. The item with the 6th NC had an 'x' beside 'Spottsylavia, Va' in the captured column. All items stated that Tanner died 10 July 1864 of chronic diarrhea at Fort Delaware.

note: based on the above notes C. Tanner of co I, 6 NC should be deleted.

39)-rost-**Doctor G. Fields**, co K, 20 NC. Capt Wilderness, d 8 Mar 65 of disease, place of death not rep.

LMA-D.G. Fields of co K, 20 NC, d 18 Mar 1865, grave 27 Oakwood Cem., Raleigh, NC.

40)-rost- **Daniel H. Baldwin**, co F, 21 NC, reported in his company as POW Sep-Oct 64, Fed Provost Marshal do no indicate he was POW, in company rec as POW through Feb 1865.

CWPOWrec- Daniel Baldwin, co F, 21 NC, died 1 Oct 1864 in 6th Corps Hosp with gun shot wound.

41)-rost- **Archibald B. Wagner**, co F, 21 NC, res Stokes Co, enl age 19 on 29 May 61, P&A until capt Spotsylvania CH 22 May 64, conf at Pt Lookout. No further records, John Wagner in same unit age 22 when enl same day as Archibald rost- **Archibald B. Wagoner**, co F, 26 NC, born at 'Davis', occ farmer prior to enl Wake Co 30 Nov 63. P&A until capt North Anna River, Va 22 May 64, conf Pt Lookout until released 12 Oct 64 after joining US Army, assigned to co A, 4 US Vol Inf., Alex Wagner in same unit.

1850 Davie Co census- John (1839) and Archibald (1843) sons of Aaron and Susannah Wagner.

1860 Stokes co census- Arch (1842) in same parents household.

CWPOW records- A. B. Wagner, co F, 26 (3 records noted) or 21 (1 record noted) NC, capt North Anna on 22 May 64, arr 30 May 64 to Pt Lookout from Port Royal, joined US Service 12 Oct 64. (3 CWPOW rec had Archibald in the 26th and only one had 21st).

note: Believe Archibald B. Wagner same person noted in the 21st and 26th, but which unit is correct?

42)-rost- 2nd Lt. **William H. Adams**, co H, 21 NC, died 22 Aug 1861, place not reported.

FO, 9 Sep 1861- Lt. W. H. Adams, 'Mountain Tigers', 11 NC, died Camp Hardee near Falls Church on 22 ult. (22 August 1861.)

43)-rost- **Miles Wilburn**, co H, 21 NC, captured by the enemy on an unspecified date.

CWPOWrec- Miles Wilburn, co H, 21 NC, captured Gettysburg 4 July 63.

44)-rost-**John A. Fryar**, co M, 21 NC, capt Ft Stedman, 31 Mar 65, place of death not reported.

City Point National Cemetery- J. Fryar, co M, 21 NC, died 31 May 1865 in grave 3755.

45)-rost-Pvt **Joshua Joyce**, co M, 21 NC, res Stokes Co, enl age 34 on 8 Aug 62, capt Gettys 3 Jul 63, conf Fort Delaware where he died, date and cause of death not reported. See above item.

CWPOWrec- J. Joyce, co C/F, 21 NC, capt Gettysburg 3 July 63, died Fort Delaware 20 Sept 63 of bronchitis chr. (one record had J. Joyce, co M, 31 NC, capt Gettysburg July 63.)

46)-rost- (no name), Co M. 21 NC, 'Guilford Dixie Boys', in 1st battle of Manassas on 21 July 1861.

FO, 21 April 1862- **John M. Trotter**, 'Dixie Boys', died in Richmond, Va on 27 Feb 1862 of typhoid fever, age 24 and from Guilford Co., Mr. Trotter was one of the 'Dixie Boys' and was in the great battle of the 21st July last.

1860 census Guilford Co.,- John M. Trotter, age 25.

note: add John M. Trotter to co. M. 21 NC.

Cause of deaths that were not listed in the NC Roster - Volume VI

rank	name	co	unit	place of death	died	cause of death
Pvt	Bartley Y. Daily	C	16	Point Lookout	6/22/64	typhoid fever
Pvt	Samuel S. Robinson	C	16	Point Lookout	8/29/64	erysipelas
Pvt	Thomas J. Anders	D	16	Point Lookout	8/30/64	chronic diarrhoea
Pvt	John A. Green	F	16	Point Lookout	2/10/65	scurvy & chr. Diarrhoea
Pvt	E. H. Joiner	F	16	Petersburg	4/13/65	gs cranium
Pvt	J.P. Harris	G	16	Point Lookout	8/14/64	dropsy of chest
Pvt	John Amick	H	16	Fort Delaware	7/25/63	chronic diarrhoea
Pvt	Isaac W. Layton	H	16	Fort Delaware	9/25/63	bromchitis, chr./acute diarrhoea
Pvt	James Bibbey	K	16	Point Lookout	6/12/64	febris remittens
Pvt	William Melton	K	16	Point Lookout	10/24/64	chronic diarrhoea
Pvt	John C. Rhyne	M	16	Elmira	9/17/64	chronic diarrhoea
Sgt	John N. Roberts	M	16	Point Lookout	12/25/63	pneumonia
Pvt	Abraham K. Copening	C	18	Point Lookout	9/30/64	chronic diarrhoea
Pvt	Alexander McLellan	D	18	Point Lookout	7/19/64	acute diarrhoea
Pvt	Thaddeus D. Malpass	E	18	Elmira	11/23/64	hospital gangrene
Pvt	Amos W. Roper	F	18	Point Lookout	8/4/64	dysentery, acute
Corp	George M. Matheny	G	18	Point Lookout	9/16/64	acute dypenteria
Sgt	Frederick K. Nash	G	18	Point Lookout	8/2/64	dysenteria, acute
Pvt	James L. Trent	G	18	Point Lookout	8/26/64	measles
Pvt	Wesley Levi Bumgarner	H	18	Point Lookout	8/15/64	chronic diarrhoea
Mus	Joseph A. Atwell	B	20	Petersburg	4/6/65	amp of thigh/typhoid fever
Pvt	George W. Powell	C	20	Point Lookout	8/11/64	acute diarrhoea
Pvt	Samuel Cockrell	D	20	Point Lookout	4/5/64	diarrhoea
Pvt	Owen Duncan	D	20	Fort Delaware	10/12/63	febris typhoides
Pvt	Blythe Hinson	D	20	Point Lookout	10/31/63	chronic diarrhoea
Pvt	Amos Bassnight	E	20	Fort Delaware	10/6/63	chronic diarrhoea
Pvt	John C. Starr	E	20	Fort Delaware	10/4/63	chronic diarrhoea
Pvt	Jesse F. Denning	H	20	Point Lookout	7/17/64	febris typhoides
1Sgt	Elijah Gregory	H	20	Point Lookout	8/2/64	chronic diarrhoea
Pvt	Ransom G. Hawley	H	20	Point Lookout	7/15/64	acute dysenteria
Pvt	Reddick Daughtry	I	20	Fort Delaware	10/5/63	lungs, inf of
Pvt	Berry Babson	K	20	Fort Delaware	10/3/63	lungs, inf of
Pvt	James W. Yates	K	20	Point Lookout	11/3/64	epilepsy
Pvt	Apollas Watson	D	21	Point Lookout	1/11/65	chronic diarrhoea
Pvt	Daniel H. Baldwin	F	21	6 Corps hosp	10/1/64	gs wound
Pvt	John Holyfield	H	21	Point Lookout	1/26/65	chronic diarrhoea
Pvt	Philip McCarter	H	21	Point Lookout	3/2/64	pneumonia
Pvt	Thomas Poore	I	21	Point Lookout	3/27/64	pneumonia
Pvt	James I. Cooper	F	17 (1st)	Boston	11/29/61	pneumonia
Pvt	James L. Coultrain	E	17 (2nd)	Richmond	6/30/65	chronic diarrhoea
Pvt	Seborne A. Cushing	E	17 (2nd)	Point Lookout	12/24/64	apoplexy
Pvt	Septimus Corprew	G	17 (2nd)	Fort Monroe	12/31/64	intermittent fever

Volume VII 22nd - 26th Infantry

1)-rost- **James T. Gilbert**, co A, 22 NC, res Caldwell Co, enl age 27 in 62, died 22 June 62, place and cause of death not reported.

rost- J. F. Gilbert, misc. sec., 22 NC, place and enlistment not rep, died on or near Richmond on or about 22 June 62.

Hollywood Cemetery records, Richmond, Va- J. F. Gilbert, co A, 22 NC, died 25 June 62, loc in grave O297.

note: Same soldier, J. F. Gilbert in the misc. sec of the 22 NC should be deleted and Richmond as the place of death enter for James T. Gilbert of co A, 22 NC.

2)-rost- **J. G. Stallings**, co A, 22 NC, capt Jericho Mills, Va on or about 23 May 1864, died Point Lookout 22 Jun 1864.

CWPOWrec- J. G. Stallings, co A, 22 NC, capt Hanover Ch 27 May 1864, died Point Lookout 22 July 1864 of diarrhea acute.

3)-rost-**Julius A. Summers**, co A. 22 NC, died 2 May 1862, place and cause of death not reported.

LibVa-J. A. Summers, co F, 22 NC, died at Ashland, Va 28 Apr 1862, buried Woodland Cem., Ashland, Va.

4)-Co B, 22 NC – full names of those with initials, found in the 1850 and 1860 census of McDowell County with year of birth:

T. F. Barnes - **Thomas Barnes** 1842
S. B. Cox - **Silvester Cox** 1844
A. A. Gibbs - **Arch A. Gibbs** 1842
Z. D. Goodman - **Zachariah Goodman** 1836 (1850 Iredell Co)
J. B. Houghstetler - **Benson Hufstutler** 1842
J. L Ingle - **John L. Ingle** 1839
Z. T. McCall - **Zachary Taylor McCall** 1846
E. McDaniel - **Elisha P. M. McDaniel** 1840
B. H. McGlamery - **Benjamin H. McGlamery**
J. G. Nichols - **Joseph G. Nichols** 1841
W. G. Poteet - **William Poteet** 1844
B. F. Seagle - **Benjamin F. Seagle** 1833
J. M. Seagle - **Jacob M. Seagle** 1842
D. D. Walker - **David Walker**

5)-rost- **James P. Jamison**, co B, 22 NC, enl McDowell Co 15 Apr 62, capt Falling Waters 14 Jul 63, conf Old Capitol Prison in Washington, DC until trans to Point Lookout 8 Aug 63, rel 5 Feb 64 aft taking the oath and joining the U.S. Army, assigned to Co G, 1 Regt U.S. Vol Inf.

rost- **James P. Jimmison**, co B, 22 NC, enl 15 Apr 62, NC pension rec indicate he died

in prison at Washington, DC 23 Jul 63, no further records.
note: This is probably the same person.

6)-rost-Pvt **Jacob Washburn**, co B, 22 NC, capt Gettysburg and 'supposed to be dead', however Federal Provost Marshall rec do not substantiate the report of his capt and death, no further rec.
1912 book-Pvt Jacob Washburn of co B, 22 NC died 2 Sep 64 at Point Lookout.
CWPOWrec- J. Washburn, (no unit listed), died Point Lookout 2 Sep 64.

7)-rost- E. P. Horney, co E, 22 NC, born 1839.
1860 census Guilford Co – **Eli P. Horney** 1838

8)-rost-Pvt J. D. May, co E, 22 NC, enl at age 25 on 22 Feb 1862, w & c Gettysburg, died Davids Island 31 July 1863 of wounds (nine May's in this unit).
rost-Pvt J. D. May, co E, 2 NC, w & c Gettysburg, died 21 Jul 63 at Davids Island of gs wound..
CWPOWrec-J. D. May, co E, 22 NC, died 31 July 63 at Davids Island, NY of vulnus sclopit.
CWPOWrec- J. D. May, co E, 2 NC, capt Gettysburg July 63, died Davis Island, NY Harbor, 31 July 63 of g shot wound, buried 735 Cypress Hill Cem.
1912 book-**John D. May**, co F, 2 NC, died 31 July 63, buried Cypress Hills Nat. Cem. In Brooklyn, NY.
note: based on the enlistment info in the 22 NC, J. D. May of 2 NC should be deleted.

9)-rost-Pvt F. W. Sapt of co E, 22 NC, killed in RR accident near Shohola 15 Jul 64, no further rec.
rost-Pvt F. W. Sapp, co A, 2 NC Cav, enl Wake Co, capt Hanover CH 1 Jun 64, conf Point Lookout, trans to Elmira, killed or missing in RR accident at Shohola, Pa 15 Jul Jul 64.
CWPOWrec- F. W. Sapp, co E, 2 NC, capt Hanover CH 1 June 64, trans from Pt Lookout to Elmira 12 July 1864, 'supposed to have been killed en-route to Elmira July 15/64'.
CWPOWrec- F. W. Sapt, co E, 22 NC, capt Hanover CH 1 June 64, died in RR accident on Erie R.R., Pa 15 July 1864.
note: should be **Francis W. Sapp** born about 1831 according to the 1850 and 1860 census of Guilford Co., NC and the correct unit is the 2 NC Cav.
note: F. W. Sapt of co E, 22 NC should be deleted.

10)-rost- **W. A. Canby**, co F, 22 NC, p & d of enl not repoted, capt in hosp Richmond 3 Apr 65, died in hosp at Richmond 27 Apr 65 of consumption.
rost- **William A. Cumby**, co F, 22 NC, res Alleghany Co., NC, enl 1862, capt Richmond hosp 3 Apr 65, d Richmond hosp 3 or 27 Apr 65, cause of death not reported.
CWPOWrec- W. A. Canby, co F, 22 NC, died Jackson Gen Hosp in Richmond, Va 27

Apr 65 of consumption.

note: based on both Confederate and Union records he should be William A. Cumby of
   co F, 22 NC, who died 27 April 1865 in Richmond.

note: W. A. Canby of co F, 22 NC should be deleted.

11)-rost- William A. Cumby, co F, 22 NC, res Alleghany Co., NC, enl 1862, capt
   Richmond hosp 3 Apr 65, d Richmond hosp 3 or 27 Apr 65, cause of death not
   reported.

rost- W. A. Canby, co F, 22 NC, p & d of enl not repoted, capt in hosp Richmond 3
   Apr 65, died in hosp at Richmond 27 Apr 65 of consumption.

CWPOWrec- W. A. Canby, co F, 22 NC, died Jackson Gen Hosp in Richmond, Va 27
   Apr 65 of consumption.

note: based on both Confederate and Union records he should be William A. Cumby of
   co F, 22 NC, who died 27 April 1865 in Richmond.

note: W. A. Canby of co F, 22 NC should be deleted.

12)-rost-**O. Hensly**, co F, 22 NC, died 30 May 1862, place of death not reported.

LibVa-**F. Hensly**, co F, 22 NC, died at Ashland, Va 12 May 1862, buried Woodland
   Cem., Ashland, Va.

note: even with date of death discretion, this is the same soldier.

13)-rost-Pvt **George W. Tyson**, co F, 22 NC died Elmira 6 Mar 65, no further rec.

rost-Pvt George W. Tyson of 2co I, 32 NC, fm Chatham Co, prev in co M, 15 NC,
   trans to 32 NC in Jun 62, capt Spotts 10 May 64, conf Point Lookout, trans 3 Aug
   64 to Elmira, died Elmira 6 Mar 65.

note: George W. Tyson of co F, 22 NC should be deleted.

14)-rost- **Samuel Claybrook**, co H, 22 NC, res Stokes Co., enl at age 21 on 1 June 61,
   wounded in right leg and captured at Gettysburg 3 July 63, r leg ampt, d in Chester
   hospital 27 July 63 of exhaustion.

rost- **S. Brenclare**, co I, 22 NC, plac and date of enl not reported, Fed rec indicate he
   was captured at Gettysburg 3 July 63, conf at Ft Delaware until trans to Chester
   Hospital 19 July 63, no further records.

CWPOWrec- (1) S. Brenclare, co I, 22 NC, capt Gettysburg (heavy line over name).

(2) S. Brenclare, co I, 22 NC, trans to Chester hospital on 17 July 63.

(3) Samuel Claybrook, co H, 22 NC, capt Gettysburg 3 July 63, died Chester hospital
   on (many dates noted in several records) 17, 24, 27 or 30 July 63 fm exhaustion fm
   ampt, bur Philadelphia Nat Cem, left $102 Confederate script, papers and a wallet.

(4) **S. Daybrook**, co H, 22 NC, capt Gettysburg 3 July 63, died 29 Aug 63 of
   exhaustion fm amputation, bur in Philadelphia Nat Cem, left $102 in Reb money,
   papers and a wallet.

(5) VA web site- Samuel Claybrook in grave 36 in Phil Nat Cem and also list D.
   Daybrook in grave 44 in Phil Nat Cem. (believe this to be in error).

(6) 1860 NC census: Samuel Claybrook lived in Stokes Co., no such names as

Daybrook or Brenclare anywhere in North Carolina.
note: while there seems to be much confustion on names and dates, believe that all
the above are the same soldier, Samuel Claybrook of co H, 22 NC. In the POW
records Claybrook and Daybrook only are noted on the Chester hospital records,
but nothing to indicate they were first at Ft Delaware. Brenclare is noted only at Ft
Delaware before being trans to Chester hospital on 17 July 63. S. Brenclare of co I,
22 NC should be deleted.

15)-rost- **James M. Hollinsworth**, co H, 22 NC, died July 63 of disease, place of death
not reported.
Lynchburg, Old City Cemetery- James Hollingsworth, co H, 22 NC.

16)-rost- J. J. Tallah, co H, 22 NC, place and date enlistment not reported, died Elmira
12 Sept 1864.
CWPOWrec- **John J. Tallah**, co H, 26 Virginia Battalion Infantry, died Elmira 13 Sept
1864 of chr diarr.
CWPOWrec- J. J. Tallah, co H, 22 NC, capt Wilderness 5 May 1864, conf Elmira 14
Aug 64, died Elmira 13 Sept 64, buried grave 241 at Woodlawn Cem.
American CW soldiers- John J. Tulloh/Tulloch of co H, 22 Virginia Battalion.
note: with the confusion of which unit he was in, believe that the 22nd Virginia Battalion
is the correct unit and J. J. Tallah of the 22nd NC should be deleted.

17)-rost- S. Brenclare, co I, 22 NC, plac and date of enl not reported, Fed rec indicate
he was captured at Gettysburg 3 July 63, conf at Ft Delaware until trans to Chester
Hospital 19 July 63, no further records.
rost- Samuel Claybrook, co H, 22 NC, res Stokes Co., enl at age 21 on 1 June 61,
wounded in right leg and captured at Gettysburg 3 July 63, r leg ampt, d in Chester
hospital 27 July 63 of exhaustion.
CWPOWrec- (1) S. Brenclare, co I, 22 NC, capt Gettysburg (heavy line over name).
(2) S. Brenclare, co I, 22 NC, trans to Chester hospital on 17 July 63.
(3) Samuel Claybrook, co H, 22 NC, capt Gettysburg 3 July 63, died Chester hospital
on (many dates noted in several records) 17, 24, 27 or 30 July 63 fm exhaustion fm
ampt, bur Philadelphia Nat Cem, left $102 Confederate script, papers and a wallet.
(4) S. Daybrook, co H, 22 NC, capt Gettysburg 3 July 63, died 29 Aug 63 of exhaustion
fm amputation, bur in Philadelphia Nat Cem, left $102 in Reb money, papers and a
wallet.
(5) VA web site- Samuel Claybrook in grave 36 in Phil Nat Cem and also list D.
Daybrook in grave 44 in Phil Nat Cem. (believe this to be in error).
(6) 1860 NC census: Samuel Claybrook lived in Stokes Co., no such names as
Daybrook or Brenclare anywhere in North Carolina.
note: while there seems to be much confusion on names and dates, believe that all
the above are the same soldier, Samuel Claybrook of co H, 22 NC. In the POW
records Claybrook and Daybrook only are noted on the Chester hospital records,
but nothing to indicate they were first at Ft Delaware. Brenclare is noted only at Ft

Delaware before being trans to Chester hospital on 17 July 63. S. Brenclare of co I, 22 NC should be deleted.

18)-rost- Captain **Charles H. Burgin**, co K, 22 NC, resided McDowell, age 24, elected 1st Lt, promoted to captain, wounded at Shepherdstown, VA, on 20 Sept 1862, died at or near Fredericksburg on 15 Nov or 1 Dec 1862 of disease.

NCS, 24 Dec 1862- Captain Charles H. Beman(?), 22 NC, resided in McDowell, entered service as 1st Lt, upon resignation of his captain he accepted that office, slightly injured by fragments of a shell in battle before Richmond, severely wounded through the left hand at Shepherdstown, because of injury he was granted a twenty day furlough, some time in Oct he returned home (McDowell Co.) where he died of typhoid fever weeks later.

19)-rost- **Henry Breedlove**, co M, 22 NC, enl Camp Holmes 6 Feb 64, capt Jericho Mills 23 May 64, died Point Lookout 6 Jun 65 of diarrhea.

rost- **Newman Breedlove**, co M. 22 NC, place and date enl not reported, died Point Lookout 6 Jun 65, place and date capt not reported, cause of death not reported.

CWPOWrec- 1) H. Breedlove, co M, 22 NC, POW assigned to co. F, 1st Division at Point Lookout. 2) Henry Breedlove, co M, 22 NC, died Point Lookout 6 Jun 65 of chr diarr. 3) N. Breedlove, co M, 22 NC, POW assigned to co. F, 1st Division at Point Lookout. 4) Newman Breedlove, co M, 22 NC, capt North Anna River on 23 May 64, arr at Point Lookout from Port Royal on 30 May 64, died Point Lookout 6 Jun 65 of chr diarr.

1850 census of Guilford Co., NC has Henry N. Breedlove age 9 in Levi Breedlove's household.

1860 census of Randolph Co., NC has Henry Breedlove age 19 in Levi Breedlove's household. (note: in both census there is a Newman Breedlove born in the 1770s, no other person by the name Newman Breedlove.)

Ancestry.com family chart- Henry Breedlove is the son of Levi and Levi is the son of Newman.

note: .Henry and Newman Breedlove in the Roster are the same person and both their records should be combined under **Henry Newman Breedlove**.

20)-rost-**Jesse Routh**, co M, 22 NC, died 30 Apr or 16 May 1862, place and cause of death not reported.

LibVa-Jesse Routh, co M, 22 NC, died at Ashland, Va 22 Apr 1862, buried Woodland Cem., Ashland, Va.

21)-rost-Pvt E. A. Griffin, misc. section, 22 NC died 4 Jan 65 at Camp Douglas, Ill, no further rec.

rost-Pvt **Edward A. Griffin**, co F, 29 NC capt Franklin, Tn 17 Dec 64, conf at Nashville, Louisville, trans to Camp Douglas 22 Dec 64, died Camp Douglas 4 Jan 65.

1912 book-same info as misc-22 NC.

CWPOWrec-E. A. Griffin, co F, 29 NC, capt Franklin, Tenn 17 Dec 64, died Camp Douglas 3 Jan 65 of pneumonia.
note: E. A. Griffin of 22 NC should be deleted.

22)-rost- **S. W. Barrier**, co B, 23 NC, place, enlistment, promotion rec not reported, w & c Gettysburg 1 July 63, rep in hosp at Gettysburg 10 Aug 63, no further records.
rost- **George W. Barrier**, co B, 20 NC, res Cabarrus Co, enl 29 Mar 62, w in thigh & capt at Gettysburg 1-3 Jul 63, conf at various Federal hosp until paroled and trans to City Point 20 Mar 64 for exchange.
CWPOWrec- **S. W. Barrier**, co B, 23 NC, capt Gettysburg 1 July 63, trans to West Bldg Baltimore on 15 Nov 63.
CWPOWrec- G. W. Barrier, co B, 20 NC, capt Gettysburg 4 Jul 63, rel fm US hospital West's Bldg Baltimore to City Point 10 Jan 64, sent for exchange to City Point 17 Mar 64.
note: believe this is the same person and George W. Barrier of co B, 20 NC is the correct soldier.

23)-rost- N. Lewis, co C, 23 NC, place and date of enlistment not reported, 1st listed in company records 28 Oct 1862, capt Gettysburg 5 Jul 1863, conf at Ft Delaware 7-12 July 63, no further records.
rost-**Noah Lewis**, co C, 33 NC, resided in Forsyth Co. where he enlisted at age 30 on 1 July 62, capt Gettysburg on or about 4 July 63, conf at Ft Delaware until paroled 30 Jul 63, died at Salem on or about 25 Sept 1863.
CWPOWrec- N. Lewis, co I, 33 NC, capt Gettysburg 5 July 63, exchanged from Ft Delaware to City Point on 30 July 63.
CWPOWrec- Noah Lewis, co C, 23 NC, capt Gettysburg 1 July 63.
note: Noah Lewis of co C, 33 NC is the correct soldier and N. Lewis of co C, 23 NC should be deleted.

24)-rost-**William R. Smith**, co C, 23 NC, res of Stanly Co, enl 3 Sep 62, wounded Chancellorsville 2-3 May 63, died Richmond on or about 16 May 63 of wounds.
rost- W. R. Smith, co H, 23 NC, place and date of enlistment not reported, wounded Chancellorsville 2-3 May 63, died Richmond 16 May 63 of disease.
Hollywood Cemetery rec, Richmond, Va- W. R. Smith, co C, 23 NC, died 16 May 63, buried in grave T318.
note: W. R. Smith of co H, 23 NC should be deleted.

25)-rost-**Christopher Columbus Crouch**, co D, 23 NC, capt Spotsylvania 12 May 64, conf at Point Lookout until paroled and trans to Boulware's Wharf, James River, VA, where he was received 18 Mar 1865 for exchange.
Compiled Service record-C. C. Crouch, co D, 23 NC, roll of POW paroled at Point Lookout and trans to Aiken's Landing, VA, 15 Mar 1865 for exchange, entry cancelled, released 12 May 1865 from Point Lookout.
CWPOWrec- C. C. Crouch, co D, 23 NC, capt Spotsylvania 12 May 64, released from

Point Lookout on 12 May 1865 by G.O. no 85 dated 8 May 65.
note: change released date to 12 May 1865 from 18 Mar 1865 (Great-Grand Father to this complier.)

26)-rost- **J. W. S. Floyd**, co G, 23 NC, trans to Point Lookout 15 Sep 1863, paroled on an unspecified date and trans to Venus Point, GA, where he died on or about 15 Nov 64 of disease.
CWPOWrec- J. W. S. Floyd, co G, 21 NC, capt Martinsburg 10 Jul 63, trans fm Baltimore 16 Sep 63, exchanged 1 Nov 64.

27)-rost- L. J. Montague, co G, 23 NC, of Granville, died at Lynchburg or Danville 13-16 Jan 1863 of variola.
FO, 2 March 1863- Dr. **Latney J. Montague**, co G, 23 NC, of Granville, died in Danville of smallpox.

28)-rost- W. R. Smith, co H, 23 NC, place and date of enlistment not reported, wounded Chancellorsville 2-3 May 63, died Richmond 16 May 63 of disease.
rost-**William R. Smith**, co C, 23 NC, res of Stanly Co, enl 3 Sep 62, wounded Chancellorsville 2-3 May 63, died Richmond on or about 16 May 63 of wounds.
Hollywood Cemetery rec, Richmond, Va- W. R. Smith, co C, 23 NC, died 16 May 63, buried in grave T318.
note: W. R. Smith of co H, 23 NC should be deleted.

29)-rost-**Henry H. Allen**, **Josiah Allen**, **W. H. Allen**, co K, 23 NC, all from Lincoln Co.
1850 Lincoln Co., NC census has Henry (11), Joseph (10) and Wm. H. (6) Allen, all sons of Levi & Polly Allen.
1860 Lincoln Co., NC census has Joseph (20) Henderson (18) Allen as sons of Levi & Polly Allen, Henry Allen (22) married.
note: no Josiah Allen found in either 1850 or 1860 Lincoln Co., NC.
note: Josiah Allen of co K, 23 NC given name should be change to **Joseph Allen** and W. H. Allen of same unit name should be change to **William Henderson Allen**.

30)-rost- John S. Shipp, co K, 23 NC, mortally wounded at Winchester 19 Sept 64.
FO, Dec 12, 1864- **John S. Shipp**, co K, 23 NC, died 21 Sept 64 in the hands of the enemy, age 18 years, 2 months and 14 days, eldest son of Wm. T. and H. M. Shipp of Gaston Co., NC.

31)-rost- **J. Storgeal**, co K, 23 NC, place and date enl not reported, capt by enemy on an unspecified date, died Elmira 22 Jan 65, cause of death not reported.
rost- **James Sturgill**, co K, 37 NC, enl 25 Dec 63, capt Wilderness or Spotsylania 6/12 May 64, conf Point Lookout, trans to Elmira 8 Aug 64, died Elmira 19 Mar 65 of pneumonia.
CWPOWrec- J. Storgeal, co K, 37 NC (Ala struck out), capt Spotsylanvia 12 May 64, died Elmira 19 Mar 65 of pneumonia (two records noted.)

1912 Book- J. Storgeal, co K, 23 NC, died Elmira 22 Jan 65, grave 1578.

note: The 1912 book is the only source for J. Storgeal of the 23 NC. While the unit nr. and death date are different, data suggest the James Sturgill of the 37 NC is the correct soldier and J. Storgeal of co K, 23 NC should be deleted.

32)-rost- E. M. Yount, co K, 23 NC, of Lincoln Co., NC, age 25 in 1861, p & a until wounded 19 Sep 64 Winchester, Va and 'left in hands of enemy', died on unspecified date, place and cause of death not reported.

CWPOWrec- Eli Yount, co K, 23 NC, died 11 Oct 64 at Winchester of gun shot w shoulder.

1850 Lincoln Co., NC census has **Eli M. Yount** (21), son of **Samuel Yount**.

1860 Lincoln Co., NC census has Eli Yount (31), son of Samuel Yount.

note: change E. M. Yount to Eli M. Yount.

33)-rost- **George B. Bolton**, co A, 24 NC, p & a until wounded left shoulder and/or thorax & capt near Five Forks, Va on or about 1 Apr 65, hosp Washington until rel on 14 Jun 65 after oath.

CWPOWrec- Geo B. Bolton, co A, 24 NC, capt S. S. Railroad 4 Apr 65, released on O. alleg. 15 June 65. (But another Federal record stated) he died wnd (wounded?) thorax on 2 Apr 65 at 3 Div 5 Army Corps hospital, register 168 AC.

34)-rost-**Theophilus G. Scott** (no rank), co B, 24 NC, pension rec indicate he enl in Oct 64, wounded and capt in Virginia in 1865, died Fort McHenry, Md on an unspecified date of wounds.

rost- T. G. Scott (Pvt), co B, 54 NC, res Burke Co, p & d enl not rep (prob enl subsequent to 31 Oct 64), wounded left leg and capt at Harper's Farm, Va on 6 Apr 65, hosp Baltimore 22 Apr 65, died in hosp at Baltimore on or about 3 May 65 of pyaemia, Federal rec of Apr-Mar 65 give his age as 45.

CWPOWrec- T. G. Scott, co B, 54 NC, capt Harper Farm, Va 6 Apr 65, died West's Building 3 May 65 of gun shot wound, buried Loudon Park Cem, Baltimore.

1912 book- Pvt T. G. Scott, co B, 54 Va, died 3 May 65, buried Loudon Park Cem, Baltimore in grave B-2.

1860 census Burke Co., NC- Theophilus G. Scott, age 39, with wife Martha and family.

1860 Onslow- no Theophilus G. or T. G. Scott noted.

note: Theophilus G. Scott of co B, 24 NC should be deleted and his full name enter in co B, 54 NC.

35)-rost-Pvt **Jaron D. Waldrop**, co C, 24 NC, p & d enl not reported, died Point Lookout 28 May 65, cause of death not reported.

rost-Pvt **Theron D. Waldrop**, co C, 34 NC, enl 1864, capt Amelia CH 3 Apr 65, died Point Lookout 28 May 65 of chronic dysentery.

1912 book-same info as 24 NC.

CWPOWrec- Jaron D. Waldrop, co C, 34 NC, capt Amelia Ch 3 Apr 65, died Point Lookout 28 May 65 of chron. Diarrhoea. (when he was captured the 34 NC was noted as his unit, one record at Pt Lookout had 24 NC.)(no Theron D. Waldrop noted in POW records.)

1850 Rutherford Co., NC census- T. D. Waldrape (23).

1860 Polk Co., NC census- T. D. Waldrop (35), wife Cela.

note: the co C, 34 NC is a Rutherford Co. company. Jaron D. Waldrop of co C, 24 NC should be deleted.

36)-rost-Pvt **William A. Fletcher**, co D, 24 NC, p & d enl not reported, died Elmira 27 Jan 65 (only info stated.)

rost-Pvt William A. Fletcher of co D, 42 NC, res Iredell, enl 20 Oct 62, gave up at Cold Harbor 3 Jun 64, conf Point Lookout, trans Elmira 17 Jul 64, died Elmira 27 Jan 65.

note: William A. Fletcher of co D, 24 NC should be deleted.

37)-rost- **Calvin W. Pitman**, co E. 24 NC, died at Petersburg on or about 20 Feb 1862 of disease.

NCS, 12 Aug 1863- Calvin W. Pittman, 24 NC, died in the 1st NC Hospital in Petersburg on 1 March 1863 of typhoid fever, age 24.

38)-rost- 2Lt **Daniel J. Downing**, co F, 24 NC, killed Sharpsburg 17 Sep 62.

CWPOWrec- Lt. D. E. J. Downing, co F, 24 NC, died of wounds after 17 Sep 62 at Lavinia Grove Farm.

note: change from killed to wounded and captured Sharpsburg 17 Sept 62 and died of wounds.

39)-rost- **Harvey Bailey**, co G, 24 NC, pen rec indicate he enl on 27 May 64, mort wounded in Georgia on 9 July 64.

rost- Harvey Bailey, co G, 29 NC, place and date of enl not rep, wounded in left hand at or near Kennesaw Mountain, Ga. 18 Jun 64, died at Covington, Ga 9 Jul 64 of wounds.

Family rec on Ancestry.com- Harvey James Bailey, b 3 Nov 25 in Burnsville, Yancey Co, NC, died Covington, Newton, Ga 9 July 64, buried Bailey-Byrd Cem, Jacks Creek, Yancey Co., NC.

note: co G of the 29 NC was a Yancey Co unit and served in Georgia, Harvey Bailey of co G, 24 NC should be deleted.

40)-rost- **John H. Smith**, co G, 24 NC, resided in Robeson Co and enlisted in Cumberland Co 1 Mar 63, Present until Jan-Feb 1864 when he was reported absent wounded, place and date wounded not reported, died prior to 3 Feb 1865, place and cause of death not reported.

FO, 1 Aug 1864- John Henry Smith, co G, 24 NC, died at his residence in Cumberland Co on 24 June 1864 from the effects of a wound received in battle on 2 June 1864.

41)-rost-not listed.

City Point National Cemetery, Va- M. Sullivan, co G, 24 NC, died 26 Mar 1865, grave

4084.

CWPOWrec- **Michael Sullivan**, co G, 24 NC, died City Point, Va 26 Mar 1865 of gun shot wound right side.

42)-rost-**Richard A. Hill**, co I, 24 NC, present & accounted until 10 Mar 65, when he was furloughed for 60 days from Richmond hospital.
LMA-R. A. Hill of co I, 24 NC, no date, grave 251 in Oakwood Cem., Raleigh, NC.

43)-rost- **Alfred C. Campbell**, co D, 25 NC, res Cherokee Co, capt near Globe Tavern, Va 21 Aug 64, d Point Lookout 26 Feb 65 of chr diarr.
rost- A. C. Campbell, co A, 38 NC, p & d of enl not rep, capt unk, d Point Lookout 27 Feb 65, cause of death not rep.
CWPOWrec- A. C. Campbell, co A, 38 NC, capt Wilderness 6 May 64, d Point Lookout 27 Feb 65 of chr diarrhea.
CWPOWrec- A. C. Campbell, co D, 25 NC, d Point Lookout 27 Feb 65 of chr diarr.
CWPOWrec- A. C. Campbell, co D, 25 NC, capt Weldon RR 21 Apr 64, exh 18 Feb 65 fm Pt Lookout.
note: several POW rec noted for both the one in the 38 and the 25, but with the additional info on him in the 25 NC A. C. Campbell of co A, 38 NC should be deleted.

44)-rost-**Jesse P. Carter**, co G, 25 NC, capt Fort Stedman 25 Mar 65, died on board of US Hospital Steamer 'Connecticut' on 25 Mar 65 of wounds.
LMA-from Arlington to Raleigh in 1871, J. P. Carter of 25 NC.

45)-rost- **John B. Lance**, co H, 25 NC, company muster rolls of Nov 64 – Feb 65 indicate he was a POW, however, rec of Fed Provost Marshal do not substantiate that report.
rost- John B. Lance, Co K, 7 NC Cav, capt Cocke Co., Tenn 14 Jan 64, conf Knoxville 17 Jan 64, sent to Camp Chase 28 Jan 64, conf Rock Island 31 Jan 64 until released 28 May 65.
note: same soldier.

46)-rost-Pvt **J. P. McGinness**, co H, 25, p & d enl not reported, in Newport News hosp 6 May 65, died Newport News 14 May 65 of debility.
rost-Pvt **Thomas M. McGinnis**, co H, 35, res Catawba Co, enl age 19 on 3 Sep 61 in Meck, capt Richmond 3 Apr 65, died Newport News hosp 14 May 65.
note: Thomas M. McGinnis of 35 NC is the correct soldier and J. P. McGinness of 25 NC should be deleted.

47)-rost- **E. McAllister**, co H, 25 NC, place and date enlisted not reported, died at Elmira on 20 Apr 65.
CWPOWrec- E. McAllister, co H, 25 SC, capt at Ft. Fisher on 15 Jan 65, at Elmira on 30 Jan 65, died Elmira on 20 Apr 65 of vairola. (seven POW records noted on

McAllister of 25 SC.)

note: The 25 SC were at Fort Fisher, while the 25 NC were in the trenches at Petersburg during the first part of 1865. Delete E. McAllister of co H, 25 NC from the records.

48)-rost-**Joseph A. Rich**, co I, 25 NC, pension rec indicate he died in Virginia on 19 Jun 1864.

Petersburg-J. A. Rich, co I, 25 NC, died Petersburg (no date), burial Petersburg Fair Ground vicinity.

49)-rost- **Newton A. Gentry**, co K, 25 NC, company muster rolls of Nov 64 – Feb 65 indicate he was a POW, however, rec of Fed Provost Marshal do not substantiate that report.

rost- Newton A. Gentry, co K, 7 NC Cav, capt Cock Co., Tenn 14 Jan 64, conf Louisville, Ky, sent to Camp Chase 20 Jan 64, conf Rock Island 29 Jan 64 until trans for exch 2 Mar 65.

note: same soldier.

50)-rost-Pvt **James M. Maner**, co K, 25 NC, capt Globe Tavern 21 Aug 64, conf Point Lookout 24 Aug 64, no further rec.

1912 book-Pvt J. Maynard, co K, 25 NC died Point Lookout 26 Mar 65.

CWPOWrec- J. Maynard, co K, 25 NC, capt Petersburg 25 May 64, died Point Lookout 26 Mar 65 of erysipilas.

51)-rost- **Reuben P. Whitt**, co K, 25 NC, company muster rolls of Nov 64 – Feb 65 indicate he was a POW, however, rec of Fed Provost Marshal do not substantiate that report.

rost- Rueben P. Whitt, co K, 7 NC Cav, capt Cocke Co., Tenn 14 Jan 64, conf Knoxville, trans to Rock Island 27 Jan 64, trans to New Orleans and exchanged 23 May 65.

note: same soldier.

52)-rost- Major **James S. Kendall**, Field and Staff, 26 NC, died on an unspecified date of yellow fever contracted at Wilmington while on furlough.

FO, 13 Oct 1862- Major Jas. S. Kendall , 26 NC, died in Wadesboro (Anson Co) on 23rd ult. (23 Sept 1862) of yellow fever contracted at Wilmington.

53)-rost- **Tilman D. Mills**, co B, 26 NC, wounded in an unspecified battle and capt by enemy on 30 July 63, paroled and exchanged prior to 6 Sept 63.

CWPOWrec- T. D. Mills, co D, 26 NC, capt Winchester, Va hosp 30 July 63.

note: prob wounded in the Gettysburg campain and taken to Winchester by the Confederate forces before being captured.

54)-rost- **Robert Rogers**, co B, 26 NC, w & c at Gettysburg 1-3 Jul 63, died on 21 Aug 63 of wounds, place of death not reported.

CWPOWrec- R. R. Rogers, co D, 26 NC, capt Winchester on 30 Jul 63, disposition unaccounted for.

55)-rost- W. T. Triplett, co C, 26 NC, died in Petersburg of chr diarrhea.
NCS, 6 May 1863- **William T. Triplett**, co C, 26 NC, died in Petersburg of measles.

56)-rost-Pvt James Q. Adams, Co. D, 26 NC.
State Troops by Mast has on page 23 letter from **James Quincy Adams** to parents Dec 6, 1861.

57)-rost- **William H. Boothe**, co D, 26 NC, w at Gettysburg, hosp at Winchester, Va where he died on 13 Aug 63 of wounds.
CWPOWrec- **W. H. Booth**, co D, 26 NC, capt at Winchester, Va 30 Jul 63, died 31 Aug 63.

58)-rost-**John Harvell**, co D, 26 NC, p & a until capt New Bern 14 Mar 62, died in hosp at or near New Bern on or about 21 Apr 62 of disease.
CWPOWrec- John Harvel, Co D, 26 NC, died 16 July 62 at Beaufort, SC of Vulnus Sclopst.

59)-rost- **Gerry G. Brewer**, co E, 26 NC, enl 1 Jun 61, p & a until capt at Hatcher's Run on 2 Apr 65.
CWPOWrec- G. G. Brewer, co E, 26 NC, capt Winchester on 30 Jul 63.
note: need to add the new info from POW records.

60)-rost- **O. Hiram Evans**, co E, 26 NC, killed on picket at or near King's School House 25 June 1862
FO, 4 August 1862- **Orpheus H. Evans**, co E, 26 NC, felled in the battle of Seven Pines 26 June 1862.

61)-rost- **Willis R. Phillips**, co E, 26 NC, rep absent sick from Nov 62 through Dec 63, not listed in the company rec in 64 or 65, paroled at Appomattox CH 9 April 1865.
FO, 4 April 1864- Willis Philips, co E, 26 NC, age 29, died at his residence in Chatham Co 1 March 1864 from chronic diarrhea from which he suffered severely for several months, he participated in the battle of Newbern and the 7 Days fighting around Richmond.

62)-rost- **Allen R. Shields**, co E, 26 NC, res Chatham Co & enl age 25 on 15 May 62, p & a until w right leg & capt Gettysburg 1-3 Jul 63, trans to Chester about 25 Jul 63, died 29 July 63 at Chester of exh. Following ampt of right leg.
rost- K. Shields, co K, 6 NC, p & d of enl not reported, w in left thigh at Gettysburg & capt 4 Jul 63, left leg amp, died 29 Jul 63 at Chester, Pa hosp.
CW POW REC- Allen Shields, co E, 26 NC, died 29 July 63 at Chester, Pa from exh. Following ampt of rt leg.

note: K. Shields of 6 NC should be deleted.

63)-rost-**Rufus Erwin**, co F, 26 NC, Res in Burke Co, died 15 July 1863 of wounds rec at Gettysburg, place of death not reported.
ADJ General's Dept., Roll of Honor Office, Scrapbook 1861-1865 Microfilm S.1.108P, Asheville newspaper titled 'Some of our dead who died in Martinsburg-**Rufus Irving**, Happy Home P.O. Burke Co, NC, 26 NC, died in country 16 July 1863.

64)-rost-2n Lt **Abner Berge Hayes**, co F, 26 NC, wounded breast and/or right arm at Bristoe Station 14 Oct 63, died in Richmond hospital on or about 7 June 1864 of wounds.
FO, 5 Sept 1864-Lt. A. B. Hays, co F, 26 NC, died of wounds rec at Cold Harbor on 22 June 1864. He was wounded in the battle of Bristow Station and also in the Wilderness on 6 May 1864, but the fatal blow was given him on the 22 June.

65)-rost-Pvt W.E. Setser, Co F, 26 NC, res Caldwell Co., NC, age 17 in 1861.
State Troops by Mast has Pvt W. Eli Setser.
1860 Caldwell Co., NC census- Eli Setser, 15, son of W. A. & Eliza Setser.
Ancestry.com family info- **William Eli Setzer**, born abt 1842, son of William A. & Eliza J. Setzer.

66)-rost- **Archibald B. Wagoner**, co F, 26 NC, born at 'Davis', occ farmer prior to enl Wake Co 30 Nov 63. P&A until capt North Anna River, Va 22 May 64, conf Pt Lookout until released 12 Oct 64 after joining US Army, assigned to co A, 4 US Vol Inf., Alex Wagner in same unit.
rost- **Archibald B. Wagner**, co F, 21 NC, res Stokes Co, enl age 19 on 29 May 61, P&A until capt Spotsylvania CH 22 May 64, conf at Pt Lookout. No further records, John Wagner in same unit age 22 when enl same day as Archibald
1850 Davie Co census- John (1839) and Archibald (1843) sons of Aaron and Susannah Wagner.
1860 Stokes co census- Arch (1842) in same parents household.
CWPOW records- A. B. Wagner, co F, 26 NC capt North Anna on 22 May 64, arr 30 May 64 to Pt Lookout from Port Royal, joined US Service 12 Oct 64. (3 CWPOW rec had Archibald in the 26th and only one had 21st).
note: Believe Archibald B. Wagner same person noted in the 21st and 26th, but which unit is correct?

67)-rost- **Henry Goodman**, co G, 26 NC, place and date of enlistment not reported, died Elmira 21 Feb 1865.
rost- **Henry H. Goodman**, co G, 2 NC Arty, res Brunswick, mustered in 10 Feb 63, capt Ft Fisher 15 Jan 65, died Elmira 21 Feb 1865 of variola.
note: delete Henry Goodman of the 26 NC.

68)-rost-Pvt **Washington P. Nelson**, co G, 26 NC, enl Chatham age 18 on 10 Jun 61, capt Harrison's Landing, Va 1 Jul 62, exch Aug 62, capt Gettysburg Jul 63, conf Fort Delaware, released 22 Sep 63 after joining US co G, 3 Md Cav.

rost-Pvt **John Wesley Nelson**, co G, 26 NC, enl Chatham age 22 on 10 Jun 61, wounded and capt Gettys Jul 63, conf Fort Delaware, trans to Point Lookout 15 Oct 63, died Point Lookout 9 Apr 64.

1912 book-Pvt Washington P. Nelson, co G, 26 NC died Point Lookout 9 Apr 64.

CWPOWrec- W. P. Nelson, 26 NC, capt Gettysburg 3 Jul 1863, joined 3rd Md Cav. Sept 1863.

69)-rost- M. Rightsel, co G, 26 NC, died at Lynchburg 26 Apr 64.

Lynchburg, Old City Cemetery- **Millan Rightsell**, co G, 26.

70)-rost- **John B. Martin**, co H, 26 NC, wounded and captured Gettysburg 1-3 July 63, died in hosp at Winchester 20 July or 3 Aug 63 of wounds.

CWPOWrec- J. B. Martin, co H, 26 NC, capt Winchester hospital 30 July 63.

note: cancel captured at Gettysburg 1-3 July 63 and died on 20 July 63 as he was evidently wounded at Gettysburg, but was taken by his Army to Winchester where he was than captured on 30 July 63. No Fed rec noted on death.

71)-rost- **William M. Persons**, co H, 26 NC, wounded Gettysburg 1 July 63, capt by enemy 30 July 63, died at or near Winchester 2 Aug 63 of wounds.

CWPOWrec- W. M. Person, co H, 26 NC, capt Winchester hospital 30 July 63.

72)-rost-**Robert Cruise**, co I, 26 NC, wounded Gettysburg 1 Jul 1863, died of wounds at an unknown place on 31 Jul 1863.

note: List noted on the internet of Confederates buried in Mount Jackson Cemetery in Virginia states that Robert Cruise of co I, 26 NC died 31 Jul 1863.

73)-rost-G. H. Sudderth, co I, 26 NC, res Caldwell County, enl age 22 on 15 Mar 1862, p & a until killed Gettysburg 1 Jul 1863.

1850 Caldwell Co. census, George Sudderth, age 7.

1860 Caldwell Co. census, George Sudderth, age 17, his parents were James and Jane Sudderth.

Family Tree Maker web site-**George Murray Sudderth**, b 1843, d 1865 Civil War.

Cause of deaths that were not listed in the NC Roster - Volume VII

Rank	name	co	unit	place of death	died	cause of death
Pvt	Larkin Coffey	A	22	Point Lookout	8/4/64	heart, chr. Vul. Dise.
Pvt	Slighter B. Shell	A	22	Point Lookout	12/24/64	pneumonia
Pvt	J.G. Stallings	A	22	Point Lookout	7/22/64	acute diarrhoea
Pvt	Stephen Bell	E	22	Fort Monroe	9/3/62	dysentery, chronic
Pvt	William A. Cumby	F	22	Richmond	4/27/65	consumption
Pvt	William Franklin Whitaker	F	22	Point Lookout	1/24/64	chronic diarrhoea
Pvt	William H. Lewis	G	22	Elmira	9/6/64	sconbutus/chr diarrhoea
Pvt	John H. Rodgers	G	22	Point Lookout	7/17/64	febris typhoides
Pvt	John Walker	G	22	Point Lookout	12/25/63	chronic diarrhoea
Pvt	Andrew P.J. Alberty	H	22	Fort Delaware	10/11/63	febris remittens
Pvt	Eli Johnson	I	22	Point Lookout	12/30/63	acute dysenteria
Corp	Joseph L. Bradley	K	22	Point Lookout	6/2/64	dysentery, chronic
Pvt	John Washburn	K	22	Point Lookout	9/2/64	congestive intermittent fever
Pvt	James Cannon	M	22	Point Lookout	6/28/64	febris typhoid
Pvt	Caleb Leonard	B	23	Point Lookout	6/29/64	chronic diarrhoea
Pvt	Lafayette Wilson	B	23	Fort Delaware	10/17/63	Rhumatism, chr/chr. diarrh
Corp	Calvin Green	C	23	Point Lookout	10/17/63	dysenteria, chronic
Pvt	Sampson S. Parker	C	23	Point Lookout	2/24/64	pneumonia
Pvt	Hosea McKinnon	D	23	Point Lookout	2/16/64	pneumonia
Pvt	Hugh C. McLean	D	23	Point Lookout	1/13/64	dysenteria, chronic
Pvt	John Mize	E	23	Point Lookout	10/2/64	chronic diarrhoea
Pvt	Alfred F. Helton	F	23	Point Lookout	7/30/64	dysenteria, chronic
Pvt	George Johnson	F	23	Point Lookout	1/20/64	chronic diarrhoea
Pvt	David S. Suther	F	23	Point Lookout	12/22/63	chronic diarrhoea
Pvt	George C. Falkner	G	23	Point Lookout	1/16/64	dysenteria, chronic
Pvt	Jordan Finch	G	23	Point Lookout	1/15/64	chronic diarrhoea
Pvt	John S. Hicks	G	23	Point Lookout	7/27/64	chronic diarrhoea
Pvt	John A. Milling	H	23	Point Lookout	6/30/64	measles
Pvt	Robert H. Wade	I	23	Fort Delaware	10/10/63	chronic diarrhoea
Pvt	Jehu Baker	K	23	Fort Delaware	10/10/63	rhemutiums, chronic
Pvt	James W. Burch	K	23	Fort Delaware	10/14/63	diphtheria
Pvt	Cornelius L. Oliver	A	24	Point Lookout	6/27/65	chronic diarrhoea
Pvt	John T. Griffin	C	24	Point Lookout	8/14/64	chronic diarrhoea
Pvt	Needham Price	C	24	Point Lookout	6/7/65	chronic diarrhoea
2Lt	Daniel J. Downing	F	24	Antietim	9/17/62	of wounds
Pvt	Noah L. Clark	H	25	Point Lookout	10/12/64	chronic diarrhoea
Pvt	James M. Maner	K	25	Point Lookout	3/26/65	erysipelas
Pvt	John Vanover	A	26	Fort Delaware	10/14/63	lungs, inf of
Pvt	John Weaver	A	26	Point Lookout	5/20/64	chronic diarrhoea
Pvt	William F. Fox	B	26	Point Lookout	12/26/63	Rhumatism, chronic
Pvt	William A. Inman	B	26	Fort Delaware	10/2/63	chronic diarrhoea
Pvt	William Phillips	B	26	Point Lookout	11/27/63	dysenteria, chronic
Pvt	Benjamin F. Bullis	C	26	Point Lookout	2/9/64	chronic diarrhoea
Pvt	Wesley L. Combs	C	26	Point Lookout	1/4/64	chronic diarrhoea
Pvt	William H. King	D	26	Point Lookout	7/9/64	acute dysenteria
Pvt	Solomon G. Pearson	D	26	Point Lookout	11/1/63	acute dysentery

Pvt	Marshall Williams	D	26	Fort Delaware	10/9/63	lungs, inf of
Sgt	James N. Ellis	E	26	Point Lookout	1/23/64	chronic diarrhoea
Pvt	John L. Smith	E	26	Point Lookout	2/28/64	pneumonia
Pvt	Atlas J. Stanley	E	26	Point Lookout	6/24/64	scorbutus
Pvt	James Davis	F	26	Point Lookout	8/13/64	acute diarrhoea
Pvt	William R. Payne	F	26	Point Lookout	3/16/64	dropsy
Pvt	Pinkney Powell	F	26	Point Lookout	6/25/64	febris typhoides
Pvt	Andrew J. Burke	G	26	Fort Delaware	10/9/63	chronic diarrhoea
Pvt	Quimby Hicks	G	26	Fort Delaware	10/12/63	chronic diarrhoea
Pvt	John Wesley Nelson	G	26	Point Lookout	4/9/64	chronic diarrhoea
Pvt	William Overman	G	26	Point Lookout	2/21/64	chronic diarrhoea
Pvt	Elias Parish	G	26	Fort Delaware	10/7/63	chronic diarrhoea
Pvt	Christopher C. Harrison	H	26	Point Lookout	2/14/65	chronic diarrhoea
Pvt	John Friddle	I	26	Fort Delaware	9/13/63	feb. typhoid/chr diarrhoea
Pvt	Isaac S. Mayberry	I	26	Point Lookout	1/19/64	chronic diarrhoea
Pvt	Fabius Prestwood	I	26	Fort Delaware	10/1/63	chronic diarrhoea
Pvt	A.B. Edwards	K	26	Gettysburg	8/1/63	ampt leg
Pvt	Rayford Willoughby	K	26	Point Lookout	2/29/64	dysenteria, chronic

Volume VIII 27th - 31st Infantry

1)-rost- **James W. Herring**, co D, 27 NC, capt in hosp at Richmond 3 Apr 65, no further records.
CWPOWrec- James W. Herring, co D, 27 NC, died 21 Apr 65 in Richmond of disease.

2)-rost- Benjamin F. Nunn, co D, 27 NC, wounded at Sharpsburg 17 Sept 1862, died on an unspecified date prior to 1 Jan 1863 of wounds, place of death not reported.
FO, 5 Jan 1863- **Benjamin Franklin Nunn**, co D, 27 NC, wounded Sharpsburg 17 Sept 1862, died near Pike Hill, Lenoir Co., NC on 3 Dec 1862 of wounds.

3)-rost-W. A. Hoff, Private, co H, 27 NC, present and accounted for until he died on September 8, 1861. Place and cause of death not reported.
Raleigh City Cemetery-**William A. Hoff**, died Sept 8, 1861.
Confederate Veteran- William Hoff of 'Pitt Volunteers' (which is co H, 27 NC) buried Raleigh City Cemetery.

4)-rost- **Wyley A. Wyatt**, co B, 28 NC, ...returned to duty prior to 1 Mar 63, trans to C.S. Navy on 3 Apr 64.
CWPOWrec- W. A. Wyatt, co B, 28 NC, capt Winchester on 30 Jul 63, disposition unaccounted for.
note: his record should be noted that this was his third captured before joining the Navy.

5)-rost- Aaron, Abel, Emanuel, Henry C., Jordan, Logan, Marcus, Philip H., William **Bolch**, co C, 28 NC.
note: While the military records indicated surname Bolch, the correct family name is **Bolick**. Additional info: Aaron Marion, Jordan Anthony and Philip Henkle.

6)-rost- **Richard A. Morrow**, co G, 28 NC, died Fredericksburg 14 Dec 1862
FO, 12 Jan 1863- **R. Alexander Morrow**, co G, 28 NC, died Fredericksburg 14 Dec 1862.

7)-rost-**John M. Coley**, co K, 28 NC, died on or about 6 Jun 1864. Place & cause of death not reported.
LMA-J. M. Coley of co B, 28 NC, d 5 Jul 1864, grave 275 in Oakwood Cem., Raleigh, NC.

8)-rost-**James C. Newson**, co D, 29 NC, capt Atlanta, Ga 22 Jul 64, to Louisville, Ky, trans to Camp Chase 31 Jul 64, no further records.
CWPOWrec- Jas. D. Newson, co D, 29 Ala, capt Atlantic 22 Jul 64, trans to Camp Chase 31 Jul 64, died 2 or 7 Dec 64 of chronic diarrhea.
1860 Tallapoosa Co., Ala census-James D. Newsom, born ca 1822.
note: since place and date of enlistment not reported for James of the 29 NC, highly believe that the Alabama soldier is correct and there was no Newson of the 29 NC.

9)-rost-**M. Ralph**, co E, 29 NC, capt Yazoo City, Miss on or about 13 Jul 63, sent to Indianapolis, trans to Ft Delaware 22 Mar 64, died at Ft Del on an unspecified date.

CWPOWrec 'Ft Delaware register'-M. Ralph, co E, 29 NC, capt Yazoo City, Miss on 14 Jul 63, rec from Camp Morton, Ind on 22 Mar 64, died Ft Delaware May 9th, 1864.

10)-rost-Pvt **Edward A. Griffin**, co F, 29 NC capt Franklin, Tn 17 Dec 64, conf at Nashville, Louisville, trans to Camp Douglas 22 Dec 64, died Camp Douglas 4 Jan 65.

rost-Pvt E. A. Griffin, misc. section, 22 NC died 4 Jan 65 at Camp Douglas, Ill, no further rec.

1912 book-same info as misc-22 NC.

CWPOWrec-E. A. Griffin, co F, 29 NC, capt Franklin, Tenn 17 Dec 64, died Camp Douglas 3 Jan 65 of pneumonia.

note: E. A. Griffin of 22 NC should be deleted.

11)-rost- **Icem Wood**, co F, 29 NC, died 16 Apr 65 of gunshot wound of the shoulder and spine, p & d wounded not reported.

CWPOWrec- **Isom Wood**, co F, 29 NC, died New Orleans, La Barracks 17 Apr 65 of gun shot wound.

12)-rost- Harvey Bailey, co G, 29 NC, place and date of enl not rep, wounded in left hand at or near Kennesaw Mountain, Ga. 18 Jun 64, died at Covington, Ga 9 Jul 64 of wounds.

rost- Harvey Bailey, co G, 24 NC, pen rec indicate he enl on 27 May 64, mort wounded in Georgia on 9 July 64.

Family rec on Ancestry.com- **Harvey James Bailey**, b 3 Nov 25 in Burnsville, Yancey Co, NC, died Covington, Newton, Ga 9 July 64, buried Bailey-Byrd Cem, Jacks Creek, Yancey Co., NC.

note: co G of the 29 NC was a Yancey Co unit and served in Georgia, Harvey Bailey of co G, 24 NC should be deleted.

13)-rost- Joseph Beasley, co I, 29 NC, p & d enl not reported, capt near Smyna, Ga 5 Jul 64, conf Louisville, Ky, trans to Camp Douglas 26 Jul 64, no further rec.

rost- **Joseph M. Beasley**, co I, 39 NC, res Macon Co, capt Chattahoochee, Ga 5 Jul 64, conf Louisville, Ky 25 Jul 64, rec Camp Douglas 28 Jul 64, rel aft oath at Camp Douglas 16 Jun 65.

CWPOWrec- Joseph Beasley, co I, 39 NC, capt Chattahoochie, Ga, 5 Jul 64, rec Camp Douglas 28 Jul 64, discharged 16 June 65.

note: Joseph Beasley of co I, 29 NC should be deleted.

14)-rost- James N. and **Thomas C. Gibbs**, of Yancey Co., co K, 29 NC, in this company.

CWPOWrec- **Henry H. Gibbs**, co K, 29 NC, died 10 Oct 1864 in Atlanta Gen. Field hospital of dysenteria.

1860 census of Yancey Co., NC – Henry H. was brother to **James N. Gibbs**.

1850 Yancey Co census – Henry H. was brother to both James N. and Thomas C. Gibbs.

note: Henry H. Gibbs should be added to co K, 29 NC with the above CWPOWrec info.

15)-rost- **Harmon R. Robinson**, co A, 30 NC, died at Martinsburg on 19 June 1863, cause of death not reported.

FO, 15 Feb 1864- R. H. Robinson, co A, 30 NC, died at Martinsburg on 18 June 1863 of typhoid pneumonia.

ADJ-Pvt R. H. Roberson, co A, 30 NCT, died at Martinsburg 18 June 1863 of typhoid pneumonia.

16)-rost-J. N. Ballenton, co C, 30 NC, born and res in New Hanover, occ Cooper, enl age 38 on 14 Jun 1863.

1850 New Hanover census-**James N. Ballington**, age 22.

1860 New Hanover census-Jas. Ballington, age 33, Cooper.

17)-rost- Corp. **Ellis A. Benton**, co E, 30 NC, conf at Newport News 14 Apr 65, date of release not reported.

CWPOWrec- Corp. E. A. Benton, co E, 30 NC, released 28 June 65 per GO nr 109.

18)-rost- A. Crouch, co E, 30 NC, p & d enl not rep, capt in hosp at Richmond, Va 3 Apr 1865, trans to Fed Provost Marshall 14 Apr 1865, no fur rec.

rost-**Allen F. Crouch**, co E, 38 NC, born Richmond Co., NC, capt in hosp at Richmond, Va 3 Apr 1865, conf Newport News, Va 24 Apr 1865, rel 30 Jun 1865 after Oath.

note: A. Crouch of co E, 30 NC should be deleted.

19)-rost-Pvt **James J. Piner** of co E, 30 NC, res New Hanover, enl age 27 on 21 Aug 63, capt Spots 20 May 64, conf Point Lookout, trans Elmira 3 Jul 64, died Elmira 4 Mar 65.

rost-Pvt James M. Piner, co E, 3 NC, res Onslow, enl age 23 on 13 May 61, prom Corp Jun 62, reduced to Pvt Oct 62, capt Spots 20 May 64, conf Point Lookout, trans to Elmira 3 Jul 64, died Elmira 4 Mar 65.

1912 book-Pvt J. Pyner of co E, 3 NC died Elmira 4 Mar 65, grave 1964.

CWPOWrec- J. M. Piner, co E, 3 NC, paroled 20 Feb 65, morning report 5 Mar 65 Elmira, ward 27, died 4 Mar 65 of variola.

CWPOWrec- J. Pyner, co E, 30 NC, died Elmira 4 Mar 65.

1860 Onslow census- J. M. Piner, 22 (no other census found on him).

1860 New Hanover census- **John J. Piner**, 25, wife Matilda, 20.

1870 New Hanover census- James Piner, 40, wife Matilda

1880 New Hanover census- James Piner, 46, wife Matilda 39

Note: James M. Piner of 3 NC died on 4 Mar 65 at Elmira.

John James/James John Piner of 30 NC came home after the war.

Delete death date of 4 Mar 65 for James J. Piner of 30 NC.

20)-rost- **Jacob Strickland**, co E, 30 NC, d Elmira 16 May 65 (no other info).

rost-Jacob Strickland, co E, 36 Regt (2 NC Arty), enl Columbus Co, capt Ft Fisher 15 Jan 65, d Elmira 16 May 65 of chr diarrhea.

CWPOWrec- Jacob Strickland, co E, 36 NC (2 NC Arty), died Elmira 16 May 65 of chr diarr.

note: Jacob Strickland of co E, 30 NC should be deleted.

21)-rost- **John Blackwell**, co G, 30 NC, died in Richmond on July 10 or July 30, 1862, of wounds.

Oakwood Cemetery Burial records-John Blackwell, co G, 30 NC, buried Aug 1, 1862 in Oakwood Cem., Richmond, Va.

note: this would make death date as July 30.

22)-rost- **K. H. McIver**, co H, 30 NC, died in Richmond 6 June 1863.

FO, 17 August 1863- **Kenneth H. Melver** (believe newspaper meant McIver), co H, 30 NC, died Richmond 6 June 1863.

23)-rost-**William Riley Diggs**, co B, 31 NC, res Anson Co., born ca 1828, died Elmira on 26 Nov 1864 of chr diarrhoea.

rost- Pvt **Noah P. Robertson**, co H, 1 NC, res Martin Co., NC, born ca 1827, released from Elmira on 27 Jun 65 after oath.

1912 book-Pvt N. Robertson, co H, 1 NC, in grave 980, died 26 Nov 64.

VA web site- N. P. Robertson, died 26 Nov 1864, buried site 980 Woodlawn Cem, Elmira.

CWPOWrec-Pvt N. P. Robertson, co H, 1 NC, died Elmira 26 Nov 1864 of chr diarrhea, roll 629, (note: written above the death statement 'Diggs, William R. Pvt 31 N.C. Co B. came in Robertson's place and').

CWPOWrec- 'Robertson N.P. Pri 1ˢᵗ NC H (capt and when) not given (died) Elmira) (when) Nov 26, 64, chr diarrhoea (number) 954 (locality) sec 2 Woodlawn Cem (letter mar) 629 (letter mark) 629.T (effects) EntD on folio 80 as Wm R Diggs'. (note: seems this line on Robertson was penciled in at the top of the page later after the others on page were entered).

CWPOWrec- William R. Diggs, co B, 31 NC, died Elmira 26 Nov 64 of chr diarrhea, in grave 954 Woodlawn Cem, 'on rolls as W. P. Robinston 1 N.C. R. see R folio 210'.

1860 Anson Co., NC census-Riley Diggs, 48, Mary, 47, Wm, 23, Thomas, 15.

1870 Richmond Co., NC census- Wm Diggs, 43 (living along); in next household on page: Thomas E. Diggs, 30, Mary, 25.

1880 Richmond Co., NC census- William Diggs, 53 (living along).

1860 Martin Co., NC census-Noah Robason, 23, Mary, 20, wife, Leah, 65, widower.

note: did Robertson (Robason) died at Elmira and Diggs came home?

24)-rost- **Robert Matthews**, co C, 31 NC, present through April 1863, no further records.
 NCS, 18 Nov 1863- Robert Matthews, co C, 31 NC, killed at Fort Sumter on 30th ult. (30 October 1863.)

25)-rost-**W. L. Stephens**, co C, 31 NC, place and date enl not reported, capt in hosp at Raleigh 13 Apr 1865. No Fur Rec.
 LMA-W. L. Stephens of co B, 31 NC no date buried in Oakwood. He was first buried on Henry Mordecai's land in Raleigh.

26)-rost-**Samuel A. Smith**, co D, 31 NC, died on 20-24 March 1863 of disease, place of death not reported.
 NCS, 15 April 1863- S. A. Smith, Co D, 31 NC, died in Wake Co., NC on 24th ult. (24 March 1863) of typhoid fever, he was at home on furlough at time of death.

27)-rost- **John W. Wombles**, co D, 31 NC, of Wake Co, served in this unit.
 NCS, Dec 21, 1864- **William N. Womble**, co D, 31 NC, of Wake Co., killed Petersburg 3 Dec 64.

28)-rost-William H. Britton, co F, 31 NC, capt Cold Harbor 1 Jun 64, confined Point Lookout 11 Jun 64, no further records.
 Ancestry.com family info-**William Henry Britton**, born 1 Dec 1837 in Pitt Co, NC, died Jan 1908 in Bethel, Pitt Co, NC. He surv the war.

29)-rost- **Benjamin Clark**, co F, 31 NC, res Martin Co., capt Roanoke Island and paroled, capt Cold Harbor 1 June 64, died Elmira 8 Oct 64 of typhoid fever.
 rost- Benjamin Clark, co K, 5 NC Cav, capt Ashland Station 1 June 64, conf at Point Lookout, tran to Elmira where he died 8 Oct 64 of typhoid fever.
 note: Benjamin Clark of the 5 Cav should be deleted.

30)-rost- **William T. Liverman**, co G, 31 NC, capt Roanoke Island 8 Feb 62, paroled Elizabeth City 21 Feb 62, no further record.
 rost- William T. Liverman, co A, 12 Batt NC Cav, enlisted Northampton Co., NC 1 Sep 62, deserted immediately after enlistment.
 rost-William T. Liverman, co D, 4 NC Cav, enlisted Southampton Co., Va 25 Sep 62, capt Waterloo, Pa. 5 Jul 63. (see rest of this unit for his record.)
 note: This is the same William T. Liverman in all three units.

31)-rost-**William A. Horton**, co H, 31 NC, died in Columbia, SC 24 March 1863, cause of death not reported.
 NCS, 6 May 1863- W. H. Horton, co H, 31 NC, died in Columbia, SC 24 March 1863 of typhoid fever.
 note: believe newspaper account meant William A. and not W. H. (who survived the war).

32)-rost- **James Parrish**, co H, 31 NC, died in an unspecified North Carolina hospital on 12-14 May 1863.

NCS, 10 June 1863- James Parish, co B, 31 NC, died in a Wilmington hospital on 18 May 1863.

note: newspaper had James in company B, but should have been company H.

33)-rost- M. G. Scarborough, co H, 31 NC, died Wilmington 30 July 1863.

NCS, 7 Oct 1863- **Melvin G. Scarborough**, co H, 31 NC, died Wilmington 30 July 1863.

34)-rost- **John P. Dewar**, co I, 31 NC, returned to duty on 10 June 1864, nor further records.

FO, 22 Aug 1864- Sgt John P. Dewar, co I, 31 NC, was shot through the head by a sharpshooter near Petersburg and instantly killed on 30 June 1864.

Petersburg- J. P. Dewar, co c, 31 NC, killed Petersburg on 30 Jun 1864, buried Petersburg Fair Ground vicinity.

35)-rost-2nd Lt. Daniel McL. Jones, co I, 31 NC, furloughed for sixty days on 6 June 64, no further records.

FO, Nov 14, 1864- **Daniel McLean Jones**, co I, 31 NC, died near battlefield on 2 Oct 64 from wounds received in the advance of Clingman's Brigade upon Fort Harrison, Va.

36)-rost- **John H. Smith**, co I, 31 NC, died prior to 18 Dec 1864, place and cause of death not reported.

FO, 15 Aug 1864- Johnnie H. Smith, co I, 31 NC, died 3 June 1864 of a wound received at Gaines' Mills on 1 June 1864.

Cause of deaths that were not listed in the NC Roster - Volume VIII

rank	name	co	unit	place of death	died	cause of death
Pvt	William F. Chestnutt	A	27	Point Lookout	8/14/64	dysenteria, acute
Pvt	George H. Woolen	B	27	Point Lookout	9/19/64	plura, inf of
Pvt	Benaja Gray	D	27	Richmond	6/2/65	of wounds
Pvt	Levi W. Carden	F	27	Point Lookout	8/10/64	jaundice
Pvt	Jonathan May	F	27	Point Lookout	8/18/64	dysenteria, chronic
Pvt	Chesley H. Blalock	G	27	Point Lookout	8/1/64	acute dysenteria
Pvt	Lorenzo Dunnegan	G	27	Point Lookout	11/5/63	pneumonia
Pvt	Elisha A. Durham	G	27	Point Lookout	6/5/65	chronic diarrhoea
Pvt	William Bullock	H	27	Point Lookout	8/7/64	chronic diarrhoea
Pvt	Solomon G. Gates	A	28	Point Lookout	1/16/64	chronic diarrhoea
Pvt	John L.H. Cline	C	28	Point Lookout	6/19/64	measles
Pvt	Robert Stoker	D	28	Point Lookout	12/23/63	chronic diarrhoea
Pvt	Alexander Bennett	E	28	Point Lookout	6/6/64	acute diarrhoea
Sgt	Henry Brantley	E	28	Richmond	5/2/65	foot, left, gs wound
Pvt	John A. Sedberry	E	28	Point Lookout	12/27/63	chronic diarrhoea
Pvt	William D. Kelly	F	28	Point Lookout	3/10/64	chronic diarrhoea
Pvt	Charles McCollum	G	28	Point Lookout	7/8/65	chronic diarrhoea
Pvt	John W. Snipes	G	28	Point Lookout	6/30/64	febris int. cong.
Corp	Berry E. Hughes	H	28	Fort Delaware	9/25/63	rheumatism chronic
Pvt	William M. Carter	I	28	Point Lookout	8/24/64	consumption
Pvt	S.W. Jennings	I	28	Davids Island	6/30/62	pneumonia
Pvt	Redding Harwood	K	28	Point Lookout	6/2/64	febris int. cong.
Pvt	Isaac Mann	C	29	Chicago	5/9/65	pneumonia
Pvt	Jabez B. Oliver	D	29	Indianapolis	8/23/63	febris typhoides
Pvt	W.L. Ivey	A	30	Point Lookout	1/26/65	diarrhoea
Pvt	John Asken	B	30	Point Lookout	8/25/64	diphtheria
Pvt	John N. Harris	B	30	Point Lookout	8/12/64	chronic diarrhoea
Pvt	Stephen H. Kirkland	B	30	Point Lookout	8/11/64	consumption
Pvt	J.R. Pendergrass	C	30	Point Lookout	8/29/64	acute diarrhoea
Sgt	John W. Wescott	C	30	Point Lookout	1/25/65	consumption
Pvt	D. Vaughn Sollice	G	30	Point Lookout	1/23/64	dysenteria, chronic
Pvt	David W. Kelly	H	30	Point Lookout	7/13/64	acute diarrhoea
Pvt	W.H. King	H	30	Point Lookout	6/30/64	febris remit
Pvt	Nathan Matthews	H	30	Point Lookout	9/16/64	remittent fever
Pvt	Josiah J. Pridgen	I	30	Point Lookout	11/26/63	febris typhoides
Pvt	Nathan C. Williams	I	30	Point Lookout	12/28/63	anemia
Sgt	Samuel J. Boyce	K	30	Washington	11/11/63	gs amp thigh
Pvt	Elisha Simmons	K	30	Newport News	6/18/65	chronic diarrhoea
Pvt	Augustine G. Sexton	C	31	Point Lookout	7/13/64	measles
Pvt	William Carroll	D	31	White House	6/9/64	gs w leg
Sgt	Parham P. Parrish	D	31	Fort Monroe	10/9/64	exh fm amp rt thigh

Additional Information and Amendments to the North Carolina Troops 1861-1865

Volume IX - 32nd - 35th and 37th Infantry

1)-rost- Sgt. Major **Joseph J. Bridges**, Field and Staff, 32 NC, promoted to Sergeant Major in Feb-Apr 1864 and trans to the Field and Staff, no further records.

Spotsylvania Confederate Cemetery, Va.- Sgt. Major James Bridges, 32 NC, buried in row 4, grave 6.

note: while the given names is the only different between the two information, strongly suggest that this is the same person.

2)-rost- **Asbury Spruill**, co A, 32 NC, enl Raleigh 7 Sept 64, capt Cedar Ck, Va 19 Oct 64, conf Pt Lookout 28 Oct 64, no further records.

CWPOWrec- Benj. (pencil above the A.) A. Spruill, co A, 32 NC, capt Strausburg, Va 19 Oct 64, rec from Harpers Ferry 28 Oct 64, died Point Lookout 28 Apr 65 of scurey.

1860 Tyrrell census-Benj. A. Spruill age 29.

note: Company A of 32 NC was raised in Tyrrell Co., NC and have A.A., Asbury, Henry W. and Jasper Spruill in unit. No Benjamin listed.

note: name should be **Benjamin Asbury Spruill** who died 28 Apr 65.

3)-rost-**Marcus Bright**, co B, 32 NC, conf Pt Lookout 25 Sep 64, no further records.

CWPOWrec- **Mark Bright**, co B, 32 NC, released 28 Nov 64 from Pt Lookout.

4)-rost- **Archibald Taylor**, 2nd co B, 32 NC, reported absent sick at Martinsburg 19 Jun3 1863, reported absent through December 1863, no further records.

FO, 15 Feb 1864- A. F. Taylor, co B, 32 NC, died at Martinsburg on 23 July 1863 of typhoid fever.

ADJ-Pvt **A. F. Taylor**, co B, 32 NC, died at Martinsburg 23 July 1863 of typhoid fever.

5)-rost-D. Savage, co C, 32 NC, capt Gettysburg 3 Jul, conf at Fort Delaware, no fur rec.

rost-**David W. Savage**, co C, 52 NC, born Chowan Co., farmer, enlisted in Gates Co. 27 Feb 62, promoted to Sgt, report missing at Gettysburg on 3 July 63, was probably killed at Gettysburg.

CWPOWrec- D. Savage, no unit or where capt, died at Fort Delaware on 22 Oct 63 of smallpox and buried on Jersey shore (Finn Point).

CWPOWrec- D. Savage, co I, 2 Miss, died Fort Delaware on 22 Oct 63.

CWPOWrec- D. Savage, no co, regt, where capt and date captured only year '1863'. (note: the line above has J.M. Pitts of co I, 2 Miss, died Ft Delaware on 22 Oct 63.

VA site-D. Savage d Fort Delaware 22 Oct 1863 bur Finn Point.

1912 book- D. Savage, co I, 2 Miss., died Ft Delaware 22 Oct 1863.

John M. Pitts, co I, 2 Miss, died Ft Delaware 22 Oct 1863.

2nd Mississippi Regiment web site- **John Minett Pitts** died Ft Delaware 22 Oct 63. There are no 'Savage' in this unit.

note: In checking on the name Savage in any Mississippi Regt found 45 and none with a given name that started with a 'D'. Of the 2,250 soldiers in the 2nd Miss. none were

Savage. There is no D. Savage of co C, 32 NC nor in co I, 2 Miss. The corrct soldier is Sgt. David Savage of co C, 52 NC and all others should be deleted.

6)-rost-**J. J. Bayles**, co G, 32 NC, enl Raleigh 1 Jun 64. died Ral 24 Nov 64. **James W. Bayles** joined same day. They both first enl in co F, 15 NC fm Harnett Co. on 18 May 1861. J. J. was discharged Sep 1861 and James W. was discharged Mar 1863.

1850 Cumberland census-Solomon and Nancy Bales are parents of **John J. Bales**, age 16, and **James W. Bales**, age 14.

note: change J. J. Bayles of 32 NC to John J. Bayles.

7)-rost- **Freeman H. Hughes**, co G, 32 NC, capt Gettysburg, confined Ft Delaware about 7 July 63, no further records.

CWPOWrec- Freeman Hughes, co G, 32 NC, capt Gettysburg 4 July 63, released on Oath 3 May 1865.

8)-rost- **James H. Barnes**, co H, 32 NC, w at Gettysburg 2 Jul 63, no further records.

CWPOWrec- J. H. Barnes, co H, 32 NC, capt Winchester 30 Jul 63, died 1 Aug 63.

9)-rost- William H. Guthrie, 2nd co I, 32 NC, died at Harrisonburg 2 August 1864, cause of death not reported.

FO, 17 Oct 1864- **William Hugh Guthrie**, co I, 32 NC, died in Harrisburg 3 Aug 1864 from wound received from the accidental discharge of his gun.

10)-rost-Pvt **George W. Tyson** of 2co I, 32 NC, fm Chatham Co, prev in co M, 15 NC, trans to 32 NC in Jun 62, capt Spotts 10 May 64, conf Point Lookout, trans 3 Aug 64 to Elmira, died Elmira 6 Mar 65.

rost-Pvt George W. Tyson, co F, 22 NC died Elmira 6 Mar 65, no further rec.

note: George W. Tyson of co F, 22 NC should be deleted.

11)-rost- **Rufus T. Egerton**, 2nd co K, 32 NC, trans from co L, 15 NC, died 14 Aug 1862 of disease, place of death not reported.

FO, 1 Sept 1862- Rufus E. Egerton, Franklin Rifles (co L), 15 NC, died in Franklin Co., NC on 14 August 1862.

12)-rost- **John Page**, co A, 33 NC, p & a until killed at New Bern 14 Mar 1862.

CWPOWrec- John Page, 33 NC, died 17 Mar 62 at New Bern of Vulmis Sclopst?.

note: record should state that he was wounded, captured and died three days later at New Bern.

13)-rost-**Noah Lewis**, co C, 33 NC, resided in Forsyth Co. where he enlisted at age 30 on 1 July 62, capt Gettysburg on or about 4 July 63, conf at Ft Delaware until paroled 30 Jul 63, died at Salem on or about 25 Sept 1863.

rost- N. Lewis, co C, 23 NC, place and date of enlistment not reported, 1st listed in company records 28 Oct 1862, capt Gettysburg 5 Jul 1863, conf at Ft Delaware 7-12

July 63, no further records.

CWPOWrec- N. Lewis, co I, 33 NC, capt Gettysburg 5 July 63, exchanged from Ft Delaware to City Point on 30 July 63.

CWPOWrec- Noah Lewis, co C, 23 NC, capt Gettysburg 1 July 63.

note: Noah Lewis of co C, 33 NC is the correct soldier and N. Lewis of co C, 23 NC should be deleted.

14)-rost- **William H. H. Wesley**, co E, 33 NC, enl Edgecombe Co., NC 1 July 1862, capt Falling Waters 14 Jul 63, conf Pt Lookout 17 Aug 63, no further records.

rost- **William H. H. Worsley**, co E, 33 NC, enl Edgecombe Co., NC 1 July 1862, capt Falling Waters 14 Jul 63, conf Pt Lookout until trans to Elmira, arr Elmira 18 Aug 64, died Elmira 6 Nov 64 of chronic diarrhea.

CWPOWrec- W. H. Weseley of Edgecombe Co, co E, 33 NC, signed 22 Feb 64 a 'desire to be sent South as Prisoners of War for Exchange'. Trans to Elmira 16 Aug 64. (1 record on this name)

CWPOWrec- William H. Worsley, co E, 33 NC, joined Elmira station 18 Aug 64, died 6 Nov 64, in grave 842, left effects of jacket, pr pants and hat.(7 records on this name)

note: the name William Wesley appeared one time when he was transferred from Point Lookout to Elmira 16 Aug 1864.

1860 Edgecombe co, NC census-William H. H. Worsley, age 15, son of Littleberry and Harrett Worsley. (no William Wesley in 1860 NC census)

note: William H. H. Worsley is the correct name and William H. H. Wesley should be deleted from *N.C. Troops* book.

15)-rost- William H. H. Worsley, co E, 33 NC, enl Edgecombe Co., NC 1 July 1862, capt Falling Waters 14 Jul 63, conf Pt Lookout until trans to Elmira, arr Elmira 18 Aug 64, died Elmira 6 Nov 64 of chronic diarrhea.

rost- William H. H. Wesley, co E, 33 NC, enl Edgecombe Co., NC 1 July 1862, capt Falling Waters 14 Jul 63, conf Pt Lookout 17 Aug 63, no further records.

CWPOWrec- W. H. Weseley of Edgecombe Co, co E, 33 NC, signed 22 Feb 64 a 'desire to be sent South as Prisoners of War for Exchange'. Trans to Elmira 16 Aug 64. (1 record on this name)

CWPOWrec- William H. Worsley, co E, 33 NC, joined Elmira station 18 Aug 64, died 6 Nov 64, in grave 842, left effects of jacket, pr pants and hat.(7 records on this name)

note: the name William Wesley appeared one time when he was transferred from Point Lookout to Elmira 16 Aug 1864.

1860 Edgecombe co, NC census-William H. H. Worsley, age 15, son of Littleberry and Harrett Worsley. (no William Wesley in 1860 NC census)

note: William H. H. Worsley is the correct name and William H. H. Wesley should be deleted from *N.C. Troops* book.

16)-rost- **Jesse Bradshaw**, co G, 33 NC, p & a until capt at Wilderness or Spotsylvania CH, Va 5-12 May 64.

CWPOWrec- J. Bradshaw, co G, 33 NC, capt Wilderness 6 May 64.

17)-rost- **Emanuel C. Thompson**, co G, 33 NC, dest to enemy 24 Feb 65, conf Washington, DC, rel on unk date after oath.

CWPOWrec- E. C. Thompson, co G, 33 NC, died 18 May 65 at Wilmington, NC General Hospital of chronic diarrhea.

18)-rost- **William L. Long**, co I, 33 NC, died at Point Lookout prior to 1 Nov 63, cause of death not reported.

CWPOWrec-William L. Long, co I, 33 NC, died Point Lookout on 30 Oct 1863 of pneumonia.

19)-rost-Pvt **Constantine Mickey**, co I, 33 NC, born Forsyth Co, enl age 21 on 1 Jul 61, capt New Bern 14 Mar 62, died in July 62 while a POW, place and cause of death not reported.

Fort Delaware Society-Pvt C (GP) Mickey died Fort Delaware 4 Aug 62.

CWPOWrec- C. Mickey, capt New Bern 14 Mar 62, confined at Fort Columbus, New York Harbor, died Ft Delaware 4 Aug 62 (did not find when he was trans from Ft Columbus to Ft Delaware.)

20)-rost-Pvt **Abraham H. Tuttle**, co I, 33 NC capt New Bern 14 Mar 62, died in NY or Fort Delaware 29 Jul 62.

Fort Delaware Society-Pvt Abraham (L) Tuttle died Fort Delaware 29 Jul 62.

CWPOWrec- Abraham Tuttle, 27 NC Troops, capt New Bern 14 Mar 1862, conf at Fort Columbia, NY Harbor, died Ft Delaware 29 July 62 (did not find when he was trans from Ft Columbus to Ft Delaware.).

21)-rost- Sgt. **James Bartlett**, co K, 33 NC, p & a until w in back near Petersburg 21-22 Jun 1864, died 22 Jun 64 of wounds, place of death not reported.

CW POW REC- Sgt James Bartlett, Co K, 33 NC, died 22 Jun 64 of gs w back in 1st Div 2 Army Corps hospital (register 34 AC).

note: rec should note that he was wounded and captured.

note: believe this Union Corps was at City Point, Va.

22)-rost- J. T. S. Gibson, co K, 33 NC, died in camp near Gordonsville 1 Sept 1862, cause of death not reported.

FO, 25 July 1864- **James S. Gibson**, co K, 33 NC, died at Gordonsville 1 Sept 1863 of chronic diarrhea, brother to Virgil A. Gibson and William H. Gibson of same company.

23)-rost- V. A. Gibson, co K, 33 NC, died in hospital at or near Lynchburg on or about 20 Nov 1862 of phthisis pulmo.

FO, 25 July 1864- **Virgil A. Gibson**, co K, 33 NC, died at Lynchburg Hospital 19 Nov 1862 of chronic diarrhea, brother to James S. and William H. Gibson of same company.

24)-rost- W. H. Gibson, co K, 33 NC, died in camp near Gordonsville 5 Sept 1862, cause of death not reported.

FO, 25 July 1864- **William H. Gibson**, co K, 33 NC, died at Gordonsville 5 Sept 1862 of chronic diarrhea, brother to James S. and Virgil A. Gibson of same company.

25)-rost-Pvt **Theron D. Waldrop**, co C, 34 NC, enl 1864, capt Amelia CH 3 Apr 65, died Point Lookout 28 May 65 of chronic dysentery.

rost-Pvt **Jaron D. Waldrop**, co C, 24 NC, p & d enl not reported, died Point Lookout 28 May 65, cause of death not reported.

1912 book-same info as 24 NC.

CWPOWrec- Jaron D. Waldrop, co C, 34 NC, capt Amelia Ch 3 Apr 65, died Point Lookout 28 May 65 of chron. Diarrhoea. (when he was captured the 34 NC was noted as his unit, one record at Pt Lookout had 24 NC.)(no Theron D. Waldrop noted in POW records.)

1850 Rutherford Co., NC census- T. D. Waldrape (23).

1860 Polk Co., NC census- T. D. Waldrop (35), wife Cela.

note: the co C, 34 NC is a Rutherford Co. company. Jaron D. Waldrop of co C, 24 NC should be deleted.

26)-rost- J. A. Cobb, co H, 34 NC, trans to Savannah for exchange, died prior to 17 Feb 65, place and cause of death not reported.

FO, 12 Dec 1864- J. E. Cobb, co H, 34 NC, exchanged soldier who died in Savannah since 20 Nov 1864.

Csagraves.com- **James A. Cobb**, co H, 34 NC, died 20 Nov 1864, buried Laurel Grove Cemetery, Savannah, Ga.

27)-rost-**Thomas A. Williams**, co A, 35 NC, last reported in company 26 Mar 1864, no further records.

Petersburg- Thomas A. Williams, 35 NC, died Petersburg on 12 Jul 1864, burial Petersburg Fair Ground vicinity.

28)-rost- **George W. Fulwood**, co B, 35 NC, died at Raleigh or at New Bern on Jan 10 or Jan 28, 1862, cause of death not reported.

Haywood papers- G. Fulwood, co 34, died Raleigh on 14 Jan 1862 of typhoid fever. (he was number 28 on death list.)

(note: many 34 and 35 NC Infantry deaths in Raleigh noted during this period, the 35 NC is the correct unit for George.)

29)-rost- **Neill A. Patterson**, co C, 35 NC, killed near Petersburg 17 June 1864.

CWPOWrec- M. A. Patterson, co C, 35 NC, died 20 June 1864 at 1 Div 9 Corps hosp of gs w head.

note: record should show he was wounded, captured and died three days later.

30)-rost- co C, 35 NC (no Rowan noted)

FO, 18 July 1864- Richard T. Rowan, co C, 35 NC, age 19, killed near Petersburg on 17 June 1864 in a charge.

1850 and 1860 Moore Co., NC census- Richard T. Rowan, born 1845

Family records on Ancestry.com- **Richard Thomas Rowan**, born 16 Jan 1845, died 17 Jun 1864.

(note: company C was a Moore Co. unit and Richard probably joined late, but did not make the muster rolls.)

31)-rost- Duncan A. Thompson, co C, 35 NC, discharged on 23 May 1862 because of abscess in the upper part of the right lung accompanied by a cough.

FO, 6 March 1865- **Duncan Alexander Thompson**, co C, 35 NC, died 22 Jan 1865.

32)-rost- Corp. **John H. Johnson**, co D, 35 NC, last reported in the rec of this company on 25 March 1864.

NCS, 6 July 1864- John H. Johnson, co D, 35 NC, fell near Petersburg on 20 May 1864, his brother, Thomas, caught him in his arms when he fell, two days later Thomas then took his body and laid it in a grave, the father a week later removed it to the family graveyard.

note: brother to Thomas J. Johnson of same company (see below.)

33)-rost- **Thomas J. Johnson**, co D, 35 NC, last reported in the rec of this company on 25 March 1864.

NCS, 6 July 1864- Thomas Johnson, co D, 35 NC, fell on the battlefield near Petersburg 17 June 1864.

note: brother to John H. Johnson of same company (see above.)

34)-rost- **Joe Dickie**, co E, 35 NC, enlisted at age 18 on 1 Feb 1863, no further records.

Petersburg- **J. W. Dickey**, co E, 35 NC, died at Petersburg, no date, buried Petersburg Fair Ground Vicinity.

35)-rost-**R. H. McCracken**, co G, 35 NC, enl 17 Oct 1863. rep sick Nov 64-Feb 65.

LMA-**R. B. McCracken** died at Camp Holmes on 1 Jan 1865, grave 6 in Oakwood Cem, Raleigh, NC.

36)-rost- Sergeant Major **Thomas C. Wright**, Field and Staff, 37 NC, wounded at Wilderness on or about 5-6 May 1864, died on 26 May 1864 of wounds, place of death not reported.

FO, 26 May 1864- Sgt. Major C. T. Wright, 37 NC, age 18, from Wilmington, died in

Petersburg on 20 May 1864 from wound received 7 May 1864.

37)-rost-Pvt **Andrew C. Gentry**, co A, 37 NC, w and c Hanover Court House, died of
wounds, place and date of death not reported.
Interment.net-Yorktown Nat Cem-Pvt Andrew Gentry of 37 NC died 27 May 62, grave
1081.

38)-rost- **William Perry**, co A, 37 NC, died in Oct 62 of disease, place of death not rep.
CWPOWrec- **W. S. Perry**, co A, 37 NC, died 13 Nov 62 at Harrisburg, Ky.

39)-rost- **John L. Reid**, co C, 37 NC, died 3 Aug 1862, place not reported.
FO, 8 Sept 1862- John L. Reid, Capt. Brown's Company from Mecklenbrug (co C, 37
NC), died Greenwood hospital on 3 August 1862.

40)-rost- **Ambrose Lee Stearns**, co C, 37 NC, died 2 Aug 1862, place not reported.
FO, 8 Sep 1862- A. L. Stearns, Capt. Brown's Company from Mecklenburg (co C, 37
NC), died in hospital near Richmond on 1 Sept 1862.

41)-rost-Pvt **Levi Carpenter** of co I, 37 died Elmira either Mar 1 or May 9, 65.
CWPOWrec- Levi Carpenter, died 1 May 1865.
1912 book-Pvt Levi Carpenter of co I, 37 NC died Elmira 1 Mar 65, grave 2740.
note: soldiers in Elmira grave numbers 2733-2797 died in May, so his death date should
be in May 65. Date in 1912 book is wrong.

42)-rost- **Joseph McAllister**, co K, 37 NC, conf Point Lookout until rel 29 Jun 65 after
Oath.
CWPOWrec- Joseph McAllister, co K, 37 NC, died 7 Jul 65 at Danville, Va of acute
diarrhea.
note: he died eight days after released on his way home.

43)-rost- **James Sturgill**, co K, 37 NC, enl 25 Dec 63, capt Wilderness or Spotsylania
6/12 May 64, conf Point Lookout, trans to Elmira 8 Aug 64, died Elmira 19 Mar 65
of pneumonia.
rost- J. Storgeal, co K, 23 NC, place and date enl not reported, capt by enemy on an
unspecified date, died Elmira 22 Jan 65, cause of death not reported.
CWPOWrec- J. Storgeal, co K, 37 NC (Ala struck out), capt Spotsylanvia 12 May 64,
died Elmira 19 Mar 65 of pneumonia (two records noted.)
1912 Book- J. Storgeal, co K, 23 NC, died Elmira 22 Jan 65, grave 1578.
note: The 1912 book is the only source for J. Storgeal of the 23 NC. While the unit
nr. And death date are different, data suggest the James Sturgill of the 37 NC is the
correct soldier and J. Storgeal of co K, 23 NC should be deleted.

Cause of deaths that were not listed in the NC Roster - Volume IX

rank	name	co	unit	place of death	died	cause of death
Pvt	Wilson G. Cahooh	A	32	Point Lookout	2/9/64	pneumonia
Pvt	John L. Van Horn	A	32	Point Lookout	7/4/64	diarrhoea
Pvt	James B Overton	B	32	Point Lookout	7/27/64	chronic diarrhoea
Pvt	Lawson Alexander Witherspoon	B	32	Point Lookout	7/24/64	acute diarrhoea
Pvt	Marcus Clippard	E	32	Point Lookout	9/5/64	chronic diarrhoea
Pvt	Jonas Hunsucker	E	32	Point Lookout	8/27/64	chronic diarrhoea
Pvt	Joshua Cosand	F	32	Point Lookout	10/27/63	erysipelas
Pvt	Elisha Kerley	F	32	Point Lookout	10/23/64	chronic diarrhoea
Pvt	James E. Newbern	G	32	Fort Delaware	10/10/63	lungs, inf of
Pvt	Daniel C. Reardon	G	32	Newport News	5/8/65	chronic diarrhoea
Pvt	Jesse Braswell	H	32	Point Lookout	9/3/64	acute dysenteria
Pvt	James Weldon Edwards	H	32	Fort Delaware	10/1/63	chronic diarrhoea
Pvt	Higdon Harper	H	32	Point Lookout	5/24/64	chronic diarrhoea
Pvt	Elias Johnson	H	32	Point Lookout	9/7/64	lungs, inf of
Pvt	David M. Odom	H	32	Point Lookout	7/3/64	acute diarrhoea
Pvt	John E. Ricks	H	32	Point Lookout	8/5/64	Chr. Val dis of heart
Pvt	George V. Whitfield	H	32	Point Lookout	10/23/64	chronic diarrhoea
1Lt	James W. Kinsey	K	32	Boston	12/19/61	febris typhoides
Pvt	Adolphus C. Summers	A	33	Point Lookout	8/28/64	chronic diarrhoea
Pvt	Miles B. Stalls	B	33	Point Lookout	7/22/64	pericardism, inf of
Pvt	George G. Kriminger	C	33	Point Lookout	7/2/64	lungs, inf of
Pvt	Allison Stough	C	33	Point Lookout	3/4/64	febris inter.
Sgt	William J. Duke	E	33	Point Lookout	7/13/64	febris typhoides
Pvt	Calvin Gaither	E	33	Fort Delaware	10/6/63	chronic diarrhoea
Pvt	James Smith	E	33	Fort Delaware	10/3/63	chronic diarrhoea
Pvt	Isaac W. Morris	F	33	Fort Delaware	10/4/63	chronic diarrhoea
Pvt	Thomas Miller	H	33	Point Lookout	1/25/64	dysenteria, chronic
Pvt	Robinson A. Sawyer	H	33	Fort Columbus	6/30/62	febris typhoides
Sgt	James Bartlett	K	33	1 Div 2 Army Corps Hosp	6/22/64	gs w back
Pvt	Augustus Ceasar Davis	A	34	Point Lookout	6/20/64	dysenteria, acute
Pvt	John B. Williams	A	34	Point Lookout	8/15/64	acute diarrhoea
Pvt	Washington W. Blankenship	B	34	Point Lookout	7/23/64	typhoid fever
Pvt	George W. Pinson	B	34	Point Lookout	10/15/63	febris typhoides
Pvt	George W. Wright	B	34	Newport News	5/23/65	scurvy/chr diarrhoea
Pvt	G.W. Coon	C	34	Point Lookout	2/7/64	chronic diarrhoea
Pvt	Lorenzo A. Davis	C	34	Point Lookout	2/2/64	chronic diarrhoea
Pvt	Reubin R. Hill	C	34	Richmond	6/3/65	chronic diarrhoea
Pvt	James H. Hudgins	C	34	Point Lookout	2/14/64	bowels, inf of
Pvt	William Nailand	C	34	Point Lookout	1/2/64	typhoid pneumonia
Pvt	Josephus S. Gibbs	D	34	Newport News	5/28/65	dropsy/diarrhoea
Pvt	J.M. Dixon	E	34	Point Lookout	8/15/64	febris remit
Corp	Lemuel S. Self	F	34	Point Lookout	10/3/64	chronic diarrhoea
Pvt	Emory E. Warren	F	34	Point Lookout	9/7/63	chronic diarrhoea
Pvt	John L. Todd	G	34	Fort Delaware	10/8/63	dysenteria, chronic
Pvt	Perry G. Putman, Sr.	H	34	Point Lookout	8/18/64	acute diarrhoea

Pvt	Asa Hazelwood	I	34	Point Lookout	7/4/64	measles
Pvt	Freeman Hurley	K	34	Fort Delaware	10/5/63	scurvy
Pvt	Eli Russell	K	34	Point Lookout	12/27/63	dysentery, chronic
Pvt	Calvin H. Council	D	35	Point Lookout	8/2/64	dysentery, acute
Pvt	Hugh M. Hunter	H	35	Point Lookout	7/1/64	acute diarrhoea
Pvt	Elam Franklin White	H	35	Point Lookout	7/21/64	acute dysenteria
Pvt	James Holloway	A	37	Point Lookout	8/25/64	scurvy
Pvt	William R. Nelson	B	37	Point Lookout	12/23/63	chronic diarrhoea
Pvt	James Martin Hendrix	C	37	Point Lookout	6/12/65	lungs, inf of
Pvt	Milus B. Pippins	C	37	Point Lookout	8/4/64	febris typhoides
Pvt	Henry Bennett	D	37	Point Lookout	4/9/64	chronic diarrhoea
Pvt	Adam Black	D	37	Point Lookout	8/11/64	acute dysenteria
Pvt	Alexander Fox	F	37	Fort Delaware	9/13/63	febris intermittens
Pvt	Larkin J. Chapman	G	37	Newport News	5/8/65	chronic diarrhoea
Pvt	Joseph C.G. Stevenson	G	37	Elmira	8/27/64	feb. typh./chr diarrhoea
Pvt	George N. Furguson	H	37	Fort Columbus	7/14/62	phthisis pulmonalis
Pvt	Marion L. Holland	H	37	Point Lookout	8/21/64	scurvy
Pvt	Daniel H. Douglass	K	37	Point Lookout	8/24/64	chronic diarrhoea

Additional Information and Amendments to the North Carolina Troops 1861-1865

Volume X 38th - 39th and 42nd - 44th Infantry

1)-rost- A. C. Campbell, co A, 38 NC, p & d of enl not rep, capt unk, d Point Lookout 27 Feb 65, cause of death not rep.

rost- **Alfred C. Campbell**, co D, 25 NC, res Cherokee Co, capt near Globe Tavern, Va 21 Aug 64, d Point Lookout 26 Feb 65 of chr diarr.

CWPOWrec- A. C. Campbell, co A, 38 NC, capt Wilderness 6 May 64, d Point Lookout 27 Feb 65 of chr diarrhea.

CWPOWrec- A. C. Campbell, co D, 25 NC, d Point Lookout 27 Feb 65 of chr diarr.

CWPOWrec- A. C. Campbell, co D, 25 NC, capt Weldon RR 21 Apr 64, exh 18 Feb 65 fm Pt Lookout.

note: several POW rec noted for both the one in the 38 and the 25, but with the additional info on him in the 25 NC A. C. Campbell of co A, 38 NC should be deleted.

2)-rost- **William T. Lewis**, co B, 38 NC, died 20 Jan 63, place of death not reported.

note: Emory Cemetery at Emory and Henry College, Virginia has **W. F. Lew** of co B, 38 NC died 20 Jan 63.

3)-rost-**Allen F. Crouch**, co E, 38 NC, born Richmond Co., NC, capt in hosp at Richmond, Va 3 Apr 1865, conf Newport News, Va 24 Apr 1865, rel 30 Jun 1865 after Oath.

rost- A. Crouch, co E, 30 NC, p & d enl not rep, capt in hosp at Richmond, Va 3 Apr 1865, trans to Fed Provost Marshall 14 Apr 1865, no fur rec.

note: A. Crouch of co E, 30 NC should be deleted.

4)-rost- **Ahigah Macon**, co G, 38 NC, enl Raleigh 19 Aug 64, died Richmond 2 Oct 64.

1850 Randolph Co., NC census - **Ahijah Macon**, 14, son of Thomas and Rosanna Macon.

1860 Randolph Co., NC census - Ahijah Macon, 24, son of Thomas and Rosanna Macon

note: of the 80 Macon in 1860 and 71 Macon in 1850 census, Ahijah is the only name that fits this soldier. Need to note to change Ahigah Macon to Ahijah Macon, born ca 1836, resided in Randolph Co., NC.

5)-rost- **J. W. Lanier**, co H, 38 NC, age 18 in 1861, resided in Randolph Co., killed in July 1864, place of death not reported.

FO, 26 Sept 1864- Ivy W. Lenoir, co H, 38 NC, from Randolph Co., killed on picket near Petersburg on 21 July 1864.

1850 Davidson Co. census- **Ivy W. Lenair**, age 10, in Clement and Nicy Lenair's household.

6)-rost- **David Mull**, co C, 39 NC, in unit, but William E. Mull is not.

CWPOWrec- **William E. Mull**, co C, 39 NC, capt Haywood Co., NC and received at

Louisville, Ky (everyone on this list had 'Oath July 64'.)

CWPOWrec- William E. Mull, co C, 39 NC, capt Chattahoochee 28 July 64, joined station 3 Sept 64, admitted 31 March 65, died Camp Chase 18 Apr 65 of pneumonia, grave 1889.

CWPOWrec- William E. Mull, co C, 39 NC, capt Haywood Co., NC in July 1864, sent from the Dept of the Cumberland to be released N.O.R. July 31, 1865 (he was stated as a conscript).

1860 census- David M. and William E. Mull were brothers from Haywood Co., NC.

note: William E. Mull should be added to Co C, 39 NC.

7)-rost- Pvt **Charles Stiles**, co C, 39 NC, trans Fort Delaware 7 Mar 64, died Fort Delaware either 1 Jan or 1 Feb 65.

1912 book-Pvt Chas Styles of co C, 39, NC died Fort Delaware 1 Jan 65, bur Finn's Point, NJ.

CWPOWrec- Charles Stiles, co C, 39 NC, died Fort Delaware 1 Feb 65 of consumption (two records noted.)

note: The 1 Jan 65 dated in the 1912 book is wrong and his death date is 1 Feb 65.

8)-rost- A. M. Allen, co I, 39 NC, p & d of enl not reported, capt by enemy on an unspecified date, died Camp Morton 5 Mar 64, cause of death not reported.

rost- **Asa M. Allen**, co G, 29 NC, rs Yancey Co., enl 26 Jul 61, capt Yazoo City, Miss 14 Jul 63, died Camp Morton 5 Mar 64 of inf of brain.

note: Allen of the 29 NC noted in five prisoner of war records, but mistakenly recorded in the 1912 War Department book as Allen of the 39 NC. A. M. Allen of co I, 39 NC should be deleted and all data enter for Asa M. Allen of co G, 29 NC.

9)-rost- **Joseph M. Beasley**, co I, 39 NC, res Macon Co, capt Chattahoochee, Ga 5 Jul 64, conf Louisville, Ky 25 Jul 64, rec Camp Douglas 28 Jul 64, rel aft oath at Camp Douglas 16 Jun 65.

rost- Joseph Beasley, co I, 29 NC, p & d enl not reported, capt near Smyna, Ga 5 Jul 64, conf Louisville, Ky, trans to Camp Douglas 26 Jul 64, no further rec.

CWPOWrec- Joseph Beasley, co I, 39 NC, capt Chattahoochie, Ga, 5 Jul 64, rec Camp Douglas 28 Jul 64, trans to Pt Lookout 14 Mar 65.

note: Joseph Beasley of co I, 29 NC should be deleted.

10)-rost- **James Jones**, co I, 39 NC, capt Resaca, Ga 16 May 64, trans to Alton, Ill 23 May 64, no further records.

CWPOWrec- James Jones, co I, 39 NC died Alton, Ill 26 Jul 64.

11)-rost-Company A, 42 NC

1 **Burwell C. Gobble**, Co A, 42 NC, res Davidson Co, enl in Washington Co at age 18 on 1 May 1864, captured Battery Anderson at Fort Fisher on 25 Dec 1864, confined Ft Monroe on 27 Dec 1864, trans to Pt Lookout on 2 Jan 1865, released fm Pt Lookout 27 Jun 1865.

2 (**Levy S. Keller** not listed in co A, 42 NC)

3 **William Henry Keptley**, co A, 42 NC, born Davidson Co, enl at age 19 on 26 Nov 1861, captured at Battery Anderson at Fort Fisher on 25 Dec 1864, confined at Ft Monroe 27 Dec 1864, trans to Pt Lookout 31 Dec 1865, released fm Pt Lookout 15 May 1865.

4 **Henry F. Koonts**, co A, 42 NC, res Davidson Co, enl New Hanover at age 18 on 1 Mar 1864, captured Battery Anderson at Fort Fisher on 25 Dec 1864, confined Ft Monroe on 27 Dec 1864, trans to Pt Lookout on 2 Jan 1865, released fm Pt Lookout 28 Jun 1865.

-rost- Vol XVII –

1 B. C. Gobble, co A, 4 Batt NC Jr Res, place and date of enl not reported, prob enl prior to 31 Oct 1864, captured at Fort Fisher on 25 Dec 1864, confined at Ft Monroe on 29 Dec 1864, sent to Pt Lookout 31 Dec 1864, trans to co A, 3 NC Jr Res 3 Jan 1865 while POW.

2 Levy S. Keller, co A, 4 Batt NC Jr Res, place and date of enl not rep, captured at Ft Fisher on 25 Dec 1864, confined at Ft Monroe on 29 Dec 1864, sent to Pt Lookout 31 Dec 1864, may have trans to co A, 3 NC Jr Res on 3 Jan 1864 while POW. Most of his rec list him in either co A, 42 or 45 NC, co A, 45 Miss. The 45 NC was not at Ft Fisher and there was no 45 Miss. He was prob a member of co A, 42 NC, rather than co A, 4 Batt NC Jr Res or Co A, 3 NC Jr Res.

3 W. H. Keptley, co A, 4 Batt NC Jr Res, place and date of enl not reported, prob enl prior to 31 Oct 1864, captured at Ft Fisher on 25 Dec 1864, confined at Ft Monroe on 29 Dec 1864, sent to Pt Lookout on 31 Dec 1864, trans to co A, 3 NC Jr Res while POW.

4 H. F. Koonts, co A, 4 Batt NC Jr Res, place and date of enl not reported, prob enl prior to 31 Oct 1864, captured at Ft Fisher on 25 Dec 1864, confined at Ft Monroe 29 Dec 1864, sent to Pt Lookout 31 Dec 1864, trans to co A, 3 NC Jr Res.

-rost vol XVII –

1 B. C. Gooble, co A, 3 NC Jr Res, prev in co A, 4 Batt NC Jr Res, died at Pt Lookout on 27 Jun 1865, cause of death not reported.

2 Levy S. Keller, co A, 3 NC Jr Res, may have been in co A, 4 Batt NC Jr Res, died at Pt Lookout 29-30 Jun 1865 of meningitis or inflammation of brain. Most of his rec list in either co A, 42 or 45 NC, Co A, 45 Miss. The 45 NC was not at Ft Fisher and there was no 45 Miss. He was prob a member of co A, 42 NC, rather than co A, 4 Batt NC Jr Res or Co A, 3 NC Jr Res.

3 W. H. Keptley, co A, 3 NC Jr Res, prev in co A, 4 Batt NC Jr Res, released at Pt Lookout on 15 May 1865.

4 H. F. Koonts, co A, 3 NC Jr Res, prev in co A, 4 Batt NC Jr Res,

1850 census Rowan Co., NC- Levi S. Keller, age 22.

1860 census Stanly Co., NC- Levi S. Keller, age 32.

CWPOWrec (7282)-Roll of Prisoners of War at Point Lookout, page 392. The following names taken in order from the roll at those captured at Ft Fisher on Dec 25, 1864 and arr at Point Lookout from Ft Monroe Jan 2, 1865.

"Geo W. Kershaw, Pvt, 3 NC Res, co A, exch Jan 17, 1865

Jos. H. Kimse, " " "

Walker Kemp, " " co C, exch Jan 17, 1865

M. R. Kirby, " " ", do Feb 18, 1865

J. A. Keller, " " ", exch Feb 18, 1865

J. H. Koonts, Capt, 42 NC, A, trans to Washington, DC Jan 27, 1865

W. H. Keptley, Pvt, 3 NC Res, ", released May 15, 1865

L. S. Keller, " " ", died June 30, 1865

H. F. Koonts, " " ", released June 28, do

E. Keener, " " co B, released June 28, 1865"

CWPOWrec (11538)- L. S. Keller, co A, 42 NC, $10.50 Confederate money taken from him 3 Jan 1865.

(note: strongly believe the Federal clerk was wrong on the unit of the last three names after Captain J. H. Koonts and they should be listed as in the 42 NC vice 3 NC (Jr) Res.)

Note: the data above on Burwell C. Gooble, Levy S. Keeler, William Henry Keptley and Henry F. Koonts should combine into company A, 42 NC Infantry; then delete the four from the 3rd NC Jr Res. And 4 Batt. NC Jr. Res.)

12)-rost-Pvt **William A. Fletcher** of co D, 42 NC, res Iredell, enl 20 Oct 62, gave up at Cold Harbor 3 Jun 64, conf Point Lookout, trans Elmira 17 Jul 64, died Elmira 27 Jan 65.

rost-Pvt William A. Fletcher, co D, 24 NC died Elmira 27 Jan 65.

CWPOWrec- William A. Fletcher, co D, 42 NC, capt Gaines Mills 3 June 64, rec Elmira 17 July 64, died 27 Jan 65 of Variola, grave 1636.

note: William A. Fletcher of co D, 24 NC should be deleted.

13)-rost-**William W. Brantley**, co G, 42 NC, p & a through 21 Mar 1865, capt by the enemy on an unspecified date, died 15 May 1865 at Camp Chase.

CWPOWrec-Wm W. Brantley, co G, 47 NC, capt Salisbury, NC 12 Apr 1865, trans via Nashville, Tenn, Louisville, Ky to Camp Chase by 5 May 1865.

14)-rost-**William Chamberlain**, co I, 42 NC, died hosp Lynchburg 8 Aug 1862 of pneu.

LMA-William Chamberlain of 42 NC, no dates, grave 145 in Oakwood Cem., Raleigh, NC.

15)-rost-**Alexander Leonard, Jr.**, co I, 42 NC, hosp New Bern 15 Mar 65 gs of lung, place, date and capt not reported, d New Bern 18 Mar 65 of wounds.

CWPOWrec- Alexander Leonard, co I, 42 NC, capt Kinston, NC 9 Mar 65, d New Bern 18 Mar 65.

16)-rost-**Alexander Melton**, co K, 42 NC, capt by enemy on an unspecified date, d Pt Lookout 7 Jun 65 of rubeola.

CWPOWrec-**Alex Martin**, co K, 42 NC, capt Kinston 10 Mar 1865, died Pt Lookout 7 June 1865 of measles.

17)-rost-1ˢᵗ Lt **Robert B. Carr**, co A, 43 appointed 2ⁿᵈ Lt 6 Mar, 62, promoted 1ˢᵗ Lt 20 Mar 62, w in left foot 3 Jul 63 at Gettys, capt in ambulance train 4 Jul 63.

rost-1Sgt Robert B. Carr, 1stco C, 12 NC, born Duplin Co, enl age 33 on 15 Apr 61, company disbanded 18 Nov 61.

note: same soldier and data should be combined and add that he was the longest held prisoner of war.

18)-rost- **William D. Ball**, co D, 43 NC, p & a until wounded 18 July 64 at Snicker's Ferry, Va, died prior to 1 Sep 64 of wounds, place of death not rep.

CW POW REC- W. D. Ball, 43 NC, died 21 July 64 at Winchester, Va.

19)-rost-Pvt **William H. Parks**, co D, 43 NC, capt Cedar Ck, Va 19 Oct 64, conf Point Lookout 25 Oct 64, released fm PL 16 Jan 65 after oath (pension rec).

1912 book-Pvt William H. Parks of co D, 43 NC died Point Lookout 16 Nov 64.

CWPOWrec- W. H. Parks, co D, 43 NC, capt Strasburg 19 Oct 64, died 16 Nov 64 (but one record stated 'Released June 16 1865').

20)-rost- **Bryant Kellum**, co F, 43 NC, killed 19 Sep 64 at Winchester.

CWPOW REC- …. Kelly, co F, 43 NC, died 30 Sep 64 at Winchester of wounds.

note: there were no Kelly's in this unit, but Kellum is very close, in this case he was wounded and captured at Winchester.

21)-rost- **William G. Thomas**, co H, 43 NC, w & c in Sept-Oct 64, died in hands of enemy 30 Sep 64, p & cause of death not reported.

CWPOWrec- W. J. Thomas, co H, 43 NC, died 20 Sep 64 at Winchester of gun shot wound head.

22)-rost- Corp. **James A. Allen**, co I, 43 NC, w & capt Winchester 19 Sep 1864, died on an unspecified date, place and cause of death not reported.

CWPOWrec- Corp. J. A. Allen, co I, 43 NC, d 30 Sept 1864 at Winchester, Va of gs ….. lungs.

23)-rost-**Calvin S. Eddins**, co K, 43 NC, born Anson Co., deserted 16 Aug 1863, reported to be undergoing sentence for absence without leave during Nov 1863-Feb 1864, died in Virginia on 1 Mar 1864 of smallpox.

rost-C. Eddins, misc, 49 NC, place and date of enlistment not reported, died at Salisbury, NC on 1 Feb 1864 of "s?".

note: believe the two are the same soldier, even if the death date is one month off and that Calvins S. Eddins was sent to Salisbury prison under sentence. Record should state Calvin S. Eddins of co K, 43 NC died of smallpox at Salisbury on 1 Feb 1864. Another source has his burial place in Rowan Co. at the Old Lutheran Church Cemetery.

24)-rost- **Thomas B. Harrington**, co K, 43 NC, died on 25 July 1864, place and cause of death not reported.

CWPOWrec- Herrington, 43 NC, died at Winchester, Va on 1 Aug 1864.

25)-rost- **Robert Kinnian**, co I, 44 NC, c Hatcher's Run 2 Apr 65, conf Point Lookout until released 6 Jun 65 after Oath.

CWPOWrec- R. Kinin, co I, 44 NC, died 11 Jun 1865 at Jackson Gen Hosp, Richmond, Va of typhoid Fever.

note: died five days after released

26)-rost- **Bedford S. Lancaster**, co K, 44 NC, p & a through April 1864.

Hollywood Cem- B. S. Lancaster, co K, 46 NC, buried 1 May 64 in grave I-208.

note: while the units are different, the correct unit is the 44th.

Cause of deaths that were not listed in the NC Roster - Volume X

rank	name	co	unit	place of death	died	cause of death
Pvt	James N. Lanier	A	38	Fort Delaware	10/3/63	lungs, inf of
Pvt	David W. Hearn	C	38	Point Lookout	7/4/64	acute diarrhoea
Pvt	David Godwin	D	38	Point Lookout	6/8/65	lungs, inf of
Pvt	Noah R. Webb	E	38	Point Lookout	6/17/64	febris remit
Pvt	Lenas F. Fullbright	F	38	Fort Delaware	9/17/63	inf of kidneys/chr diarrhoea
Corp	Elcanah R. Hefner	F	38	Baltimore	10/14/64	chronic diarrhoea
1Sgt	Jonas N. Bradshaw	G	38	Point Lookout	8/11/64	acute dysenteria
Pvt	James Allen Lackey	G	38	Fort Delaware	10/15/63	acute dysenteria
Sgt	William C. Hamrick	I	38	Point Lookout	8/18/64	acute diarrhoea
Pvt	Wiley Keen	K	38	Fort Delaware	10/14/63	chronic diarrhoea
Sgt	Daniel McMillan	K	38	Point Lookout	3/14/64	pneumonia
1Lt	John S. Ray	K	38	Johnson's Island	11/18/63	smallpox
Pvt	Joseph Hayes	D	42	Point Lookout	7/30/64	acute dysenteria
Mus	Lewis U. Bass	A	43	Point Lookout	3/8/64	pneumonia
1Corp	Solomon S. Broom	B	43	Washington	7/14/64	gs neck & shoulders
Pvt	Wilson L. Stowe	B	43	Point Lookout	6/16/64	febris remit
Pvt	George W. Duncan	D	43	Point Lookout	7/17/64	acute diarrhoea
Pvt	W.H. Thompson	D	43	Winchester	10/10/64	gs thigh
Pvt	Benjamin D. Bell	F	43	Fort Delaware	10/8/63	dysenteria, chronic
Pvt	Bythel Bell	F	43	Point Lookout	2/24/64	chronic diarrhoea
Pvt	Bryant Kellum	F	43	Winchester	9/30/64	of wounds
Pvt	Andrew Hooks	H	43	Point Lookout	10/21/64	chronic diarrhoea
Pvt	George W. Thomson	B	44	Point Lookout	1/17/65	chronic diarrhoea
Corp	Alexander Congleton	C	44	Point Lookout	1/3/64	chronic diarrhoea
Sgt	Woody M. Smith	D	44	Point Lookout	6/22/65	chronic diarrhoea
Pvt	C. B. Dismukes	E	44	Point Lookout	12/11/64	chronic diarrhoea
Pvt	John E. Hammond	E	44	Elmira	11/23/64	pleuro pnumonia
Pvt	Matthew D. Wicker	E	44	Point Lookout	8/23/64	febris typhoides
Pvt	Robert Kinnian	I	44	Richmond	6/11/65	typhoid fever
Pvt	Arthur Tucker	I	44	Point Lookout	6/23/64	lungs, inf of
Pvt	Burwell Burnett	K	44	Point Lookout	2/1/64	chronic diarrhoea
Pvt	William L.F. Merritt	K	44	Point Lookout	3/11/64	debility
Pvt	Lewis W. Snider	K	44	Point Lookout	6/25/64	acute diarrhoea
Corp	Simeon Swanson	K	44	Washington	1/12/64	febris remittent/variola

Volume XI 45th - 48th Infantry

1)-rost-Pvt **Nicholas Gibson**, co A, 45 NC, died Elmira 14 May 65.
1912 book-Pvt N. Gipson of co A, 45 died Elmira 14 Mar 65, grave 1662. note: soldiers
  in graves 1661 to 1732 died in Mar 65.
CWPOWrec- N. Gipson, died 14 Mar 1865.
note: change death month from May to March.

2)-rost- T. Small, co A, 45 NC, died in hosp at Lynchburg 5 May 64.
Old City Cemetery, Lynchburg, Va- **Thomas Small**, co A, 45 NC.

3)-rost- **Andrew E. Milloway**, co B, 45 NC, died on or about July 2 or 12, 1863, place
  and cause of death not reported.
FO, 27 Jan 1864- A. E. Millaway, co B, 45 NC, died at Martinsburg on 2 July 1863 of
  typhoid fever.

4)-rost-**Thomas J. Durham**, co D, 45 NC, capt Petersburg, d Fed Hosp 26 Mar 65 of
  wounds.
VA web stie- T. J. Durham, co D, 45 NC, died 26 Mar 65, buried City Point Cemetery
  in grave 3658.

5)-rost- **William W. Lovins**, co E, 45 NC, w Gettysburg 1-3 Jul 63, rtn to duty Jan-Feb
  64.
CWPOWrec- William W. Lovins, co E, 45, capt Winchester 30 Jul 63, disposition
  unaccounted for.

6)-rost- Richard Williams, co G, 45 NC, res Rockingham, enl age 36 on 2 Mar 63, p &
  a until he died in Danville hospital on 12/5/63 of measles.
rost- **Richard D. Williams**, co I, 45 NC, res Rockinham, enl age 36 on 2 Mar 63, p & a
  until he died in Danville hospital on 12/5/63 of measles.
Danville, Va Confederate Hospital deaths- R. D. Williams, co G, 45 NC.
note: Richard Williams of co I, 45 NC should be deleted.

7)-rost-**Lewis R. Compton**, co I, 45 NC, p & a until died hosp Petersburg 7 Aug 1862.
Born and res of Caswell, enl age 18 on 5 Mar 1862.
LMA-Lewis R. Compton of 45 NC, d 18 Aug 1864, grave 136 in Oakwood Cem.,
  Raleigh, NC.

8)-rost- **Marine Oakley**, co K, 45 NC, p & a until he deserted at Kinston on 2 May 63,
  hosp at Richmond 2 Sept 63 with a gunshot wound, place and date wounded not
  reported.
CWPOWrec- M. Oakly, co K, 45 NC, capt Winchester 30 Jul 63, disposition
  unaccounted for.

note: Marine Oakley rejoined his company prior to the Gettysburg campaign, he was prob wounded at Gettysburg before being captured at Winchester, he was released at an unknown date and sent to the Richmond hospital.

9)-rost- **Elijah T. Pope**, co K, 45 NC, rep sick in hosp during May-Dec 64, dropped from rolls of the company in Jan-Feb 65, no further records.
Lynchburg, Old City Cemetery- E. T. Pope, co K, 45 NC.

10)-rost- **Henry L. Meares**, co A, 46 NC, w near Spotsylvania Ch 10 May 1864, died of wounds, place and date of death not reported.
Geocities.com/CollegePark/Grounds/7235/spot-nr – Register of names of men buried in the Confederate Cemetery Spotsylvania C.H., Va- H. L. Merrs, co A, 46 NC.

11)-rost-Pvt **William Wallace**, co A, 46 NC, res Wayne Co, enl Robeson 8 Feb 62, AWOL Apr 62, dropped fm rolls Sep-Oct 62.
CWPOWrec- Pvt William Wallace, co F, 46 NC, capt Five Forks 1 Apr 1865, died Harts Island 16 Jun 1865 of chr diarroea.
1912 book-Pvt William Wallace, co A, 46 NC died NY Harbor 16 Jun 1865, bur Cypress Hill Nat Cem, Brooklyn, NY, grave 3011.
note: drop fm co rolls in 62, but he died 3 yrs later while in same co, so he evidently came back to his unit and was capt.

12)-rost-**Allen Wilkinson**, co A, 46 NC, dest 18 Jul 63, returned to duty 1 Aug 64, died 24 Jan 65 of spinal meningitis, place of death not reported.
rost-Allen Wilkinson, co E, 46 NC, absent wounded or sick until 11 Dec 64 when he was hosp at Petersburg with chronic diarrhea, died at Petersburg on 24 Jan 1865.
Petersburg-A. Wilkerson, co A, 46 NC, killed at Petersburg 10 Sep 1864, buried Petersburg Fair Ground vicinity.
note: change Allen Wilkinson (Davidson Co.) of co A, 46 NC killed at Petersburg on 10 Sep 1865 and Allen Wilkinson (Granville Co.) of co E, 46 NC died at Petersburg on 24 Jan 1865 of spinal meningitis

13)-rost- **Thomas Upton West**, co B, 46 NC, sent to hosp 20 Dec 62, never returned to company and supposed to have died prior to 1 Nov 64, place, date, and cause of death not reported.
Lynchburg, Old City Cemetery- Thomas West, co B, 46 NC.

14)-rost-**Daniel Campbell**, co D, 46 NC, enl Orange CH, Va age 19 on 23 Mar 1864. p & a through 17 Feb 1865.
LMA-D. Campbell, co D, 6 NC, died 16 Jan 1865, grave 32 in Oakwood Cem., Raleigh, NC.

15)-rost- **A. Spinks Wright**, co G, 46 NC, died Lynchburg 18 May 64.
Lynchburg, Old City Cemetery- **Alfred Wright**, co G, 46 NC.

16)-rost- Sgt **William Hicks**, co K, 46 NC, capt unk, conf Ft Monroe, conf Newport News 1 May 65, no further records.

CWPOWrec-Sgt William Hicks, co K, 46 NC, rec from Ft Monroe 1 May 65, released 30 June 1865 per G.O. nr 109.

17)-rost- **Reuben Sigman**, co K, 46 NC, killed 17 Sep 62 at Sharpsburg.

CWPOWrec- R. Sigmon, 46 NC, died 17 Sep 62 at Sharpsburg.

note: POW record indicates that he was mort wounded and captured.

18)-rost- **Edmond F. Bass**, ca A, 47 NC, capt Burgess' Mill 27 Oct 64, conf Pt Lookout 31 Oct 64, paroled 13 Feb 65 and rel Cox's Landing, James River, Va 15 Feb 65 for exchanged.

Hollywood Cemetery- E. T. Bass, co E, 47 NC, died 2 Mar 65, bur Hollywood Cem in grave w333.

19)-rost- **John Whitey**, co A, 47 NC, died 9 May 62 of disease, place of death not reported.

Haywood papers- Whitley, 47 NC, died May 62 in Raleigh, NC.

20)-rost-**Nathaniel Gay**, co B, 47 NC, released at Hart's Island 17 Jun 65 after oath.

VA web site-N. Gay, d 23 Jun 1865, buried Cypress Hills Cem, New York, NY.

1912 book- N. Gay, C.S.A., died 23 Jun 1865, grave 3044, Brooklyn, NY.

CWPOWrec- Nathaniel Gay, co B, 47 NC, of Edgecomb Co., NC, capt South Side RR 2 April 1865, rec from City Point 7 April 1865, released 17 June 1865 from Hart's Island, NY Harbor.

note: he died six days after taking the oath and since he is buried in Brooklyn, he was kept because of sickness.

21)-rost-**Nathaniel Jean**, co B, 47 NC, d Ral hosp 1 Apr or 6 Apr 1862. cause of death not reported.

LMA-M. Jean of Crudup's Company, d 3 Apr 1862. (note:Capt Crudup was Commander of co B, 47).

Haywood papers- N. Jean, of Col Rogers (Commander of the 47th NC), died April 1st, 1862 of pneumonia.

22)-rost- D. E. Powell, co C, 47 NC, died at Greenville on 1 or 17 April 1863, cause of death not reported.

NCS, 15 July 1863- **Durrell E. Powell**, 47 NC, died in Greenville on 17 April 1863 from typhoid pneumonia..

23)-rost-**Rufus P. Daniel**, co D, 47 NC, present Mar-Apr 1864, no further record.

Petersburg-R. P. Daniel, co D, 47 NC, killed Petersburg on 12 Aug 1864, buried Petersburg Fair Ground vicinity.

24)-rost-**Rufus Holmes**, co F, 47 NC, born and reside in Franklin Co., enl at age 25 on 8 Mar 62, killed at Gettysburg on or about 3 July 1863.

rost-B. Holmes, co F, 57 NC, place and date of enl not reported, Fed med rec indicate that he was wounded in the thigh and capt at Gettysburg 1-3 July 1863, died in a Gettysburg hosp 17 July 1863 following ampt of leg.

note: believe B. Holmes and Rufus Holmes are the same soldier. The correct entry should be Pvt Rufus Holmes of co F, 47 NC, wounded in the thigh at Gettysburg and captured, died in a Gettysburg hospital on 17 July 1863 following ampt of leg. (his company thought he was killed while the Federal records indicate his captured and death.)

25)-rost-**Thomas J. Jackson**, co G, 47 NC, killed on an unspecified date (probably prior to September 1, 1864). Place of death not reported.

Geocities.com/CollegePark/Grounds/7235/spot-nr – Register of names of men buried in the Confederate Cemetery Spotsylvania C.H., Va- T. J. Jackson, co G, 47 NC.

26)-rost-**James Joyner**, co H, 47 NC, was prob killed Gettysburg 1-3 Jul 1863.

LMA-James Joiner of 47 NC, no dates, grave 466 in Gettysburg sec of Oakwood Cem., Raleigh, NC.

Edward Richter papers- Pvt James Joyner, co H, 47 NC, died 10 July 1863 at Gettysburg and buried on J. Rife's farm at Cashtown, Pa.

27)-rost-1ˢᵗ Sgt. A. D. Royster, co H, 47 NC, born Wake and res as a clerk.

Oakwood Cemetery, Raleigh- full name is **Arkansas Delaware Royster**.

28)-rost- **Thomas B. Meaiton**, co I, 47 NC, born Wake Co, res as farmer, enl age 21 on 3 Mar 62, died Raleigh hospital 25 Apr 62 of disease.

Haywood papers- **Thomas Martin**, 47 NC, died Raleigh 24 Apr 62 of pneumonia.

note: the name Meaition not found in any records, but could not find Thomas Martin in the census for Wake county. Possibly the correct name is Martin.

29)-rost- **Zwean Forshee**, co K, 47 NC, enl 22 Apr 62, no further records.

Haywood papers- Z. Foushee, 47 NC, died in Raleigh on 17 Jun 62 of typhoid fever.

30)-rost- **Franklin Strayhorn**, co K, 47 NC, died in hospital in Raleigh on April 4 or in May, 1862, of disease.

Haywood papers- F. Strayhorn, 43 NC, died in Raleigh 3 April 1862 of pneumonia.

note: unit wrong in Haywood papers but the same soldier.

31)-rost- **Daniel Whitsel**, co K, 47 NC, born in Alamance Co., enlisted age 21 on 5 Mar 62, died in hospital at Raleigh on May 1 or June 5, 1862 of typhoid pneumonia.

Haywood papers- **Daniel Whitesell**, 47 NC, died in Raleigh 5 June 1862.

1860 Alamance Co., NC census- Daniel Whitesell, age 18, son of William and Sarah.

1850 Alamance Co., NC census- Daniel Whitesell, age 7, son of William and Sarah.

Family Tree- Daniel Whitesell, born 8 Jul 1841, died 5 Jun 1862, son of William Whitesell and Sarah Clapp.

note: last name should be change to Whitesell and death date is 5 June 1862.

32)-rost- **John L. Brown**, co C, 48 NC, present in March-April 1864, no further records.

Geocities.com/CollegePark/Grounds/7235/spot-nr – Register of names of men buried in the Confederate Cemetery Spottsylvania C.H., Va- J. L. Brown, co C, 48 NC.

33)-rost- **Daniel Morris**, co D, 48 NC, died in Raleigh in May, 1862, of disease.

Haywood papers- D. Morris, 48 NC, died in Raleigh 14 May 1862.

34)-rost- **C. S. Curlee**, co E, 48 NC, died at Lynchburg on or about 4 Jan 63.

Lynchburg, Old City Cemetery-**Calvin Curles**, co E, 48 NC

35)-rost- Captain **Hugh Wilson**, co F, 48 NC, ca 1827 and from Union Co, resigned 9 July 1862 for reason of disease of the lungs and general debility.

FO, 1 Feb 1864- Hugh Wilson, age 37, died at his residence in Walkersville, Union Co. died 17 Sept (1863), brother to Captain William Wilson killed at Gettysburg.

36)-rost-Pvt **W. Loggett**, co G, 48 NC place and date of enl not rep, capt Gettys 3 Jul 63, died Fort Delaware 11 Oct 63.

CWPOWrec- W. Doggett, co G, 48 NC, capt Gettysburg 5 July 1863, died Ft. Delaware 31 Oct 1863 of typhoid fever.

note: 48 NC not at Gettysburg, not sure if this soldier was from North Carolina or another state.

37)-rost- **A. J. Koontz**, co H, 48 NC, killed 17 Sept 62 at Sharpsburg.

CWPOWrec- **A. J. Koons**, 48 NC, died 17 Sept 62 at Antietim.

note: POW record indicates that he was mort. Wounded and captured, not killed.

38)-rost-**William Scott**, co I, 48 NC, last reported in comp records on 17 Jun 1864.

Petersburg-William Scott, co J, 48 NC, died at Petersburg on 9 Aug 1864, buried Petersburg Fair Ground vicinity, Va.

39)-rost- Sgt **A. Frank Motsinger**, co K, 48 NC, died Point Lookout 5 Mar 65.

1850 census Davidson-**Abram F. Motsinger** age 18.

1860 census Davidson-A.F. Motsinger.

note: Abram is first named.

Cause of deaths that were not listed in the NC Roster - Volume XI

.

rank	name	co	unit	place of death	died	cause of death
Pvt	William W. Corum	B	45	Point Lookout	12/23/63	chronic diarrhoea
Pvt	John M. Parker	B	45	Point Lookout	8/6/64	febris typhoides
Pvt	John B. Lee	C	45	Raleigh	4/27/62	pneumonia
Pvt	Nimrod Shoe	C	45	Point Lookout	4/19/65	chronic diarrhoea
Pvt	Haywood Chamberlan	E	45	Point Lookout	7/18/64	dysenteria, acute
Pvt	Robert E. Coleman	E	45	Point Lookout	6/22/64	vulnus sclopst
Pvt	William T. Meador	E	45	Point Lookout	8/6/64	Paralysis
Pvt	Thomas B. Carter	F	45	Point Lookout	2/4/64	pneumonia
Pvt	Edward J. Covington	F	45	Fort Delaware	10/11/63	rhumatisme, chr.
Pvt	L. Osborne	F	45	Fort Delaware	9/27/63	chr rhumatism/anemia
Pvt	John W. Jones	H	45	Point Lookout	8/8/64	febris typhoides
Pvt	Aaron Saunders	H	45	Elmira	2/3/65	variola
Pvt	David N. Walker	H	45	Point Lookout	1/26/64	chronic diarrhoea
Pvt	E.B. Tramwell	I	45	Fort Delaware	10/13/63	smallpox
Pvt	Robert Walker	I	45	Point Lookout	9/6/64	acute diarrhoea
Pvt	William Dunn	B	46	Point Lookout	1/16/64	chronic diarrhoea
Pvt	Murdock Skipper	D	46	Baltimore	10/14/64	chronic diarrhoea
Pvt	Reuben Sigmon	K	46	Sharpsburg	9/17/62	of wounds
LtCol	John Azariah Graves	-	47	Johnson's Island	3/1/64	apoplexy
Pvt	William T. Bass	A	47	Point Lookout	3/28/64	typhia dysenteria
Pvt	Jackson J. Bissett	A	47	Point Lookout	12/19/63	pneumonia
Pvt	Lemuel T. Braswell	A	47	Point Lookout	12/11/63	dysentery, chronic
Pvt	W.H. Ward	A	47	Harts Island	6/9/65	pneumonia
Pvt	Nathaniel Jean	B	47	Raleigh	4/1/62	pneumonia
Pvt	Joseph W. Higgins	D	47	Point Lookout	12/30/63	gs w l femur
Pvt	Chesley Searles	E	47	Point Lookout	2/20/64	pneumonia
Pvt	James N. Harper	G	47	Point Lookout	6/28/65	chronic diarrhoea
Pvt	William A. Stone	G	47	Point Lookout	12/20/63	smallpox
Pvt	Wiley P. Allmond	I	47	Point Lookout	5/3/64	lungs, inf of
Pvt	G.A. Boyette	I	47	Fort Delaware	10/1/63	chronic diarrhoea
Pvt	Calvin Broughton	I	47	Fort Delaware	10/2/63	chronic diarrhoea
Pvt	Asbury Marshall	I	47	Fort Delaware	10/11/63	chronic diarrhoea
Pvt	Thomas B. Meaiton	I	47	Raleigh	4/24/62	pneumonia
Corp	William H. Shepherd	I	47	Point Lookout	3/24/64	dysenteria typhoid
Pvt	Michael R. Sharp	K	47	Fort Delaware	10/8/63	febris remittent
Pvt	Franklin Strayhorn	K	47	Raleigh	4/3/62	pneumonia
Pvt	W. Loggett	G	48	Fort Delaware	10/11/63	febris typhoids
Pvt	Samuel H. Scarlett	G	48	Point Lookout	8/23/64	acute dysenteria

Volume XII 49th - 52nd Infantry

1)-rost- S. R. Rollins, co B (2ⁿᵈ), 49 NC, wounded in head and capt Drewry's Bluff 16 May 64, sent to Ft Monroe, no further rec.

CWPOWrec- **Summie R. Rollins**, co B, 47 NC, died Ft Monroe 20 Jun 64 of v.s. fract of skull.

note: while the prison rec has his unit wrong this is the same soldier Summie R. Rollins of the 49 NC.

2)-rost- **Hugh B. Monroe**, co D, 49 NC, w rt ankle and capt 2 Jun 1864 at Bermuda Hundred, no further records.

CWPOWrec- Hugh B. Monroe, co D, 49 NC, died 10 Aug 1864 at Fort Monroe of exhaustion fm amp right foot.

3)-rost-**J. A. McArthur**, co H, 49 NC, capt Ft Stedman, d Fed Field Hosp 1 Apr 65 of wounds.

VA web site- J. A. McArthur, co H, 49 NC, died 1 Apr 65, buried in City Point National Cemetery in grave 3881.

4)-rost-**Joseph Lenhardt**, co K, 49 NC, present through Aug 1864 (was prob wounded slightly at or near Petersburg May-Aug 1864.)

Petersburg- **J. W. Lenhardt**, co K, 49 NC, died Petersburg (no date), burial Petersburg Fair Ground vicinity.

5)-rost- **Even Simpson**, co K, 49 NC, killed 17 Sept 62 at Sharpsburg.

CWPOWrec- ... Simpson, 49 NC, died 17 Sept 62 at Antitam.

note: indicates Simpson was wounded and capt vice killed.

6)-rost- C. Eddins, misc, 49 NC, place and date of enlistment not reported, died at Salisbury, NC on 1 Feb 1864 of "s?".

rost- **Calvin S. Eddins**, co K, 43 NC, born Anson Co., deserted 16 Aug 1863, reported to be undergoing sentence for absence without leave during Nov 1863-Feb 1864, died in Virginia on 1 Mar 1864 of smallpox.

note: believe the two are the same soldier, even if the death date is one month off and that Calvins S. Eddins was sent to Salisbury prison under sentence. Record should state Calvin S. Eddins of co K, 43 NC died of smallpox at Salisbury on 1 Feb 1864. Another source has his burial place in Rowan Co. at the Old Lutheran Church Cemetery.

7)-rost- **Thomas Dicken**, co F, 50 NC, died (presumably at Wilmington) on 7 March 1864 of disease.

FO, 28 March 1864- Thomas Dicken, co F, 50 NC, died at the Marine Hospital in Wilmington on 7 March 1864 of small pox.

8)-rost-Pvt William King, co G, 50 NC died near Hopewell, Va 25 Mar 65.

rost-Pvt **William J. King**, co G, 56 NC, enl Henderson Co 1 Jan 64, w and capt Fort Stedman 25 Mar 65, died Federal Field Hosp 26 Mar 65.

City Point Nat Cem-Pvt William King of co G, 50, died 25 Mar 65, grave C3758.

note: with the enlistment and capt info on King in the 56 NC, William King of the 50 NC should be deleted.

9)-rost- **W. Henry B. Prevo**, co A, 51 NC, deserted Sullivan's Island, SC 23 July 1863.

FO, 14 Sept 1863- Henry W. B. Provo, co A, 51 NC, died at his residence in Randolph Co., NC on 24 August 1863 of typhoid fever.

10)-rost- Saul McMercer, co. D, 51 NC died Elmira Jul 27, 1864.

rost- **John Picket Mercer** and Miles V. Mercer, co D, 51 NC, (same unit as Saul McMercer.)

CWPOWrec- F. Mercer, co D, 51 NC, died 27 July 1864

Family Tree- Saul McRibben Mercer (not McMercer), born 1846 of Robeson Co. is brother to John Picket and Miles Vanburen Mercer. He is listed at Woodlawn Nat Cem as F. Mercer in Grave 149, CSA section with same death date.

1850 Robeson Co., NC census- Miles V. (13), John (10) and Saul M. (7) were sons of Saul and Catharine Mercer.

note: no McMercer in NC census. note: Change Saul McMercer to **Saul McRibben Mercer** and change Miles V. Mercer to **Miles Vanburen Mercer**, both of co D, 51 NC.

11)-rost- William Gregory, co E, 51 NC, capt Petersburg 16 Jun 64, conf Point Lookout, trans Elmira 9 Jul 64, released 19 Jul 65 after oath.

rost- **William A. Gregory**, co I, 45 NC, res Person Co., NC, age 37 in 1862, capt Spotsylvania CH 10 May 64, trans fm Pt Lookout to Elmira 3 Aug 64, d Elmira 11 or 17 Sept 64 of 'hospital gangrene'.

CWPOWrec- William Gregory, co E, 51 NC, capt near Petersburg 16 Jun 64, rec at Elmira 17 July 64, died 17 Sept 64 of hospital gangrene, buried in grave 326.

CWPOWrec- William Gregory, co E, 56 or 26 (penciled in over 56 or 26 is 'on dead roll as 51 NC'), capt near Petersburg 16 May 64, from Pt Lookout to Elmira 14 July 64, died 17 Sept 64, rols 31 T.

CWPOWrec-William Gregory, co I, 45 NC, died Elmira 17 Sept 64 of hospital gangrene.

1912 book-Pvt William Gregory of co E, 51 NC died Elmira 17 Sep 64, grave 318.

1860 Person Co., NC census- William Gregory (34) with family Mary (29), John (2) and James (1).

1870 Person Co., NC census- John H. Walker (19), Mary Walker (39), John Gregory (12), James Gregory (10) and Rebecca (8).

note: seems William A. Gregory of 45 NC died at Elmira, but officials stated that he was in co. E, 51 NC. The NC Roster is correct and the VA and Woodlawn Cemetery should be notified of error.

12)-rost- **Daniel Ward**, co G, 51 NC, conf at Pt Lookout 20 May 64, died on an unspecified date while POW.

FO, 12 Dec 1864- Daniel Ward, 51 NC, The Richmond Ambulance Committee furnishes a list of soldiers who died in going to Savannah for exchange.

13)-rost-**Doctor W. Pope**, co I, 51 NC, capt Cold Harbor 1 Jun 64, conf Point Lookout 11 Jun 64, released 17 Jun 65 after oath (pension rec).

1912 book-Pvt D. W. Pope of co I, 51 NC died 15 Jul 64 in train wreck (on way to Elmira).

CWPOWrec- D. W. Pope, co I, 51 NC, (one rec had him being rel 17 Jun 65, but several other rec had him killed in the Sholhola, Pa RR accident on their way to Elmira from Point Lookout.)

Family info on Ancestry.com- Doctor W. Pope, b 25 Dec 1832 in Cumberland Co., NC, d 5 May 1919 in Harnett Co., NC.

note: seems Doctor W. Pope survived the war. (Was he involved in the RR accident, but survived?) The *NC Roster* is correct and the VA and Woodlawn Cemetery should be notified of error.

14)-rost- Jeremiah Robinson, co C, 52 NC, enl Gates 10 May 62, des Camp Mangum 6 Jun 62.

Gettysburg death Roster- Cpl **Jeremiah B. Robinson** of co C, 52 NC.

CWPOWrec- Corp. J. B. Robinson, co G, 52 NC, capt Gettysburg, died in Letterman Hospital, 9 Sept 1863, buried in Oakwood Cemetery, Raleigh, NC, grave 476.

note: believe J. B. Robinson is Joseph B. Robinson of same unit and prob should be for him in the Krick book.

15)-rost- **David W. Savage**, co C, 52 NC, born Chowan Co., farmer, enlisted in Gates Co. 27 Feb 62, promoted to Sgt, report missing at Gettysburg on 3 July 63, was probably killed at Gettysburg.

rost-D. Savage, co C, 32 NC, capt Gettysburg 3 Jul, conf at Fort Delaware, no fur rec.

CWPOWrec- D. Savage, no unit or where capt, died at Fort Delaware on 22 Oct 63 of smallpox and buried on Jersey shore (Finn Point).

CWPOWrec- D. Savage, co I, 2 Miss, died Fort Delaware on 22 Oct 63.

CWPOWrec- D. Savage, no co, regt, where capt and date captured only year '1863'. (note: the line above has J.M. Pitts of co I, 2 Miss, died Ft Delaware on 22 Oct 63.

VA site-D. Savage d Fort Delaware 22 Oct 1863 bur Finn Point.

1912 book- D. Savage, co I, 2 Miss., died Ft Delaware 22 Oct 1863.

John M. Pitts, co I, 2 Miss, died Ft Delaware 22 Oct 1863.

2nd Mississippi Regiment web site- John Minett Pitts died Ft Delaware 22 Oct 63. There are no 'Savage' in this unit.

note: In checking on the name Savage in the Mississippi Regt found 45 and none with a given name that started with a 'D'. Of the 2,250 soldiers in the 2nd Miss. none were Savage. There is no D. Savage of co C, 32 NC nor in co I, 2 Miss. The corrct soldier is Sgt. David Savage of co C, 52 NC and all others should be deleted.

16)-rost- **William E. Hutchinson**, co F, 52 NC. Killed at Gettysburg 3 Jul.

Wasted Valor- A NY publ report in 1864 on relief of wounded and sick soldiers after battle of Gettysburg--in a Federal field hosp.-'..a young boy trying to follow some Confederate troops, came towards us and laid down at our feet in his exhaustion--the little fellow was fed--place in a comfortable bed and well nursed; but at end of 3 days, without a wound, he died of exhaustion. His name is William Hutchinson'.

17)-rost- **Adam Miller Hager**, co G, 52 NC, res Lincoln Co., NC, enl 62, capt Gettys 3 Jul 63, conf on or about 10 Jul 63 at Fort Delaware, no further rec.

rost- A. M. Hager of 2nd co C, 2 NC, capt Gettys 3 Jul 63, died Fort Delaware 26 Oct 63 (only info entered).

1912 book-Pvt A. M. Hager of co C, 2 NC died Fort Delaware 26 Oct 63, bur Finn's Point, NJ.

note: Hager of 2 NC should be deleted after combining info to Adam Miller Hager..

18)-rost- **Julius A. Kendall**, co I, 52 NC, enl Stanly Co age 33 on 1 Mar 63, left at Gettys 3 Jul 63.

rost- **J. A. Kindall**, co I, 52 NC, res Stanly Co, enl age 33 on 1 Mar 63, killed Gettys 3 Jul 63.

note: same soldier

19)-rost- **Ezekiel Martin**, co I, 52 NC, prob killed at Gettys about 3 Jul 63.

rost- **Ezekiel Morton**, co I, 52 NC, res Stanly Co, farmer, enl Camp French age 33 on 25 Sep 62, killed Gettys 3 Jul 63.

note: same soldier with Morton as correct name.

20)-rost- **George Thomas Yeates**, co K, 52 NC, capt Gettysburg, conf Fort Delaware 10 Jul 63, rec of Fed Provost Marshal indicate both he died while POW and he was exchanged, no further records.

CWPOWrec- G. T. Yeates, co K, 52 NC, capt Gettysburg 3 July 63, send to Ft Delaware July 63, trans to Point Lookout Oct 1863, exchanged 25 Dec 1863 fm Point Lookout, died 16 Jan 1864 of smallpox.

note: poss set to be exchanged on 25 Dec 63, but died before the exchanged completed.

Cause of deaths that were not listed in the NC Roster - Volume XII

rank	name	co	unit	place of death	died	cause of death
Pvt	Fate Calk	G	49	Point Lookout	6/13/65	chronic diarrhoea
Pvt	Even Simpson	K	49	Antietim	9/17/62	of wounds
Pvt	John A. Shaw	D	51	Baltimore	10/14/64	Chronic diarrhoea
Pvt	Nelson Snipes	E	51	Point Lookout	5/28/64	chr. Diarr./of wounds
Pvt	Bryant Page	I	51	Washington	9/3/64	gs hip joint & foot
Pvt	John F. Hamilton	A	52	Point Lookout	5/28/64	chronic diarrhoea
Pvt	Monroe Hurlocker	A	52	Point Lookout	9/9/64	chronic diarrhoea
Pvt	Leroy Smith	B	52	Fort Delaware	10/7/63	chronic diarrhoea
Pvt	William Ferrell	C	52	Point Lookout	9/9/64	acute diarrhoea
Pvt	Joshua Jones	C	52	Fort Delaware	2/3/64	typhoid malarial fever
Pvt	David H. Bowman	D	52	Point Lookout	11/18/63	gs rt leg
Pvt	John Richard Francis Wall	D	52	Point Lookout	10/9/63	febris typhoides
Sgt	Samuel C. Crouch	E	52	Point Lookout	8/10/64	dysentery, acute
Pvt	John L. Brown	F	52	Point Lookout	7/28/64	acute dysenteria
Pvt	John S. Hix	F	52	Point Lookout	1/13/64	chronic diarrhoea
Pvt	Joseph Woods	F	52	Point Lookout	1/5/64	chronic diarrhoea
Pvt	Henry Davis	G	52	Point Lookout	8/6/64	measles
Pvt	William F. Munday	G	52	Fort Delaware	10/10/63	bronchitis
Pvt	William T. Potts	G	52	Point Lookout	12/26/63	pneumonia
Pvt	John Frank Sifford	G	52	Point Lookout	2/20/64	chronic diarrhoea
Pvt	William Lafayette Bynum	H	52	Point Lookout	1/11/64	dysenteria, chronic
Sgt	John C. McCall	H	52	Point Lookout	3/6/65	lungs, inf of
Pvt	Lafayette Stroup	H	52	Point Lookout	2/17/64	chronic diarrhoea
Pvt	Robert B. Stroup	H	52	Point Lookout	2/13/64	chronic diarrhoea
Pvt	George E. Kirk	I	52	Point Lookout	3/13/64	diarrhoea
Pvt	Archibald C. Lowder	I	52	Point Lookout	9/16/64	acute diarrhoea
Pvt	Martin Morgan	I	52	Point Lookout	9/14/64	scurvy
3Lt	Willis Randall	I	52	Johnson's Island	12/31/64	typhoid fever
Pvt	William Browning	K	52	Point Lookout	5/3/64	chronic diarrhoea
Pvt	John W. McKnight	K	52	Point Lookout	5/25/64	chronic diarrhoea
Pvt	Alexander R. Merritt	K	52	Fort Delaware	10/6/63	dysentery, chronic
Corp	William R. Pratt	K	52	Point Lookout	3/6/64	dysenteria typhoid

Volume XIII - 53rd - 56th Infantry

1)-rost-**John W. Rierson**, Major, Field and Staff, 53 NC, capt Ft Stedman, d Field Hosp near Petersburg 26 Mar 65.

VA web site- J. W. Rierson, Maj., 53 NC, died 26 Mar 65, buried in City Point Cemetery in grave 3750.

2)-rost- **Robert G. Crumpler**, co C, 53 NC, died on or about 18 May 1862 of disease, place of death not reported.

Haywood papers- hospital death number 122, R. G. Crumpler, 53 NC, died in Raleigh hospital on 17 May 1862.

3)-rost-Sgt. **Laurister L. Marshall**, co E, 53 NC, killed Gettysburg 2-3, 1863.

1912 book-Corp. Lauriston L. Marshall, Corp., co E, 53 NC died Point Lookout on 7 Apr 1864.

4)-rost-**Tobias Fogleman**, co F, 53 NC, capt by enemy on an unspecified date. Hosp Point Lookout 6 Jun 1865, d Point Lookout 27 Jun 1865.

CWPOWrec-Tobias Fogleman, co F, 53 NC, capt Petersburg 2 Apr 1865, rec at Pt Lookout from City Point, Va 4 Apr 65.

5)-rost-**William Bennett, Jr.**, co H, 53 NC, rep absent sick in Mar 64-Feb 65. (rec of Fed Provost Marshal indicate that he died at Ft Del 4 Jan 64.)

rost-**James W. Bennett**, co I, 53 NC, conf Ft Del on or about 9 July 63. died at Ft Del 4 Jan 64 of inf of pleura.

1912 book- William Bennett Jr., co H, 53 NC, died Ft Delaware 4 Jan 64.

CWPOWrec- W. Bennett, co I, 53 NC, capt Gettysburg 5 July 63, died 4 Jan 64 of inf of pleura at Ft Del.

note: believe James W. Bennett died at Ft Del and not William Bennett Jr.

6)-rost-**James G. Austin**, co I, 53 NC, died near Weldon 8 Aug 62.

LMA-J. G. Austin, co I, 53 NC, no dates, grave 88 in Oakwood Cem., Raleigh, NC.

7)-rost- **William L. Forney**, co B, 54 NC, hosp at Charlottesville 9 Jan 1863 with chronic diarrhea, furloughed for 30 days on 7 Mar 1863, died on 22 Mar 1863, place and cause of death not reported.

NCS, 20 May 1863- William L. Forney, Captain McDowell's Company (co B, 54 NC), after the Fredericksburg battle he became disease and was in the Charlottesville hospital, about 1 March 1863 he was found by a kind friend in Salisbury in such a low condition that he was unable to tell how he got there, he was brought home on 8 March 1863 and died on 15 March 1863.

FO, 13 May 1863- William Forney, 1 NC, age 24, died in Burke Co., NC of chronic diarrhea. (note: William Forney, age 21 of Burke Co., first served in the 1 NC (6 months).)

8)-rost- T. G. Scott, co B, 54 NC, res Burke Co, p & d enl not rep (prob enl subsequent to 31 Oct 64), wounded left leg and capt at Harper's Farm, Va on 6 Apr 65, hosp Baltimore 22 Apr 65, died in hosp at Baltimore on or about 3 May 65 of pyaemia, Federal rec of Apr-Mar 65 give his age as 45.

rost-**Theophilus G. Scott** (no rank), co B, 24 NC, pension rec indicate he enl in Oct 64, wounded and capt in Virginia in 1865, died Fort McHenry, Md on an unspecified date of wounds.

CWPOWrec- T. G. Scott, co B, 54 NC, capt Harper Farm, Va 6 Apr 65, died West's Building 3 May 65 of gun shot wound, buried Loudon Park Cem, Baltimore.

1912 book- Pvt T. G. Scott, co B, 54 Va, died 3 May 65, buried Loudon Park Cem, Baltimore in grave B-2.

1860 census Burke Co., NC- Theophilus G. Scott, age 39, with wife Martha and family.

1860 Onslow- no Theophilus G. or T. G. Scott noted.

note: Theophilus G. Scott of co B, 24 NC should be deleted and his full name enter in co B, 54 NC.

9)-rost- **Samuel H. Stafford**, co I, 54 NC, capt North Anna River, Va 22 May 64, died Point Lookout 27 July 1864 of disease.

CWPOWrec- S. H. Stafford, co I, 54 NC, capt Spottsylvania 22 May 64, trans fm Port Royal to Pt Lookout 30 May 64, died 27 July 64 of measles.

CWPOWrec- Z. J. Stafford, co I, 54 NC, capt Spottsylvania 22 May 64, trans fm Port Royal to Pt Lookout 30 May 64, died 3 July 1864 Point Lookout of chronic diarrhea.

1850 Forsyth Co census- Samuel H. (17) and Zadok J. (4) Stafford were sons of Zadok J. & Hanah Stafford.

1860 Forsyth Co census- Samuel H. (25) and Zadok J. (14) Stafford were sons of Zadok A. & Hannah Stafford.

note: **Zadok J. Stafford** prob enlisted late in the war and should be added to co I, 54 NC.

10)-rost- **James H. Taylor**, miscellaneous, 54 NC, served in co D, 12 NC (2 NC Vol), was reported trans to this regiment (54 NC) on an unspecified date; however, rec of this regt do not indicate that he served herein, no further records.

NCS, 20 August 1862-James H. Taylor, 2 Regt N.C.V., died on the 23rd ult. (23 July 1862), age 23, soon after battle of Hanover he was trans to the Comm Dept of Col Wimbish's Regt (54 NC), he was taken ill at Camp Mangum soon after his tran and returned home (Granville Co) where he expired just four weeks after his attack.

11)-rost- **David Marlow**, co B, 55 NC, mort wounded & capt 7/1/63 Gettysburg, place and date of death not rep.

CWPOWrec- **D. F. Marlow**, co B, 55 NC, died 7/5/63 Gettysburg.

12)-rost- **J. J. Edwards**, co E, 55 NC, w Gettysburg 1-3 July 63, rep in Hagerstown hosp Aug 63, died prior to 1 July 1864, p & d & c of death not reported.

CWPOWrec- J. J. Edwards, 55 NC, capt 'Funetown', in Seminery Hospital at

Hagerstown.

Southern Historical Soc papers, vo XXVII, page 242-250, Sick and Wounded Conf soldiers at Hagerstown and Williamsport- Pvt J. J. Edwards, 55 NC, w 14 July, died 9 August.

13)-rost- **Noah J. Canipe**, co F, 55 NC, capt Gettysburg 1 July 63, trans fm Ft Delaware to Pt Lookout 20 Oct 63, paroled on an unspecified date, died at Petersburg in winter of 63, cause of death not reported.

CWPOWrec- **L. Caipe**, co F, 55 NC (5 records noted), capt Gettysburg 2 July 63, trans to Hammond General Hospital at Pt Lookout between 11 and 30 Nov 63, died at Pt Lookout 8 Dec 63 of acute diarrhea.

note: all POW rec indicate co F, 55 NC. There were eight 'Canipe' soldiers from Cleveland County. Believe L. Caipe is the same as Noah J. Canipe and he died at Pt Lookout vice Petersburg.

14)-rost-**Sidney Gay**, co I, 55 NC, present in May-June 1864, no further records.

Petersburg-S. Gay, co I, 55 NC, died Petersburg on 14 Sep 1864, buried Petersburg Fair Grounds vicinity.

15)-rost- **Benjamin Franklin Kendrick**, co B, 56 NC, died in Richmond on or about 30 July 1864, presumably of wounds.

FO, 5 Sept 1864- Benjamin F. Kendrick, co B, 56 NC, died in Winder Hospital in Richmond on 30 July 1864 of typhoid fever.

16)-rost- Charles Miller, co B, 56 NC, deserted on 27 August 1864.

FO, 27 Feb 1865- **Charles W. Miller**, co B, 56 NC, age 24, died at his father's residence in Cumberland Co., NC on 18 February 1865.

17)-rost- **David A. Clements**, co E, 56 NC, killed 14 Jul 1864, place of death not reported.

Petersburg- D. A. Clements, co E, 56 NC, killed Petersburg 15 Jul 1864, burial Petersburg Fair Ground vicinity.

18)-rost-**Louis Justice**, co F, 56 NC, capt Globe Tavern, d 24 Aug 64 of wounds at unk place.

VA web site- L. Jestive, co F, 56 NC died 24 Aug 64, buried City Point National Cemetery, Va in grave 4092.

19)-rost-Pvt **William J. King**, co G, 56 NC, enl Henderson Co 1 Jan 64, w and capt Fort Stedman 25 Mar 65, died Federal Field Hosp 26 Mar 65.

rost-Pvt William King, co G, 50 NC died near Hopewell, Va 25 Mar 65.

City Point Nat Cem-Pvt William King of co G, 50, died 25 Mar 65, grave C3758.

note: with the enlistment and capt info on King in the 56 NC, William King of the 50 NC should be deleted.

20)-rost- **William G, Kuykendall**, co G, 56 NC, born Henderson Co, res farmer, enl age 20 on 12 Apr 62, died in Raleigh on 21 Nov 62 of disease.

rost- **G. W. Kirkendoff**, co F, 7 Batt NC Cav, died in hosp at Raleigh 21 Nov 1862.

note: G. W. Kirkendoff of 7 Batt NC Cav should be deleted.

21)-rost-Pvt **Calvin C. Tabor**, co G, 56 NC, pre in co F-14 NC, trans 4 Jan 65, w in head and capt Petersburg 27 Mar 65, died hosp Washington 16 Apr 65 (note Alexander Taber of Henderson Co. in unit.)

rost-Pvt Calvin C. Taber, co G, 5 NC, place and date enl not rep, w in head and capt Petersburg 27 Mar 65, held City Point, trans to Washington, DC 9 Apr 65, died hosp in Washington 16 Apr 65 of wounds.

note: Calvin C. Taber of 5 NC should be deleted.

The next five items (22 to 26) concerns Company H, 56 NC and Company C, 68 NC. They are the same five soldiers of the 56 and 68 NC Inf. Data should be combine into Company C, 68 NC Inf.

22)-rost- Pvt. **Ambrose Jones**, co H, 56 NC, res of Camden Co., NC, place and date enl not reported, capt Camden Co., NC 1 Dec 63, confined Norfolk and Ft. Monroe, trans to Point Lookout 5 Feb 64, rel from Point Lookout 28 Jun 65.

rost- Corp. **Amos Jones**, co C, 68 NC, enl Camden 31 Aug 63, capt 10 Dec 63, rep POW through 30 Jun 64, no further record.

23)-rost- **Daniel McCoy**, co H, 56 NC, place and date of enl not reported, capt Camden Co. 1 Dec 63, sent to Norfolk, Va, trans to Fort Monroe, Va, where he arr on 1 Feb 64, tran to Point Lookout where he arr 3 Feb 64, died Point Lookout 22 Feb 64 of smallpox.

rost- **Daniel Macoy**, co C, 68 NC, enl Currituck Co. on 31 Aug 63, capt by enemy on an unspecified date, died in a Fedral prison on 20 Feb 64, place and cause of death not reported.

24)-rost- **John R. Perkins**, co H, 56 NC, res of Caswell Co., NC, enl at age 24 on 8 Nov 64, capt Five Forks, Va on 1 Apr 65, rel from Point Lookout 16 Jun 65.

rost- John Perkins, co C, 68 NC, enl Camden Co., NC 31 Aug 63, while serving in co G, 59 NC, on receipt roll 30 Sep 64, no further record.

25)-rost- **William Sawyer**, co H, 56 NC, place and date enl not reported, capt Camden Co., NC 1 Dec 63, trans from Ft. Monroe to Point Lookout 3 Feb 64, exchanged 17 Mar 64, no further record.

rost- William Sawyer, co C, 68 NC, enl Camden Co., NC 31 Aug 63, listed as paroled prisoner on 30 Apr 64, present 30 Jun 64, name on receipt roll 30 Sep 64, no further record.

26)-rost- **Nathaniel Wright**, co H, 56 NC, date and place enl not reported, capt Currituck Co., NC on unspecified date, sent to Norfolk, hosp at Portsmouth, Va 2 Jan 64, died Portsmouth on 6 Feb 64 of typh fever.

rost- Nathaniel Wright, co C, 68 NC, enl Camden Co., NC 31 Aug 63, capt 10 Dec 63, reported as POW through 30 Jun 64, no further record.

27)-rost- **William K. Jackson**, co K, 56 NC, died in Richmond 9 June 1864 of disease.

FO, 29 Aug 1864- W. K. Jackson, co K, 56 NC, died in Richmond 9 June 1864 of black measles.

Cause of deaths that were not listed in the NC Roster - Volume XIII

rank	name	co	unit	place of death	died	cause of death
Pvt	John H. Kiser	D	53	Fort Delaware	10/10/63	scurvy
Pvt	Francis M. Amburn	G	53	Point Lookout	6/19/64	chronic diarrhoea
Pvt	William Bennett, Jr.	H	53	Fort Delaware	1/4/64	lungs, inf of
Pvt	Anannias Brigman	I	53	Washington	8/8/64	exh. amp left anke
Pvt	George F. Owens	A	54	Point Lookout	2/15/64	acute diarrhoea
Corp	James A. McGalliard	B	54	Point Lookout	1/6/64	pneumonia
Pvt	John M. Coble	D	54	Point Lookout	6/17/64	febris remit
Pvt	James A. Jones	D	54	Point Lookout	2/23/64	pneumonia
Pvt	Reuben R. Dickens	F	54	Point Lookout	8/26/64	chronic diarrhoea
Pvt	William Harris	F	54	Point Lookout	2/10/64	febris typhoides
Pvt	John Wilborn	H	54	Point Lookout	9/8/64	febris remit
Pvt	A. Crofford Greenway	I	54	Point Lookout	3/6/64	chronic diarrhoea
Pvt	Andrew Padgett	I	54	Point Lookout	2/19/64	chronic diarrhoea
Pvt	Samuel H. Stafford	I	54	Point Lookout	7/27/64	measles
Corp	A.L. Bunn	K	54	Point Lookout	4/7/64	chronic diarrhoea
Pvt	J.B. Kittle	K	54	Point Lookout	11/13/63	pneumonia
Pvt	James W. Ferrell	A	55	Fort Delaware	10/6/63	acute dysenteria
Pvt	Henry Lucas	A	55	Fort Delaware	10/2/63	febris typhoides
Corp	Robert M. Pittman	A	55	Point Lookout	11/13/63	chronic diarrhoea
Pvt	Jackson Price	A	55	Point Lookout	3/7/64	diarrhoea
Pvt	Calvin Raper	A	55	Point Lookout	2/4/64	dropsy, Idiapathie?
Sgt	Edmond J. Greer	B	55	Point Lookout	2/13/64	chronic diarrhoea
Sgt	Thomas S. Pearson	B	55	Point Lookout	12/26/63	febris typhoides
Sgt	Asa Rash	B	55	Point Lookout	11/4/63	dysentery, chronic
Pvt	Jeremiah Heavener	C	55	Fort Delaware	10/5/63	dysentery, chronic
Pvt	Michael White	C	55	Fort Delaware	10/9/63	scurvy
Pvt	William F. Bryson	D	55	Fort Delaware	10/15/63	mumps
Pvt	John P. Green	D	55	Point Lookout	6/9/65	chronic diarrhoea
Pvt	Isaac Hamrick	D	55	Point Lookout	2/27/64	chronic diarrhoea
Pvt	Willis G. Lovelace	D	55	Point Lookout	9/13/64	acute dysenteria
Pvt	William G. Lovelace	D	55	Point Lookout	7/30/64	febris remit
Pvt	George W. Mooney	D	55	Point Lookout	12/28/63	chronic diarrhoea
Corp	James L. Fleming	E	55	Fort Delaware	9/14/63	act. dysenteria/typh fever
Pvt	John Sr. Mills	E	55	Point Lookout	2/22/64	chronic diarrhoea

rank	name	co	unit	place of death	died	cause of death
Pvt	Peter M. Bivens	F	55	Point Lookout	2/19/64	chronic diarrhoea
Pvt	David A. Bumgarner	F	55	Point Lookout	8/10/64	fetris remitten
Pvt	David W. Turner	F	55	Chester	8/2/63	gen. dibility/chr diarrhoea
Pvt	John W. Brock	G	55	Fort Delaware	10/1/63	lungs, inf of
Pvt	William Fields	G	55	Point Lookout	1/11/64	pneumonia
Pvt	John D. Strickland	G	55	Fort Delaware	10/10/63	anemia
Pvt	Josiah J. Thompson	G	55	Point Lookout	1/25/64	dysenteria, chronic
Pvt	J.B. Barefoot	I	55	Fort Delaware	10/9/63	acute diarrhoea
Corp	William H. Moore	I	55	Fort Delaware	10/13/63	erysipelas
Pvt	Thomas Neal	I	55	Fort Delaware	10/8/63	chronic diarrhoea
Pvt	John Dallas Yancey	K	55	Fort Delaware	10/10/63	chronic diarrhoea
Pvt	Myamin Haynes	F	56	Federal Field Hosp	8/21/64	gs abdomin
Pvt	John Thomas Lee	H	56	Point Lookout	6/19/64	vulnus sclopst
Pvt	Silas Smith	H	56	Point Lookout	7/27/64	acute dysenteria

Volume XIV 57th - 58th and 60th - 61st Infantry

1)-rost- **Raymond Gibson**, co D, 57 NC, res Stokes Co, enl Forsyth Co 4 July 62 at age 31. Capt Gettysburg, paroled, capt Rappahanock Station, paroled, prior to 22-23 Aug 64 capt near Charlestown, WVa, conf Elmira, released 16 Jun 65.

rost- Rayman Gibson, co D, 6 NC, capt Charles Town, WVa 22 Aug 64 and conf at Fort Delaware. No further records.

CWPOWrec- Raymond Gibson, co D, 57 NC, capt Charlestown, WVa 22 Aug 64 and released 19 Jun 65.

note: delete Rayman Gibson of co C, 6 NC.

2)-rost- **H. R. Curtis**, co E, 57 NC, capt Williamsport 6 Jul 63, after he was left behind as a nurse for the wounded, no further records.

CWPOWrec- H. R. Curtis, Med. Dispeser, 57 NC, capt Williamsport, at the Seminary Hospital in Hagerstown, Md (no date).

3)-rost-**Jacob Lantz**, co E, 57 NC, p & d enl not rep, rec of Fed Prov Mars ind he died at Point Lookout 29 Apr 1864. No fur rec.

CWPOWrec- Jacob Lantz, Co E, 57 NC, capt Rappahannoch on 7 Nov 1864 (along with many others), d Pt Lookout 29 Apr 1864 of diarrhea.

4)-rost-Pvt **Edmund Cress** of co F, 57 NC, res Cabarrus Co., NC, capt Gettysburg, died at Fort Delaware, date and cause of death not rep.

1912 book-Pvt Edmund Cress of co F, 57 Va, died 17 Sep 63, bur Finn's Point, NJ (prob died at Fort Delaware.)

CWPOWrec- Pvt Edmund Cress, co F, 57 NC or Va, capt Waterloo, Pa. 5 July 1863, died 17 Sept 1863.

5)-rost-**B. Holmes**, co F, 57 NC, place and date of enl not reported, Fed med rec indicate that he was wounded in the thigh and capt at Gettysburg 1-3 July 1863, died in a Gettysburg hosp 17 July 1863 following ampt of leg.

rost-**Rufus Holmes**, co F, 47 NC, born and reside in Franklin Co., enl at age 25 on 8 Mar 62, killed at Gettysburg on or about 3 July 1863.

note: believe B. Holmes and Rufus Holmes are the same soldier. The correct entry should be Pvt Rufus Holmes of co F, 47 NC, wounded in the thigh at Gettysburg and captured, died in a Gettysburg hospital on 17 July 1863 following ampt of leg. (his company thought he was killed while the Federal records indicate his captured and death.)

6)-rost- 1st Lt **John C. Green**, co B, 58 NC, resided in Mitchell or Yancey Co, died at Jacksboro, Tenn on or about 28 Jan 1863, cause of death not reported.

NCS, 12 Aug 1863- 1st Lt John C. Green, co B, 58 NC, citizen in Mitchell Co, died at Jacksborough, Tenn on 28 June 1863 of typhoid fever.

The following list of (four) names was extracted from the Atlanta newspaper, the *Southern Confederacy*, dated March 25, 1864, and was preceded by the following notation:

"Below is appended a list of all deaths occurring among the soldiers at this post in the Newsom, Frank Ramsay, University and Flewellan Hospitals, from the 12th of October, 1863, to March 16th, 1864. By giving this list publicity some bereaved family may possibly receive the first tidings that a loved member of the home circle has gone to his last sleep, and to them is given the consolation that nothing was left undone by experienced and humane and attentive physicians to arrest the destroyer."

7)- **Harvey H. Gregg**, company E, 58th North Carolina, January 20, 1864.
(NC Roster - Harvey H. Gragg, co D, 58 NC – died prior to Jan 1, 1865. Place, date, and cause of death not reported.)

8)- **S.G. Brown**, company B, 60th North Carolina, January 27, 1864.
(NC Roster – S. G. Brown, co B, 60 NC – died at Cassville, Georgia, Jan 18 or Jan 27, 1864.)

9)- **Abraham B. Bradley**, company D, 60th North Carolina, January 4, 1864.
(NC Roster – Abraham B. Bradley, co D, 60 NC – died on Jan 4, 1864. Place and cause of death not reported.)

10)- James Clack, company D, 60th North Carolina, November 17, 1863.
(NC Roster – **James A. Clark**, co D, 60 NC – died on an unspecified date in 1864. Place and cause of death not reported.)

11)-rost- **Payton Rash**, co M, 58 NC, enlisted Watauga Co. 26 Sept 62, deserted fm camp at Jacksboro, Tn 29 Dec 62, ret to duty 20 Mar 63, tran to co G of this regiment in May 63, deserted at Clinton, Tn prior to 1 July 63, died at Ft Delaware 10 Sep 63 of measles.
rost- **Payton Rash**, co I, 6 NC Cav, while in the 5 Batt he was capt at Hawkins Co., Ky 20 June 63 and conf at Camp Chase, Oh, trans fm co C, 5 Batt NC Cav 8 Aug 63 while POW at Ft Delaware, died Ft Delaware 10 Sep 63.
note: on CWPOWrec there are 11 rec for P. or Peyton Rash, 7 listed him in the 65 NC (6 Cav) while 2 had the 58 NC, and one rec had '65' written above '58' under unit, capt Hickory Co., Tn 20 June 63, tran fm Lexington, Ky to Camp Chase 29 June 63, tran fm Camp Chase to Ft Delaware 14 July 63, died Ft Delaware 10 Sept 63, he was 24 at time of death, 6 ft, blue eyes and sandy hair. While confused as to the correct unit this is the same man listed in both cases.

12)-rost- **William P. Benison**, Co D, 60 NC, capt Missionary Ridge 25 Nov 63, trans to Rock Island, Ill 11 Dec 1863, no further records.
CWPOWrec- William P. Bennison, co D, 60 NC, capt Missinary Ridge 25 Nov 63, enlisted in U. S. Navy and sent to Naval R...... Camp Douglas, Ill 25 Jan 64.

13)-rost- **Jordan F. Russell**, co D, 60 NC, captured, trans from Nashville to Louiseville, was ordered to Camp Chase, Ohio on 25 Feb 63, but was 'not able to go', died (presumably at Louiseville) on an unspecified date.

Confederate Section of Cav Hill Cemetery, Louiseville, Ky- J. F. Russell (only info), died 28 Feb 63, buried in CS lot 256 nr 98.

14)-rost-**Solomon W. Faison**, co A, 61 NC, killed at Drewry's Bluff 13-16 May 1864.

CWPOWrec- Solomon W. Faison, co A, 61 NC, died 23 May 1864 at Fort Monroe of gun shot wound left lung.

note: Faison was wounded and captured.

15)-rost-Pvt **John Dawson** of co C, 61 NC, born Craven, res in Lenoir Co, enl in Craven 62, capt Globe Taven, Va 19Aug 64, conf Point Lookout 24 Aug 64, died at Point Lookout 22 Feb 65.

rost-Pvt John Dawson of co C, 6 NC, place and date of enlistment not reported, died Point Lookout 22 Feb 65.

note: John Dawson of co C, 6 NC should be deleted.

Cause of deaths that were not listed in the NC Roster - Volume XIV

rank	name	co	unit	place of death	died	cause of death
Pvt	A.M. Kennerly	A	57	Point Lookout	1/15/64	dysentery, chronic
Pvt	P.A. Overcash	B	57	Point Lookout	11/26/63	smallpox
Pvt	William H.H. Mathews	D	57	Point Lookout	8/12/64	chronic diarrhoea
Pvt	John Marcus Hefner	E	57	Point Lookout	7/27/64	acute diarrhoea
Pvt	Carlos Elphonse Lowrance	E	57	Washington	11/16/63	gs back/asthenia
Pvt	Benjamin Sigman	E	57	Point Lookout	6/4/64	febris typhoides
Pvt	R.W. Caldwell	F	57	Fort Delaware	10/12/63	febris typhoid
Pvt	William N. Ritchie	F	57	Point Lookout	3/21/64	diarrhoea
Pvt	William Mooneyham	H	57	Newport News	6/19/65	typhoid fever
Pvt	William B. Priddy	H	57	Point Lookout	5/15/65	chronic diarrhoea
Pvt	Henry D. Smith	H	57	Point Lookout	4/5/64	febris continues
Pvt	William Atkins	I	57	Point Lookout	2/14/64	dysenteria, chronic
Pvt	James M. Foster	I	57	Point Lookout	2/7/64	chronic diarrhoea
Pvt	Austin W. Harder	I	57	Point Lookout	12/22/63	acute diarrhoea
Pvt	Jefferson H. Walker	I	57	Point Lookout	12/29/63	chronic diarrhoea
Pvt	John Brand	E	58	Knoxville	7/29/64	gs w thigh flesh
Pvt	Housen Newton Bridges	A	60	Murfreesboro	2/23/63	vulnus sclopst
Pvt	W.G. Brown	B	60	Indianapolis	10/20/63	febris remittens
1Lt	Henry Clay Lowrance	D	60	Point Lookout	8/11/64	chronic diarrhoea
Pvt	Isaac Ledford	F	60	Nashville	2/26/63	consumption/smallpox
Pvt	John Dawson	C	61	Point Lookout	2/22/65	debilitas
Corp	Allen Grimsley	E	61	Point Lookout	1/24/64	chronic diarrhoea
Pvt	Sherwood Hines	E	61	Point Lookout	12/22/63	chronic diarrhoea
Pvt	Linville Joines	I	61	Hampton	8/31/64	chronic diarrhoea

Volume XV - 62nd - 64th and 66th - 68th Infantry

1)-rost- **J. F. Reece**, co I, 62 NC, NC pension rec indicate that he served in this company.

CWPOWrec- **James Reece**, Co I, 62 NC, capt Cumberland Gap 9 Sept 1863, received at Camp Douglas 26 Sept 1863, died Camp Douglas on 14 Oct 1864 of consumption, buried Chicago City Cemetery.

2)-rost-Pvt **Gideon Low**, co K, 62 NC, res Jackson Co, farmer, enl Transylvania at age 29 on 14 Jul 62, capt Knox Co., Ky 9 Aug 63, conf Rock Island, Ill 24 Jan 64, died Rock Island on 2 Feb 64, (in Roster statement 'Contray to 2:512 of this series, he never served in Company K, 65th Regiment NC Troops, 6th Regiment NC Cavalry.)

rost-Pvt **Gideon Lowe**, co K, 6 NC Cav, capt Knox Co, Ky 9 Aug 63, conf Camp Chase, Ohio, trans to Rock Island, Ill 22 Jan 64, no further rec as of 24 Jan 64.

CWPOWrec- Gideon Lowe, co K, 62 NC, capt Knox Co., Ky 9 Aug 63, rec Louisville, Ky 25 Aug 63, sent to Camp Chase 1 Sep 63, died Rock Island 29 Feb 64 of variola.

note: Gideon Lowe of 6 NC Cav should be deleted.

3)-rost- **Marion L. Buckner**, co A, 64 NC, rel fm Camp Douglas 12 Jun 65 after Oath.

CWPOWrec- Marion L. Buckner, co A, 64 NC, died 17 Jun 1865 at General Hospital Chattanooga, Tn, burial records.

note: died 5 days after his released from prison.

4)-rost-**John Coggins** and **Enoch Cutrell**, co A, 66 NC, both capt near Fairfield, NC 20 Feb 1864 and exchanged 18 March 1865.

CWPOWrec-John Coggins, Enoch Curtell; plus, **David Calhoun** and **Eleaser Curtell** all of 66 NC were capt near Fairfield, NC 20 Feb 1864, arrival at Point Lookout from Fort Monroe on 26 Feb 1864, Enoch Curtell and John Coggins were exchanged in March 11 and 15 1865, David Calhoun died at Point Lookout 8 May 1864 and Eleaser Curtrell died at Point Lookout 3 Sept 1864.

CWPOWrec-'desire to be sent South as Prisoners of War for exchange'-

E. Cutrell of Hyde Co,

E. Cutrell of Hyde Co,

J. Coggins of Edgecombe Co

1850 Hyde Co., NC census- 1) Enoch Cutrell (11) in Asbay Cox household.

2) David Cahoon (9) John T. (34) Nancy (24) William

H. (5) Charles E.(5/12)

1850 Pitt Co., NC- John Coggins (3) Willaim (39) Lucenda (36)

1860 Hyde Co., NC census- Eleaza Cutrel (40) Selinia (25) Jane (7) Mary (4)

1860 Edgecombe Co., NC census- John H. Coggins (13)

note: David Calhoun, born abt 1841 of Hyde Co. and Eleaser Curtrell, born abt 1820 of Hyde Co. should be added to co A, 66 NC.

5)-rost- Company A, 66 NC Inf.—list members of Spencer's Rangers that were transferred to this company on an unspecified date (probably in February-September, 1864) while Prisoners of War. (note: this list has nineteen men that were captured at Fairfield, NC on 20 Feb 1864.)

rost-Captain Spencer's Ind. Comp. NC Cav.- Capt. Spencer, Lt. **S. P. Sparrow**, and twenty-six men of this company were captured on 20 Feb 1864 at Fairfield, NC. (note: this roster list eighteen of them.)

CWPOWrec- all the follow prisoner of war records on the above men and those not listed in the two volumes of *NC Troops*, were recorded as being in the 66 NC, with a few noted as being in company A of that unit. This indicates that Spencer's Rangers were transferred to Co. A, 66 NC before 20 Feb 1864.

1) Those listed in Spencer's Company, but not in co. A, 66 NC: Capt. **William H. Spencer** and Pvt. **David R. O'Neal**.

2) Those listed in Co. A, 66 NC, but not in Spencer's Company. Pvt. **James T.(or J.) Midgett**, Pvt. **William J. Brooks** and Pvt. **William P. Bryan**

3) **Leroy Smith**, no rank, listed in Spencer's on bounty roll dated 4 Apr 63 to 29 Aug 63 and listed in Co. A, 66 NC with a pension record of being wounded in the arm and hand. CWPOWrec has Corp. Leroy Smith, 66 NC, capt Fairfield, NC on 20 Feb 64 and exchanged 14 Mar 65.

4) The following soldiers were not listed in either Spencer's Company nor co. A of the 66 NC. They were all captured at Fairfield, NC on 20 Feb 64:

a. Pvt **David Calhoun** died at Point Lookout on 8 May 64,

b. Pvt **Elaser Curtrell** (see miscellaneous section of 66 NC) died at Point Lookout on 3 Sep 64,

c. Pvt **Tillman Dunbar** was released on Oath 25 Apr 64,

d. Pvt **William G. Murray** was exchanged at Aikens Laning on 30 Oct 64

e. Pvt **William Sawyer** was released on 14 May 65.

5) The six names in items 3 and 4 should be added to Co. A, 66 NC.

6)-rost- **Arthur Allgood**, co G, 66 NC, both legs shot off at Hair's House, Va on an unspecified date (prob in the summer of 1864), died in Richmond on an unspecified date of wounds.

Hollywood Cem., Richmond, Va rec- A. Allgood, co G, 66 NC, died 7/11/64, buried in grave U644.

7)-rost-**Hendersons** in co H, 67 NC, Elza, Isaac N., J. L., Lewis Hill, Nixon, Stephen and Thomas.

LMA-**John Henderson** of co H, 67 NC, no dates, grave 9 in Oakwood Cem, Raleigh, NC..

Poss J. L. Henderson on bounty payroll 20 Oct 64. No fur rec.

The next five items (8 to 12) concerns Company H, 56 NC and Company C, 68 NC. They are the same five soldiers of the 56 and 68 NC Inf. Data should be combined into Company C, 68 NC Inf.

8)-rost- Corp. **Amos Jones**, co C, 68 NC, enl Camden 31 Aug 63, capt 10 Dec 63, rep POW through 30 Jun 64, no further record.

rost- Pvt. **Ambrose Jones**, co H, 56 NC, res of Camden Co., NC, place and date enl not reported, capt Camden Co., NC 1 Dec 63, confined Norfolk and Ft. Monroe, trans to Point Lookout 5 Feb 64, rel from Point Lookout 28 Jun 65.

9)-rost- **Daniel MaCoy**, co C, 68 NC, enl Currituck Co. on 31 Aug 63, capt by enemy on an unspecified date, died in a Fedral prison on 20 Feb 64, place and cause of death not reported.

rost- Daniel McCoy, co H, 56 NC, place and date of enl not reported, capt Camden Co. 1 Dec 63, sent to Norfolk, Va, trans to Fort Monroe, Va, where he arr on 1 Feb 64, tran to Point Lookout where he arr 3 Feb 64, died Point Lookout 22 Feb 64 of smallpox.

10)-rost- John Perkins, co C, 68 NC, enl Camden Co., NC 31 Aug 63, while serving in co G, 59 NC, on receipt roll 30 Sep 64, no further record.

rost- **John R. Perkins**, co H, 56 NC, res of Caswell Co., NC, enl at age 24 on 8 Nov 64, capt Five Forks, Va on 1 Apr 65, rel from Point Lookout 16 Jun 65.

11)-rost- **William Sawyer**, co C, 68 NC, enl Camden Co., NC 31 Aug 63, listed as paroled prisoner on 30 Apr 64, present 30 Jun 64, name on receipt roll 30 Sep 64, no further record.

rost- William Sawyer, co H, 56 NC, place and date enl not reported, capt Camden Co., NC 1 Dec 63, trans from Ft. Monroe to Point Lookout 3 Feb 64, exchanged 17 Mar 64, no further record.

12)-rost- **Nathaniel Wright**, co C, 68 NC, enl Camden Co., NC 31 Aug 63, capt 10 Dec 63, reported as POW through 30 Jun 64, no further record.

rost- Nathaniel Wright, co H, 56 NC, date and place enl not reported, capt Currituck Co., NC on unspecified date, sent to Norfolk, hosp at Portsmouth, Va 2 Jan 64, died Portsmouth on 6 Feb 64 of typh fever.

13)-rost- **William N. Mitchell**, company F, 68 NC, dropped from the company rolls prior to June 30, 1864. Reason he was dropped not reported.

Haywood papers- William Mitchell of 68 NC, died March 9, 1863 in Raleigh hospital of pneumonia. Not listed on the Oakwood Cemetery roster, buried site unknown.

Cause of deaths that were not listed in the NC Roster - Volume XV

rank	name	co	unit	place of death	died	cause of death
Pvt	Harvey Hannah	A	62	Chicago	10/12/64	-
Pvt	Thomas Jones	B	62	Chicago	3/4/65	pneumonia
Pvt	John E. Fincher	C	62	Chicago	5/12/64	rheumatism, acute
3Lt	Henderson Criswell	D	62	Johnson's Island	9/12/64	typhoid fever
Pvt	Enos Gray	D	62	Indianapolis	10/16/63	chronic diarrhoea
Pvt	James E. Tomberlin	F	62	Indianapolis	10/31/63	lungs, inf of
Corp	James T. Carson	G	62	Chicago	7/28/64	dysentery, acute
Pvt	Cornwell Herren	H	62	Chicago	4/28/64	smallpox
Pvt	William Stephen Cook	B	66	Point Lookout	5/6/65	chronic diarrhoea
Pvt	Joseph J. Leonard, Jr.	B	66	Point Lookout	10/3/64	acute dysenteria
Pvt	William Henry McKeel	D	67	Point Lookout	9/9/64	acute diarrhoea
Pvt	William S. Shivers	D	67	New Bern	7/7/64	gs lt lung
Pvt	Alexander Gray	E	67	Point Lookout	9/13/64	dropsy
Pvt	Henry Stocks	I	67	Point Lookout	6/8/64	lungs, inf of
Pvt	John M. Cartwright	A	68	Point Lookout	2/9/64	febris typhoid
Pvt	Joseph T. Leyden	A	68	Point Lookout	5/1/64	congestive chill
Pvt	Ebenezer W. Sawyer	A	68	Point Lookout	3/26/64	diarrhoea
Pvt	Henry A. Jackson	B	68	Elmira	12/4/64	chronic diarrhoea
Pvt	Charles Taylor	B	68	Baltimore	10/20/64	chronic diarrhoea
Pvt	Jonathan Tillett	B	68	Point Lookout	7/29/64	febris remit
Pvt	William M. Whitehurst	B	68	Fort Monroe	1/13/64	chronic diarrhoea

Volume XVI - Thomas Legion

1)-rost- 1ˢᵗ Sgt **Goodson M. Cole**, co A. Walker's Battalion, Thomas Legion, capt Winchester 19 Sep 64, conf at Point Lookout on or about 26 Sep 64, paroled on or about 1 Nov 64.
rost- Sgt. G. M. Cole, co A, 1 NC, capt Winchester 19 Sep 64, sent to Pt Lookout 23 Sep 64 (only info).
CWPOWrec- Sgt. Goodson M. Cole, co A, Thomas Legion, capt Winchester 19 Sep 64, trans fm Harpers Ferry to Pt Lookout 26 Sept 64, trans to Aikens Landing for exchange 1 Nov 64.
note: G. M. Cole of 1 NC should be deleted.

2)-rost- Sgt **Rufus L. Cooper**, co A, Walker's Battalion, Thomas Legion, capt Winchester 19 Sep 64, conf Point Lookout 26 Sep 64, paroled 15 Mar 65.
rost- Sgt. R. L. Cooper, co A, 1 NC, capt Winchester 19 Sep 64, sent to Pt Lookout 23 Sep 64 (only info).
CWPOWrec- Sgt. R. L. Cooper, co A, Thomas Legion, capt Winchester 19 Sep 64, trans fm Harpers Ferry to Pt Lookout 26 Sept 64, exchange 13 Mar 65, rec at Aiken Landing 15 Mar 65.
note: R. L. Cooper of 1 NC should be deleted.

3)-rost- **John M. Thurman**, co A, Walker's Battalion, Thomas Legion, name appears on rec rolls for clothing 15 Mar and 4 Jun 64, no further records.
Lynchburg, Old City Cemetery- J. M. Thurman, co A, Thomas Legion, NC.

4)-rost-Pvt **Moses I. Hall**, co B, Walker's Batt, Thomas Legion, enl Cherokee Co 19 Jul 62, rep absent sick from 15 Feb to 31 Dec 63. Listed as deserter 29 Feb 64.
1912 book-Pvt Moses J. Hall of co B, Thomas Legion Cav, died Fort Delaware 31 Mar 64, bur Finn's Point, NJ.
Fort Delaware Society-Pvt Moses J. Hall of co B, Thomas Legion, capt Cherokee Co, NC 18 Feb 64, died Fort Delaware 31 Mar 64 of smallpox.

5)-rost-Pvt Asaph W. Sherill, co C, Indian Battalion, Thomas Legion.
Ancestry.com-**Asaph Wilson Sherrill**, b 1818 Haywood, d 2 Mar 1865 Ft Delaware.

6)-rost- **Jonas Talley**, co D, Indian Battalion, Thomas Legion, died Camp Chase on 21 Nov 64 probably of diarrhea.
CWPOWrec- Jonas Talley, co D, Thomas Batt, died Camp Chase on 21 Nov 64 of Jaundice and diarrhea.

Volume XVII – Junior Reserves

1)-rost-**Merideth C. Davis**, co A, 1 Batt NC Jr Res, rep on detached service on 11 June 64, capt by enemy on unspecified date and conf at Elmira, died Elmira on 20 Dec 64, cause not reported.

rost-**Michael C. Davis**, co A, 1 NC, capt Spotsylvania CH 12 May 64, trans from Pt Lookout to Elmira 6 Aug 64, died Elmira 20 Dec 64 of pneumonia.

CWPOWrec-M. C. Davis, co A, 1 NC, capt Spotsylvania (or some reports 'Wilderness') on 12 May 64, trans from Pt Lookout to Elmira 3 Aug 64, died Elmira on 20 Dec 64 of pneumonia.

note- 'no further records' should be entered for Merideth C. Davis of 1 Batt NC Jr Res and died at Elmira should be deleted.

2)-rost- J. W. Armstead, co B, 1 Jr Res, p & d of enl not rep, d Point Lookout on 6 Mar 65 of typhoid fever.

rost- **James W. Olmstead**, co B, 1 Jr Res, born Michigan, enl Camp Holmes on 21 May 64, capt Hamilton, Va on 12 Dec 64, trans fm Camp Hamilton, Va to Pt Lookout on 27 Dec 64, died at Pt Lookout on 6 Mar 65, cause of death not rep.

note: J. W. Armstead should be deleted and add typhoid fever as cause of death for James W. Olmstead.

3)-rost-**David Hauss, Eli Hauss, Joseph Hauss, William T. Hauss**, co C, 2 NC Jr Res (see page 260)

rost-**David Huss** (20 Sep 46) , **Eli C. Huss** (about 28 Mar 47), **Joseph H. Huss** (about 20 Aug 46), **William T. Huss** (about 16 Jun 46), co C, 2 NC Jr Res (see page 262)

1850 and 1860 Lincoln Co., NC census-David and Joseph Hauss, age 14, were twins of Peter and Barbara Hauss.

NC Death Cert.-**David C. Huss**, born 20 Sep 46, died 2 May 1920, son of Peter and Barbara Huss.

NC Death Cert.-**Elias Calvin Huss**, born 1 Feb 47, died 10 Feb 1838

NC Death Cert- Joseph Huss, born 25 (prob should be 20) Sep 46, died 21 May 1926, son of Peter Huss.

NC Death Cert- **William Theodare Hauss**, born 6 Jun 46, died 5 Apr 1931.

note: the four names noted on page 260 and 262 of the Roster are the same four soldiers and while David, Elias and Joseph had Huss on their death cert., William had Hauss as his last name. David C. and Joseph H. (family members stated his middle name was Franklin) were twins born on 20 Sep 1846 to Peter and Barbara Hauss/Huss.

note: The four names on page 260 and also 262 are the same soldiers and the names Hauss and Huss were interchangeable

4)-rost-company A, 3 NC Jr Res

1 **B. C. Gooble**, co A, 3 NC Jr Res, prev in co A, 4 Batt NC Jr Res, died at Pt Lookout on 27 Jun 1865, cause of death not reported.

2 **Levy S. Keller**, co A, 3 NC Jr Res, may have been in co A, 4 Batt NC Jr Res, died at

Pt Lookout 29-30 Jun 1865 of meningitis or inflammation of brain. Most of his rec list in either co A, 42 or 45 NC, Co A, 45 Miss. The 45 NC was not at Ft Fisher and there was no 45 Miss. He was prob a member of co A, 42 NC, rather than co A, 4 Batt NC Jr Res or Co A, 3 NC Jr Res.

3 **W. H. Keptley**, co A, 3 NC Jr Res, prev in co A, 4 Batt NC Jr Res, released at Pt Lookout on 15 May 1865.

4 **H. F. Koonts**, co A, 3 NC Jr Res, prev in co A, 4 Batt NC Jr Res.

-rost-Company A, 4 Batt NC Jr Res.

1 B. C. Gobble, co A, 4 Batt NC Jr Res, place and date of enl not reported, prob enl prior to 31 Oct 1864, captured at Fort Fisher on 25 Dec 1864, confined at Ft Monroe on 29 Dec 1864, sent to Pt Lookout 31 Dec 1864, trans to co A, 3 NC Jr Res 3 Jan 1865 while POW.

2 Levy S. Keller, co A, 4 Batt NC Jr Res, place and date of enl not rep, captured at Ft Fisher on 25 Dec 1864, confined at Ft Monroe on 29 Dec 1864, sent to Pt Lookout 31 Dec 1864, may have trans to co A, 3 NC Jr Res on 3 Jan 1864 while POW. Most of his rec list him in either co A, 42 or 45 NC, co A, 45 Miss. The 45 NC was not at Ft Fisher and there was no 45 Miss. He was prob a member of co A, 42 NC, rather than co A, 4 Batt NC Jr Res or Co A, 3 NC Jr Res.

3 W. H. Keptley, co A, 4 Batt NC Jr Res, place and date of enl not reported, prob enl prior to 31 Oct 1864, captured at Ft Fisher on 25 Dec 1864, confined at Ft Monroe on 29 Dec 1864, sent to Pt Lookout on 31 Dec 1864, trans to co A, 3 NC Jr Res while POW.

4 H. F. Koonts, co A, 4 Batt NC Jr Res, place and date of enl not reported, prob enl prior to 31 Oct 1864, captured at Ft Fisher on 25 Dec 1864, confined at Ft Monroe 29 Dec 1864, sent to Pt Lookout 31 Dec 1864, trans to co A, 3 NC Jr Res.

-rost-Company A, 42 NC

1 **Burwell C. Gobble**, Co A, 42 NC, res Davidson Co, enl in Washington Co at age 18 on 1 May 1864, captured Battery Anderson at Fort Fisher on 25 Dec 1864, confined Ft Monroe on 27 Dec 1864, trans to Pt Lookout on 2 Jan 1865, released fm Pt Lookout 27 Jun 1865.

2 (Levy S. Keller not listed in co A, 42 NC)

3 **William Henry Keptley**, co A, 42 NC, born Davidson Co, enl at age 19 on 26 Nov 1861, captured at Battery Anderson at Fort Fisher on 25 Dec 1864, confined at Ft Monroe 27 Dec 1864, trans to Pt Lookout 31 Dec 1865, released fm Pt Lookout 15 May 1865.

4 **Henry F. Koonts**, co A, 42 NC, res Davidson Co, enl New Hanover at age 18 on 1 Mar 1864, captured Battery Anderson at Fort Fisher on 25 Dec 1864, confined Ft Monroe on 27 Dec 1864, trans to Pt Lookout on 2 Jan 1865, released fm Pt Lookout 28 Jun 1865.

1850 census Rowan Co., NC- Levi S. Keller, age 22.

1860 census Stanly Co., NC- Levi S. Keller, age 32.

CWPOWrec (7282)-Roll of Prisoners of War at Point Lookout, page 392. The following names taken in order from the roll at those captured at Ft Fisher on Dec 25, 1864 and arr at Point Lookout from Ft Monroe Jan 2, 1865.

"Geo W. Kershaw, Pvt, 3 NC Res, co A, exch Jan 17, 1865

Jos. H. Kimse, " " "

Walker Kemp, " " co C, exch Jan 17, 1865

M. R. Kirby, " " ", do Feb 18, 1865

J. A. Keller, " " ", exch Feb 18, 1865

J. H. Koonts, Capt, 42 NC, A, trans to Washington, DC Jan 27, 1865

W. H. Keptley, Pvt, 3 NC Res, ", released May 15, 1865

L. S. Keller, " " ", died June 30, 1865

H. F. Koonts, " " ", released June 28, do

E. Keener, " " co B, released June 28, 1865"

CWPOWrec (11538)- L. S. Keller, co A, 42 NC, $10.50 Confederate money taken from him 3 Jan 1865.

(note: strongly believe the Federal clerk was wrong on the unit of the last three names after Captain J. H. Koonts and they should be listed as in the 42 NC vice 3 NC (Jr) Res.)

Note: the data above on Burwell C. Gooble, Levy S. Keeler, William Henry Keptley and Henry F. Koonts should combine into company A, 42 NC Infantry; then delete the four from the 3rd NC Jr Res. And 4 Batt. NC Jr. Res.)

5)-rost-Pvt **J. A. Smith**, co A, 3 NC, capt at Fort Fisher on 25 Dec 64, conf at Fort Monroe, Va 29 Dec 64. (no further info).

note: The 3 NC Inf was not at Fort Fisher on 25 Dec 64, but the 3 NC Jr Res was capt on that date at Fort Fisher.

6)-rost- **J. G. Hooser**, co B, 3 NC Jr Res, capt Ft Fisher on 25 Dec 64 while in co B, 4 Batt NC Jr Res (Alamance and Forsyth Co., NC unit), died Pt Lookout on 10 May 65 of unk cause.

CWPOWrec- Isaac Hooser, co B, 3 NC Res, died Pt Lookout on 10 May 65 of acc diarr.

CWPOWrec- **Isaac G. Huser**, co B, 3 NC, on 'List of valuables taken from POW on 2 Jan 65'-$20 Confederate script.

1850 Forysth Co., NC census- Isaac G. Hauser, born 1848

1860 Forysth Co., NC census- two 'Isaac G. Hauser' noted, one born 1846 and the other 1848.

note: J. G. Hooser should be changed to Isaac G. Hauser and add cause of death as acute diarrhea.

7)-rost- **Haynes L. Powell**, co C, 7 Batt NC Res, enlisted near Wilmington 1 Jun 64, no further records.

FO, 24 Oct 1864-Haynes L. Powell, co C, 7 Battalion Junior Reserves, age 17 years, 6 months, from Robeson Co, died in hospital at Smithville, NC on or about the 10 August 1864.

Cause of deaths not reported in volume XVII - Junior Reserves

rank	Name	co	unit	place of death	died	cause of death
Pvt	James W. Olmstead	B	1 Jr Res	Pt Lookout	3/6/65	typhoid fever
Pvt	D. E. Lane	H	1 Jr Res	Pt Lookout	7/7/65	chr diarrhoea
Pvt	Isaac Holyfield	D	2 Jr Res	Pt Lookout	1/26/65	chr diarrhoea
Pvt	Isaac G. Hauser	B	3 Jr Res	Pt Lookout	5/10/65	acc diarrhoea
Pvt	Alfred M. Staly	B	3 Jr Res	Pt Lookout	2/13/65	chr diarrhoea
Pvt	Alexander Porterfield	C	3 Jr Res	Pt Lookout	6/16/65	chr dysentery
Pvt	Elias George Goforth	F	3 Jr Res	Pt Lookout	2/13/65	typhoid fever

Additional information noted in bold italicized names/dates

co	unit	rank	name	from	birth
A	1 Batt Jr Res	Sgt	*John S.* Dobson	McDowell	1847
A	1 Batt Jr Res	Pvt	*Samuel B.* Gillespie	McDowell	1847
D	1 Batt Jr Res	Pvt	*James M.* Bowden	Davie	1846
D	1 Batt Jr Res	Pvt	*Thomas J.* Canter	Wilkes	1846
D	1 Batt Jr Res	Corp	*George W.* Roseman	Alexander	1847
E	1 Batt Jr Res	1stLt	James B. Douthit	Davie	*1847*
A	1 Jr Res	Pvt	*Philander* Batchelor	*Nash*	*1846*
B	1 Jr Res	Pvt	James W. Olmstead	*Granville*	*1847*
B	1 Jr Res	Pvt	*N. David* Winston	*Granville*	*1847*
C	1 Jr Res	Pvt	*David A.* Bodenhamer	*Davidson*	*1846*
C	1 Jr Res	Pvt	Moses L. Headrick	*Davidson*	*1847*
C	1 Jr Res	Pvt	*John* Redwine	*Davidson*	*1847*
C	1 Jr Res	Corp	*Romulus G.* Roberts	Davidson	*1847*
D	1 Jr Res	Pvt	*Silas W.* Bell	Wake	1846
D	1 Jr Res	Pvt	*George P.* Brassfield	Wake	1847
D	1 Jr Res	Pvt	*Ferdinand D.* Moring	Wake	1847
D	1 Jr Res	Pvt	*William A.* Parish	Wake	1847
D	1 Jr Res	Pvt	*John Dallas* Thrower	*Wake*	1847
E	1 Jr Res	Pvt	*Murdock* Bethune	*Montgomery*	*1846*
E	1 Jr Res	Pvt	*Daniel R.* Monroe	Moore	1847
F	1 Jr Res	Pvt	*Wiley M.* Pugh	Randolph	1847
I	1 Jr Res	Pvt	*John* Crabtree	*Orange*	*1847*

I	1 Jr Res	Pvt	*John J.* Russell	Anson	*1847*
I	1 Jr Res	Corp	*Manly* Snipes	Orange	1846
B	2 Jr Res	Pvt	*William A.* Beaver	*Rowan*	*1846*
B	2 Jr Res	Pvt	John C. Corzine	Rowan	*1847*
C	2 Jr Res	Pvt	John Wright	Gaston	*1847*
D	2 Jr Res	Pvt	*Reubin B.* Condry	*Cleveland*	*1847*
D	2 Jr Res	Pvt	*John M. B.* Hopper	Cleveland	1847
F	2 Jr Res	Pvt	*William A.* Long	Union	1847
G	2 Jr Res	Pvt	Marmaduke Gay	*Edgecombe*	*1847*
H	2 Jr Res	Pvt	*James P.* Wallace	Johnston	1847
A	3 Jr Res	Pvt	*Burrell C.* Gobble	*Davidson*	*1847*
B	*3 Jr Res*	*Pvt*	*Isaac G. Hauser*	*Forsyth*	*1847*
C	3 Jr Res	Pvt	*Henry M.* Boyles	*Stokes*	*1847*
C	3 Jr Res	Pvt	Zachariah Crabtree	*Orange*	*1847*
D	3 Jr Res	Pvt	*Daniel* Cain	*Bladen*	*1846*
E	3 Jr Res	Pvt	David F. Eckard	*Catawba*	*1847*
F	3 Jr Res	Pvt	Richard O. Hodge	*Iredell*	*1848*
F	*3 Jr Res*	*Pvt*	*Reason S. Lazenby*	*Iredell*	*1847*
G	*3 Jr Res*	*Pvt*	*Benedict B.* Hood	*Caldwell*	*1847*
H	3 Jr Res	Pvt	*Marshal A.* Edwards	Cumberland	1847
H	3 Jr Res	Sgt	*Evander* McAlpin	Cumberland	1847
I	*3 Jr Res*	*Pvt*	*Peter McArthur*	*Robeson*	*1847*
I	3 Jr Res	Pvt	*H. Purdie* Prevatt	Robeson	1846
B	4 Batt Jr Res	Pvt	John P. Lewis	*Forsyth*	*1847*
C	4 Batt Jr Res	Sgt	*John Tyler* Brooks	Person	1846
C	4 Batt Jr Res	Pvt	Zachariah Crabtree	*Orange*	*1847*
B	7 Batt Jr Res	Pvt	*David James* Cook	*New Hanover*	*1846*
C	7 Batt Jr Res	Pvt	*Hector L.* McNeill	Robeson	1847
B	8 Batt Jr Res	Pvt	Stanhope H. Fisher	Catawba	*1847*
B	8 Batt Jr Res	Pvt	*George S.* Jones	*Catawba*	*1848*
B	8 Batt Jr Res	Pvt	*James P.* Weatherspoon	*Catawba*	*1847*

Additional Information and Amendments to the North Carolina Troops 1861-1865

Items for the Senior Reserves

1)-Nat Archives file-Pvt P. B. Wood, co C. 5 NC Sr Res, enlisted in Dobson (a Surry Co town). Absent-detailed as farmer.

CWPOWrec- **Peter B. Wood**, co C, NC Reseres, capt Burke Co., NC 28 Jun 64, 54ans to Nashville 10 Jul 64, died Camp Douglas 9 Dec 1864 of chr diarr.

1912 book-P. B. Wood of co 5 NC Sr Res died 9 Dec 64 at Camp Douglas.

1860 Surry Co census at Hotell had P. B. Wood, age 13, son of Henry and Prudence.

1850 Surry Co census at Hotell had Peter Wood, age 3, son of Henry and Prudence.

2)-Nat Arch file-Pvt **William Baker**, co E, 6 NC Sr Res, enlisted in Chatham Co.

1912 book-Pvt William Baker of co E, 6 NC Sr Res died at Camp Douglas, Chicago on 10 Jan 1865 (no Riley Baker noted.)

CWPOWrec- **Riley Baker**, co E, NCR, capt Kenasaw Mt 24 Jun 64, died Camp Douglas on 10 Jan 1865 of scorbutic.

3)-Nat Arch file-Pvt **Robert K. Worly**, McNeill's Co, 8 NC Sr Res, fm Richmond Co, enlisted at Wilmington, NC 10 Nov 1864.

1912 book-Pvt Robert K. Worly of McNeill's Co, 8 NC Sr Res died at Point Lookout on 28 Apr 1865.

CWPOWrec- R. K. Worley, 8 NC, capt Rockingham 7 Mar 65, died Point Lookout 28 Apr 65 of acute diarrhoea.

note: Worly must have been captured by Sherman's Army when they entered North Carolina on their march.

Other Notes of Interest

1) Note of interest to how North Carolina citizens (Quakers) were captured at NC State salt works at Wilmington: The USS *Fort Jackson*, **a** wooden side wheel steeamer in the United States Navy during the War, was assigned in December 1863 to the North Atlantic Blockading Squadron to cruise off the Western Bar, Cape Fear. The following month she helped in destroying the grounded blockade runner *Bendigo* at Folly Inlet. In April, Captain Benjamin F. Sands, her commanding officer, organized a boat expedition in which her crew crossed the bar to Masonboro Sound just east of Wilmington, North Carolina, and destroyed valuable State salt works, and seized a number of prisoners.

2) The following North Carolina soldiers were captured in a Winchester, Virginia, Hospital on 30 July 1863. Most if not all were wounded in the Gettysburg Campaign. They evidently were taken by the Confederate forces to Winchester before being captured. The *NC Roster* mentions in a few cases as being captured at Winchester on 30 July 63. Most were noted in Federal records as 'disposition unaccounted for' in the remarks section, but evidently were released prior to September 1863.

Name	Co	Unit	Remarks
Richard Amos		Manley's Batt	
Rufus Atkinson	G	13	
J. H. Bisset	A	47	
W. H. Booth	D	26	died 31 July 1863
G. G. Brewer	E	26	
J. H. Burnes	H	32	died 1 Aug 1863
M. Burns	E	57	
R. H. Burns	E	2	
A. L. Caddell	H	26	
J. N. Caddell	H	26	
James Campbell	I	4	
C. O. Chenartt		Latham's Batt	
J. H. Clounts	F	26	
B. M. Coffery	H	11	
J. J. Dumming	F	1	
James W. Flowers	A	1 Arty	
G. W. Garmon	D	26	trans to Jackson before name was taken
R. C. Honeycutt	E	47	
S. M. King	D	5 Cav	

William W. Lovins	E	45	
M. Manger	K	45	trans to Ft Jackso before name was taken
J. B. Martin	H	26	
T. D. Mills	D	26	
R. H. Morrison	B	2 Cav	
M. Oakly	K	45	
G. W. Partin	D	26	
W. M. Person	H	26	
William C. Quinn	D	2 Cav	
R. R. Rogers	D	26	
Isaac Strickland	A	20	died 31 July 1863
J. M Thomas	F	26	mistake name taken after trans to Mt Jackson
Jackson Towery		NC Arty	(should be co C, 1 NC Arty)
W. C. Warner	H	3 Cav	
W. H. Williams	D	11	
W. A. Wyatt	B	28	

More Research Needed

Following soldiers buried in City Point National Cemetery

1- **J. Nichols**   C 34 NC 7 Apr 65, grave 3964-rost-not listed in Roster.
2- **J. McKinney**   B 48 NC 4 Apr 65, grave 4085-rost-not listed in Roster.

Data for futher volumes of NC Roster

1)-rost-misc section-Capt **Robert F. Shearer**, 8 NC, res Caldwell Co, capt in Caldwell 14 Apr 65, conf Camp Chase until released 14 June 65, Fed Provost Marshal records indicate that he served in 'three company', no further records.
CWPOWrec-Capt **Robert T. Sheaver**, 8 NC, 3rd, capt Caldwell Co., NC 14 Apr 65, trans to Camp Chase 2 May 1865.
note: This was prob Sgt Robert F. Shearea, co B, 7 NC, born Watauga Co., NC, res Cabarrus Co, farmer, enl at age 30 on 12 Jul 61 and discharged 14 Feb 64. The above mention 8 NC poss meant for a reserve/milita unit.

2)-rost-Sgt **Paul Farthing**, co A, 11 NC died Camp Chase, Ohio or Camp Dennison, Ohio 11 Apr 65, place and date capt not reported.

CWPOWrec- 1st Sgt Paul Farthing, co A, 11 Batt, capt Watauga Co., NC 2 Feb 65, sent to Chattanooga than to Louisville, Ky by 19 Feb 65, trans to Camp Chase 3 Mar 65, died Camp Chase 11 Apr 1865 of erysipelas.

www.37nc.org/11th.php3- "Watauga Co, NC", 11 NC Battalion Home Guard had 2 companys (A and B), poss 200 to 250 men served in this unit. Only about 120 names have surfaced. "Paul Farthing and his nephew, Reuben P. Farthing, were captured 5 Feb 1865 at Camp Mast and died at Camp Chase, Ohio."

note: Paul Farthing of 11 NC should be deleted and info added to future volume on 11 NC Battalion Home Guard.

3)-rost-Pvt **Reuben P. Farthing** of co A, 11 NC Batt, died Camp Chase or Camp Dennison, Ohio 24 Apr 65, date and place of capt not reported.

CWPOWrec- R. P. Farthing, co A, 11 NC Batt, capt Watauga Co., NC 2 Feb 65, sent to Chattanooga than to Louisville, Ky by 19 Feb 65, trans to Camp Chase 3 Mar 65, died Camp Chase, Ohio 24 Apr 65 of pneumonia.

www.37nc.org/11th.php3- "Watauga Co, NC", 11 NC Battalion Home Guard had 2 companys (A and B), poss 200 to 250 men served in this unit. Only about 120 names have surfaced. "Paul Farthing and his nephew, Reuben P. Farthing, were captured 5 Feb 1865 at Camp Mast and died at Camp Chase, Ohio."

note: Reuben P. Farthing of 11 NC Batt. should be deleted and info added to future volume on 11 NC Battalion Home Guard.

4)-*Fayetteville Observer,* 24 Oct 1864- 1stLt **James B. Usher**, Co C, 32 Battalion North Carolina Home Guards, ca 1827, from Montgomery Co, killed in Moore Co., NC 1 Sept 1864 by deserters. The fatal ball struck him, passing just above the heart, killing him instantly.

5)-FO, 3 Feb 1862- **Captain Rogers**, company militia from Martin Co., committed suicide by shooting himself through the heart at Fort Hill on Sunday evening last (2 Feb 1862).

NC Conf Militia Officers Roster, page27- Captain **William B. Rogerson**, 10 Regiment, 3rd Brigade, of Martin Co., killed himself.

6)-Co D, 12th Battalion Virginia Light Artillery-- the following 38 soldiers were noted on the web site '*memers.aol.com/jweaver300/grayson/harr-art.htm*' as being in Co A, 13th Battalion North Carolina Light Artillery, but were not listed in the NC Roster (except for the two officers, Horne and McNeill). The *'American Civil War Soldiers'* site on *'Ancestry.com'*, these men were noted in Co. D, 12th Battalion Virginia Light Artillery. The Co. D, 12th Batt Va L Arty was trans to Co. A, 13th Batt NC L Arty on 4 Nov 1863. They should be added in a further volume on North Carolinians in other State's units.

BARRENTINE, CHARLES: Enl. 5/8/62 in Richmond Co., NC. Died on 7/16/62 of rubeola.

BARBER, BENJAMIN: Enl. on 4/28/62 in Richmond Co., NC. Pres. on 6/62 roll. Exchanged to Co. E, 38th NCT for Thomas H. Waters on 7/15/62.

BARRENTINE, SILAS L.: Enl. on 3/15/62 in Wilmington, NC. "Died in camp suddenly by visitation of God in the line of duty." per 6/62 roll.

BATTON, WILLIAM: Enl. on 3/15/62 in Richmond Co., NC. AWOL on 6/62 roll.

BRISTOW, JOHN: Enl. on 5/5/62 in Richmond Co., NC. Died of measles on 7/17/62.

BRISTOW, RICHARD: Enl. on 5/5/62 in Richmond Co., NC. Died of measles on 6/11/62.

BUTLER, JOHN E.: Enl. on 3/15/62 in Richmond Co., NC. Died on 7/30/62 of typhoid fever.

FREEMAN, JAMES L.: Enl. on 5/6/62 in Richmond Co., NC. AWOL on 7/1/62. Deserted on 8/20/63.

HALL, WILLIAM: Enl. on 5/23/62 in Rockingham Co., NC. Died on 5/27/62 with typhoid pneumonia.

HORNE, HENRY R.: 2nd Lt./1st Lt./Adjutant. Pres. on 6/62 and 2/63 rolls. Pres. on 2/64. Discharged from Gen. Hosp. #3, Goldsboro, NC on 9/12/64. Status not stated on 12/64 roll. Pres. on 2/65.

LIVINGSTON, JOHN: Enl. on 5/8/62 in Richmond Co., NC. AWOL on 6/62 roll.

McKETHAN, SANBORN: Enl. on 3/15/62 in Wilmington, NC. Died in hospital per 6/62 roll.

McKINNON, CHARLES E.: Enl. on 3/23/62 in Richmond Co., NC. Pres. on 6/62 and 2/63 rolls. NFR.

McNEILL, ARCHIBALD: 1st Sgt./2nd Lt., Enl. on 5/14/62 in Richmond Co., NC. Pres. on 6/62 and 2/63 rolls. Pres. 2/64. Status not stated on 12/64. Pres. on 2/65 roll.

McNEILL, DUNCAN: Corp., Enl. on 3/17/62 in Wilmington, NC. Promoted to Corp. on 5/16/62. Pres. on 6/62 roll. NFR.

McNEILL, MALCOLM D., Sr. 1st Lt., Enl. on ?. Pres. on 6/62 rolls. Absent sick on 9/11/62. res. on 2/63 roll. Furloughed for 30 days on 7/23/63 from Gen. Hosp. #10, Richmond, VA, or remittent fever. Pres. on 2/64. Status not stated on 12/64 roll. Pres. on 2/65 roll. Res. of Springfield, NC.

MOODY, THOMAS W., Jr. 1st Lt., Pres. on 6/62, 9/62 and 2/63 rolls. Resigned on 5/28/63.

NORTON, ANDREW: Enl. on 4/28/62 in Richmond Co., NC. Never reported for duty, listed as AWOL on 6/62 roll.

NORTON, LODERICK: Enl. on 4/28/62 in Richmond Co., NC. Never reported for duty, listed as AWOL on 6/62 roll.

NORTON, WILLIAM: Enl. on 4/28/62 in Richmond Co., NC. Never reported for duty, listed as AWOL on 6/62 roll.

PATE, ALEXANDER: Enl. on 3/15/62 in Wilmington, NC. Discharged for disability due to phthisis on 7/7/62. Described as born in Richmond Co., NC, age 20, 5'11", light comp., blue eyes, red hair, occ. farmer.

PATE, ELDRIDGE: Enl. on 4/28/62 in Richmond Co., NC. Pres. 6/62. NFR.

PEELE, JOHN: Enl. on 4/28/62 in Richmond Co., NC. Never reported for duty, listed as AWOL on 6/62 roll.

PRICE, MOSES: Enl. in 5/63, conscript. Deserted on 6/15/63 on march from Franklin, VA to Petersburg, VA.

PRICE, ZACHARIAH: Enl. in 5/63, conscript. Deserted on 6/15/63 on march from Franklin, VA to Petersburg, VA.

SMITH, CAMERON: Enl. on 3/17/62 in Wilmington, NC. Pres. on 6/62 roll. NFR.

SMITH, CLEMENT: Enl. on 3/20/62 in Rockingham, NC. Discharged per 6/62 roll.

SNEAD, ISRAEL: Enl. on 9/8/62 in Richmond, VA. Died in hosp. at Jerusalem, VA on 2/23/63 of pneumonia.

SNEAD, JOSHUA JORDAN: Enl. on 5/3/62 in Richmond Co., NC. Pres. on 6/62 roll. Died on 9/16/62 of typhoid fever at Farmville, VA Gen. Hosp.

TAYLOR, JAMES P.: Enl. on 3/15/62 in Wilmington, NC. Pres. on 6/62. NFR.

TAYLOR, THOMAS H.: Enl. on 4/22/62 in Richmond Co., NC. Pres. on 6/62 roll. Discharged on 9/27/62 for disability. Born in Richmond Co., NC, age 21, 5'4", dark comp., light hair, blue eyes, occ. farmer.

WATERS, DAVID: Enl. on 4/28/62 in Richmond Co., NC. Never reported for duty, listed as AWOL on 6/62 roll.

WATERS, JOHN: Enl. on 4/28/62 in Richmond Co., NC. Never reported for duty, listed as AWOL on 6/62 roll.

WEBB, LEWIS (LOUIS) H.: Capt., Pres. on 6/62 roll. Pres. in arrest on 9/62 roll. Pres. on 2/63 roll. Pres. on all rolls thru 2/65. Res. of Richmond Co., NC. B. 1827. Living in Franklin, VA in 1901. D. 1902. Buried in the Poplar Springs Cem., Franklin, Isle of Wight Co., VA.

WRIGHT, CAMERON G.: Enl. on 4/28/62 in Richmond Co., NC. Pres. on 6/62 and 2/63 rolls. NFR.

WRIGHT, GEORGE P.: Enl. on 3/31/62 in RIchmond Co., NC. Pres. on 6/62 and 2/63 rolls. Admitted to Chimborazo Hosp. #1 6/28/63 with parotitis. Died on 7/2/63, "murdered at Rocketts."

WRIGHT, JAMES: Enl. on 3/17/62 in Wilmington, NC. Died on 6/18/62 or measles.

WRIGHT, THOMAS M.: Enl. on 5/14/62 in Richmond Co., NC. Pres. on 6/62 and 2/63 rolls.

Cause of deaths for further Volumes of NC Roster

Rank	name	co	unit	place of death	died	cause of death
Sgt	**Paul Farthing**	A	11 Batt Home Guard	Columbus	4/11/65	erysipelas
Pvt	**Reuben P. Farthing**	A	11 Batt Home Guard	Columbus	4/24/65	pneumonia
Pvt	**Robert K. Worly**	-	8 Sr Res	Point Lookout	4/28/65	acute diarrhea
Pvt	**Lee Tanner**	-	NC Res	Chicago	7/31/64	acute dysenteria

Last Minute Findings

Vol 2 & 3)-rost- **James Baisden**, co I, 1 NC Cav, res in Duplin Co., enlisted at age 29 on 17 Jun 1861, capt Gettysburg 3 July 1863, died Ft Delaware on 18 Oct 1863.

rost- **J. Basscloud**, co I, 1 NC, capt Gettysburg 3 July 1863, died Ft Delaware on 18 Oct 1863 of diphtheria.

CWPOWrec- J. Basdon, co I, 1 NC Cav, died Ft Delaware on 18 Oct 1863 of diphtheria.

Note: delete J. Basscloud of 1 NC.

Vol 2 & 9)-rost- **Charles Shadgate**, co G, 4 NC Cav, enl Bertie Co. on 1 Oct 1862, on muster rolls through Mar 63, but not rep as present or absent.

rost- Charles Shadgate, co G, 32 NC, pre in co F, 4 NC Cav, died in Richmond hosp on 2 Mar 1865.

Southerners at Rest- **Charles W. Shadgett**, unid Conf. unit, died Feb 1865, buried unk in Hollywood Cem., Richmond, VA.

1850 & 1860 census Bertie Co.- Charles Shadgett, born ca 1845.

Note: changed name to Shadgett vice Shadgate.

Vol 4)-rost- Z. G. Pattishall, co E, 8 NC, died in Richmond hosp 15 Mar 1865.

Southerners at Rest- **Zachariah G. Pattishall**, co E, 8 NC, died 17 Mar 1865, buried grave W230 in Hollywood Cem., Richmond, VA.

Vol 7 & 13)-rost- ____ **Ebbs**, co B, 23 NC, p & d of enlistment not reported, wounded and capt at Gettysburg 1-3 July 63, died Gettysburg 4 July 1863 of wounds.

Rost- **William D. Epps**, co B, 53 NC, enlisted in Mecklenburg Co., NC 20 Mar 1862, wounded in the abdomen at Gettysburg 1 July 1863, died at Gettysburg on 4 July 1863 of wounds.

Note: delete ____ Ebbs of the 23 NC.

Vol 10)-rost- **Jesse Bradshaw**, co D, 38 NC, enlisted in Sampson Co. on 22 Oct 1861, enlisted as Private in Co G, 33 NC Troops on 2 Nov 1861.

CWPOWrec- J. Bradshaw, co B, 38 NC, captured at Gettysburg 5 Jul 1863, trans fm Ft Delaware to Point Lookout 15 Oct 1863, died Point Lookout on 11 Aug 1864.

note: Jesse of the 33 and 38 NC Troops are two different soldiers.

Vol 13 & 14)-rost- Sgt. **Daniel McCollum**, co I, 53 NC, from Union Co., enl at age 33 on 20 Mar 62, w Spotsylvania CH 10 May 64, capt in Richmond hospital 3 Apr 1865, died in hosp at Richmond on 3 May 1865, cause of death not reported.

rost- Sgt. **D. McCullom**, co I, 58 NC, place and date of enlistment not reported, capt (prob in hosp) Richmond on 3 Apr 1865, died in Richmond hosp on 2 May 1865 of chronic diarrhea.

note: delete D. McCullom of co I, 58 and add chronic diarrhea as cause of death to Daniel McCollum of co I, 53 NC.

Vol 15)-rost- Sgt **John A. Russell**, co A, 62 NC, died Richmond hosp on or about 1 Apr 1865.

Southerners at Rest- Sgt J. A. Russell, co A, 62 NC, died 21 Apr 1865, buried grave W623 in Hollywood Cem., Richmond, VA.

Index

A

Abernathy, Ben F. 57
Abernathy, Franklin D. 50
Abernathy, John R. 50
Adams, George F. 20
Adams, James Q. 76
Adams, James Quincy 76
Adams, W. H. 63
Adams, William H. 63
Adcock, Elvis A. 50
Adcock, Elvis Green 50
Adderton, W.S. 55
Alberty, Andrew P.J. 79
Alexander, Erasmus B. 57
Alexander, L. D. 57
Alexander, L. Dowe 57
Alexander, Lorenzo D. 57
Allen, A. M. 100
Allen, Asa M. 100
Allen, Henry H. 71
Allen, J. A. 103
Allen, James A. 103
Allen, Josiah 71
Allen, Levi & Polly 71
Allen, W. H. 71
Allen, William Henderson 71
Allgood, A. 130
Allgood, Arthur 130
Allman, Leonard 47
Allmond, Wiley P. 112
Amburn, Francis M. 123
Amick, John 64
Amos, Richard 142
Anders, Thomas J. 64
Anton, J. G. 37
Armstead, J. W. 135
Asken, John 87
Atkerson, A. H. 35
Atkins, William 127
Atkinson, Alvin 35
Atkinson, Rufus 142
Atwell, Joseph A. 64
Austin, J. E. 37
Austin, J. G. 119
Austin, J. J. 37
Austin, James G. 119
Austin, Joseph B. 21

B

Babson, Berry 64
Bailey, Harvey 73, 82
Bailey, Harvey James 73, 82
Bains, Henderson 47
Baisden, James 21, 146
Baker, Jehu 79
Baker, Riley 141
Baker, William 141
Baldwin, Daniel 62
Baldwin, Daniel H. 62, 64
Baldwin, David W. 33
Bales, James W. 90
Bales, John J. 90
Bales, Solomon and Nancy 90
Ball, W. D. 103
Ball, William D. 103
Ballenton, J. N. 83
Ballington, James N. 83
Barber, Benjamin 8, 145
Barefield, Gabriel 44
Barefoot, J.B. 124
Barfield, Gabriel 44
Barnes, Christopher C. 10
Barnes, J. H. 90
Barnes, J. N. 35
Barnes, James H. 90
Barnes, John N. 35
Barnes, N. P. 15, 36
Barnes, T. F. 65
Barnes, Thomas 65
Barnes, W. P. 15, 36
Barnes, William 51
Barnes, William P. 14, 15, 36
Barrentine, Charles 8, 145
Barrentine, Silas L. 8, 145
Barrier, G. W. 61, 70
Barrier, George W. 61, 70
Barrier, John A. 45
Barrier, Levi C. 45
Barrier, S. W. 61, 70
Barrier, Tobias A. 45
Barriere, T. A. 45
Bartlett, James 92, 96
Basnight, Amos 61
Bass, E. T. 109
Bass, Edmond F. 109
Bass, Lewis U. 105
Bass, William T. 112

Basscloud, J. 146
Bassnight, Amos 61, 64
Batchelor, James E. 47
Batchelor, Philander 138
Batton, William 8, 145
Bayles, J. J. 90
Bayles, James W. 90
Bean, B.F. 38
Bean, Benjamin F. 38
Beasley, Joseph 82, 100
Beasley, Joseph M. 82, 100
Beasley, William R. 55
Beaver, William A. 139
Bell, Benjamin D. 105
Bell, Bythel 105
Bell, N. R. 51
Bell, Samuel 30
Bell, Silas W. 138
Bell, Stephen 79
Beman, Charles H. 69
Benison, William P. 126
Bennett, Alexander 87
Bennett, Henry 97
Bennett, James W. 119
Bennett, W. 119
Bennett, Jr., William 119, 123
Bennison, William P. 126
Benton, E. A. 83
Benton, Ellis A. 83
Beofford, Wesley 2, 3
Berry, George W. 47
Bethune, Murdock 138
Bibbey, James 64
Bigham, John R. 55
Birney, S. B. 5
Bisset, J. H. 142
Bissett, Jackson J. 112
Bivens, Peter M. 124
Black, Adam 97
Black, W.W. 55
Blackburn, J.C. 33
Blackwell, John 84
Blalock, Chesley H. 87
Blankenship, Washington W. 96
Blount, Hosea G. 58
Blue, Daniel S. 15
Bodenhamer, David A. 138
Bolch, Aaron, Abel, Emanuel, Henry C.,
       Jordan, Logan, Marcus, Philip H.,
       William 81
Bolick, Sidney 55
Bolton, George B. 72

Boon, Augustus N. 50
Boone, A. N. 50
Booth, W. H. 76, 142
Boothe, William H. 76
Bostick, John 13, 29
Bostick, John C. 13, 29
Bouse, George F. De 60
Bowden, James M. 138
Bowers, J. A. 49
Bowers, John 53
Bowers, John A. 49
Bowman, David H. 117
Boyce, Samuel J. 87
Boyett, William S. 11
Boyette, G.A. 112
Boyette, George T. 32
Boyles, Henry M. 139
Bradley, Abraham B. 126
Bradley, Joseph L. 79
Bradshaw, J. 92, 146
Bradshaw, Jesse 92, 146
Bradshaw, Jonas N. 105
Brady, Nathan M. 46
Brafford, Wesley 2, 3
Brakefield, Henry N. 33
Brand, John 127
Brandon, James C. 21
Brantley, Henry 87
Brantley, William W. 102
Brassfield, George P. 138
Braswell, Jesse 96
Braswell, Lemuel T. 112
Breedlove, H. 69
Breedlove, Henry 69
Breedlove, Henry Newman 69
Breedlove, N. 69
Breedlove, Newman 69
Brenclare, S. 67, 68
Brett, Everett J. 59
Brewer, G. G. 76, 142
Brewer, Gerry G. 76
Bridgers, Clement 19
Bridgers, Clements 18
Bridges, Housen Newton 127
Bridges, James 89
Bridges, Joseph J. 89
Bright, Marcus 89
Bright, Mark 89
Brigman, Anannias 123
Briner, T. A. 45
Bristow, John 8, 145
Bristow, Richard 8, 145

Britt, Alexander A. 33
Britt, E. J. 59
Britt, George W. 32
Britton, William H. 85
Britton, William Henry 85
Brock, John W. 124
Brooks, John Tyler 139
Brooks, William J. 20, 130
Broom, Solomon S. 105
Broughton, Calvin 112
Brown, A. 30, 38
Brown, Anderton 30, 38
Brown, Archibald 10
Brown, Elisha 7
Brown, J. L. 111
Brown, J. M. 39
Brown, John L. 111, 117
Brown, John Moore 39
Brown, John T. 53
Brown, John Thomas 53
Brown, John W. 32
Brown, S.G. 126
Brown, W.G. 127
Brown, William A. 45
Browning, William 117
Bruce, R. E. 32
Bryan, George Pettigrew 13
Bryan, Thomas P. 60
Bryan, William P. 20, 130
Bryson, William F. 123
Buckner, Marion L. 129
Bullard, John Isom 5, 7
Bullis, Benjamin F. 79
Bullock, William 87
Bumgarner, David A. 124
Bumgarner, W. 25
Bumgarner, Wesley Levi 64
Bumgartner, W. 25, 26
Bungarner, William 25
Bunn, A.L. 123
Burch, James W. 79
Burden, Zachob J. 21
Burgin, Charles H. 69
Burke, Andrew J. 80
Burnes, J. H. 142
Burnett, Burwell 105
Burnett, Drew D. 17
Burney, Shipman 5
Burney, Shipman B. 5
Burns, M. 142
Burns, R. H. 142
Burton, Blaney W. 11

Butler, John E. 8, 145
Bynum, William Lafayette 117

C

Caddell, A. L. 142
Caddell, J. N. 142
Caddell, S. J. 27
Cahooh, Wilson G. 96
Cahoon, David 129
Cain, Daniel 139
Caipe, L. 121
Caldwell, R.W. 127
Calhoun, David 20, 129, 130
Calk, Fate 117
Cameron, J. F. 29
Cameron, John F. 29
Campbell, A. C. 74, 99
Campbell, Alfred C. 74, 99
Campbell, D. 108
Campbell, Daniel 108
Campbell, James 36
Campbell, James 142
Canby, W. A. 66, 67
Canipe, Noah J. 121
Cannon, James 79
Canter, Thomas J. 138
Canup, Benjamin F. 47
Caps, J.M. 37
Caps, James M. 37
Caps, James N. 37
Carden, Levi W. 87
Carpenter, David 55
Carpenter, Levi 49, 95
Carr, Robert B. 50, 103
Carroll, William 87
Carson, James T. 132
Carswell, M.H. 47
Carter, J. P. 74
Carter, James H. 33
Carter, Jesse P. 74
Carter, Thomas B. 112
Carter, William M. 87
Cartwright, John M. 132
Carver, James M. 33
Cash, William 38
Caudle, S. J. 27
Chamberlain, William 102
Chamberlan, Haywood 112
Chambers, Jesse 47
Chapel, H. O. 12
Chapman, Larkin J. 97
Chatham, William 40

Chatham, Willliam 47
Chenartt, C. O. 142
Chestnutt, William F. 87
Clack, James 126
Clamps, W. C. 2, 25
Clamps, W. C. C. 2, 25
Clapp, Wesley 2, 25
Clapp, William Whitesell and Sarah 111
Clark, Benjamin 16, 17, 85
Clark, James A. 126
Clark, John B. 44
Clark, Noah L. 79
Claybrook, Samuel 67, 68
Clements, D. A. 121
Clements, David A. 121
Cline, John L.H. 87
Clippard, Marcus 96
Close, Robert A. 21
Clounts, J. H. 142
Cobb, J. A. 93
Cobb, J. E. 93
Cobb, James A. 93
Cobble, George 11, 26
Coble, G. 11, 26
Coble, John M. 123
Cobler, Edmond 32
Cobler, Greenville 32
Cockrell, Samuel 64
Coffery, B. M. 142
Coffey, Larkin 79
Coggins, J. 129
Coggins, John 129
Coggins, John H. 129
Coghill, George 55
Cogleman, P.L. 42
Cole, G. M. 23, 133
Cole, Goodson M. 23, 133
Coleman, Robert E. 112
Coley, J. M. 81
Coley, John M. 81
Coley, Wesley 52
Colley, Leroy C. 46
Collins, J. W. 26
Colvard, Jesse A. 20
Combs, Wesley L. 79
Compton, Lewis R. 107
Conder, William 55
Condry, Reubin B. 139
Congleton, Alexander 105
Congleton, Henry 3
Congleton, Owen 3
Cook, David James 139

Cook, William Stephen 132
Cooley, Wesley 52
Cooley, William 52
Coolie, C. 52
Coon, G.W. 96
Cooper, Giles 44
Cooper, Giles H. 43, 44
Cooper, Hiram B. 10
Cooper, James I. 64
Cooper, R. L. 23, 133
Cooper, Rufus L. 23, 133
Copening, Abraham K. 64
Corprew, Septimus 64
Corum, William W. 112
Corzine, John C. 139
Cosand, Joshua 96
Coughton, O. 3
Coultrain, James L. 64
Council, Calvin H. 97
Covington, Edward J. 112
Cowan, George H. 33
Cowan, Jr., Thomas 33
Cox, Gabriel 21
Cox, S. B. 65
Cox, Silvester 65
Crabtree, John 138
Crabtree, Zachariah 139
Cranfield, J. H. 35, 46
Cranford, J. M. 53
Crawford, John Milton 53
Creecy, James E. 55
Crepps, J. 37
Crepps, Monroe 37
Cress, Edmund 125
Criswell, Henderson 132
Croom, David F. 1
Cross, Thomas 30
Crouch, A. 83, 99
Crouch, Allen F. 83, 99
Crouch, C. C. 70
Crouch, Christopher Columbus 70
Crouch, Samuel C. 117
Cruise, Robert 78
Crumpler, R. G. 119
Crumpler, Robert G. 119
Cumby, William A. 66, 67, 79
Curlee, C. S. 111
Curles, Calvin 111
Curtell, Eleaser 129
Curtis, H. R. 125
Curtrell, Elaser 20, 130
Cushing, Seborne A. 64

Cutrel, Eleaza 129
Cutrell, E. 129
Cutrell, Enoch 129

D

Daily, Bartley Y. 64
Daniel, Rufus P. 109
Dardin, Henry 46
Darnell, William E. 55
Daughtry, Reddick 64
Davenport, Benjamin S. 32
Davis, Augustus Ceasar 96
Davis, Calvin 33
Davis, Henry 117
Davis, Hiram 10
Davis, Hugh J. 14
Davis, Hugh Johnston 14, 21
Davis, James 80
Davis, Lorenzo A. 96
Davis, M. C. 23, 135
Davis, Merideth C. 23, 135
Davis, Michael C. 23, 135
Davis, Peter F. 21
Dawson, John 39, 127
Daybrook, S. 67, 68
Denning, Jesse F. 64
Dennis, J.O. 32
Dewar, J. P. 86
Dewar, John P. 86
Dick, Edmond F. 46
Dicken, Thomas 113
Dickens, Reuben R. 123
Dickey, J. W. 94
Dickie, Joe 94
Diggs, Riley 27, 84
Diggs, Thomas E. 84
Diggs, William 27, 84
Diggs, William R. 26, 84
Diggs, William Riley 26, 84
Dismukes, C. B. 105
Dixon, J.M. 96
Dixon, W. O. 52
Dixon, William 46
Dobson, John S. 138
Doggett, W. 111
Dorman, John 47
Dough, John C. 44, 47
Dough, Thomas T. 44
Douglass, Daniel H. 97
Douthit, James B. 138
Downing, D. E. J. 73
Downing, Daniel J. 73, 79

Doxy, John V. 47
Drake, H. 40
Drake, H. J. 40
Dry, Tobias A. 47
Duckett, Joseph N. 33
Duckworth, J. L. 15, 18
Duckworth, Jonathan L. 15, 18
Duke, Nash 47
Duke, Ransom H. 46
Duke, William J. 96
Dula, William T. 41
Dumming, J. J. 142
Dunbar, Tillman 20, 130
Duncan, George W. 105
Duncan, Owen 64
Dunn, J. M. 7
Dunn, Joseph M. 7
Dunn, William 112
Dunnegan, Lorenzo 87
Durham, Elisha A. 87
Durham, T. J. 107
Durham, Thomas J. 107
Dyon, William 52

E

Eckard, David F. 139
Eddins, C. 113
Eddins, Calvins S. 113
Eddins, Calvin S. 103, 113
Edwards, A.B. 80
Edwards, J. J. 120, 121
Edwards, James Weldon 96
Edwards, Marshal A. 139
Egerton, Rufus E. 90
Egerton, Rufus T. 90
Ellis, Charles S. 1, 4, 10
Ellis, Charles Stephen 1, 4
Ellis, Charles T. 1, 3
Ellis, James N. 80
Ellis, Wiley Jones 21
Emerson, David 10
Epps, William D. 146
Erwin, Rufus 77
Erwin, William Randolph 21
Etheridge, Samuel A. 21
Evans, J. A. 59, 60
Evans, James A. 59, 60
Evans, Joseph 50
Evans, O. Hiram 76
Evans, Orpheus H. 76
Evans, R. 50
Evans, Robert 11, 24, 32

Evans, W.W. 11, 24

F

Faison, Solomon W. 127
Falkner, George C. 79
Fanney, William 46
Farthing, Paul 49, 144, 146
Farthing, R. P. 49, 144
Farthing, Reuben P. 49, 144, 146
Ferrell, James W. 123
Ferrell, William 117
Fields, D.G. 62
Fields, Doctor G. 62
Fields, William 124
Finch, Jordan 79
Fincher, John E. 132
Fisher, J.A. 33
Fisher, Stanhope H. 139
Flake, Hyman 47
Fleming, James L. 123
Fletcher, James 50
Fletcher, William A. 73, 102
Flowers, J. W. 2
Flowers, James W. 2, 142
Floyd, Henry 55, 62
Floyd, J. W. S. 71
Fogleman, P.L. 42
Fogleman, Peter L. 42
Fogleman, Tobias 119
Fooshee, R.B. 55
Forney, William 119
Forney, William L. 119
Forshee, Zwean 110
Fort, W. H. 53
Fort, William H. 53
Foster, James M. 127
Foushee, Z. 110
Foust, Jr., John 10
Fouts, John 17
Fowler, Joseph S. 2
Fowler, M.S. 2
Fowler, Simon W. 46
Fox, Alexander 97
Fox, Miles 60
Fox, William F. 79
Frazier, James M. 26
Frederick, E. 29
Frederick, Elisha 29
Freeman, James L. 8, 145
Friddle, John 80
Fryar, John A. 63
Fulford, Anson B 33

Fullbright, Lenas F. 105
Fulwood, G. 93
Fulwood, George W. 93
Furgerson, J. T. 44
Furguson, George N. 97
Furguson, J. T. 44
Furr, Allison 47

G

Gaither, Calvin 96
Garmon, G. W. 142
Garrett, James F. 46
Garver, J.M. 46
Gates, Solomon G. 87
Gay, Marmaduke 139
Gay, N. 109
Gay, Nathaniel 109
Gay, S. 121
Gay, Sidney 121
Gee, Nevil 46
Gentry, Andrew 95
Gentry, Andrew C. 95
Gentry, Newton A. 75
Gibbs, A. A. 65
Gibbs, Arch A. 65
Gibbs, Henry H. 82, 83
Gibbs, James N. 82
Gibbs, Josephus S. 96
Gibbs, Thomas C. 82, 83
Gibson, J. T. S. 92
Gibson, James S. 92
Gibson, John A. 47
Gibson, Nicholas 107
Gibson, Rayman 39, 125
Gibson, Raymond 39, 125
Gibson, V. A. 92
Gibson, Virgil A. 92, 93
Gibson, W. H. 93
Gibson, William H. 92, 93
Gilbert, J. F. 65
Gilbert, James T. 65
Gill, Thomas 36
Gill, Thomas H. 36
Gillespie, Carter W. 21
Gillespie, James R. 21
Gillespie, Samuel B. 138
Gipson, N. 107
Givens, David A. 21
Gladson, John M. 32
Glimps, J. L. 18, 39
Glimps, James L. 18, 39
Glimpse, J. L. 18, 39

Additional Information and Amendments to the North Carolina Troops 1861-1865

Glimpse, James Leonard 18, 39
Glimpse, Leonard J. 18, 39
Gobble, B. C. 101, 136
Gobble, Burrell C. 139
Gobble, Burwell C. 100, 136
Godwin, David 105
Goforth, Elias George 138
Gooble, B. C. 135
Gooble, Burwell C. 102, 137
Gooding, William 31
Goodman, Henry 6, 77
Goodman, Henry H. 6, 77
Goodman, Z. D. 65
Goodman, Zachariah 65
Goodwin, B.F. 55
Gordon, William W. 51
Gore, William K. 59
Gossett, Abraham 55
Gower, Henry S. 5
Grady, Frederick 19
Gragg, Harvey H. 126
Graves, John Azariah 112
Gray, Alexander 132
Gray, Benaja 87
Gray, Enos 132
Green, Calvin 79
Green, John A. 64
Green, John C. 125
Green, John P. 123
Greenway, A. Crofford 123
Greer, Edmond J. 123
Gregg, Harvey H. 126
Gregory, Elijah 64
Gregory, James 114
Gregory, John 114
Gregory, William 114
Gregory, William A. 114
Griffin, Charles P. 39
Griffin, Claudius P. 39, 40
Griffin, E. A. 69, 70, 82
Griffin, Edward A. 69, 82
Griffin, Jane 40
Griffin, John T. 79
Griffin, Thomas B. 40
Grimsley, Allen 127
Gurkin, James 21
Guthrie, Thomas C. 10
Guthrie, William H. 90
Guthrie, William Hugh 90

H

Hackeman, Gerhard D. 58, 59

Hager, A. M. 28, 116
Hager, Adam Miller 28, 116
Hall, David 32
Hall, Jeptha 23
Hall, Moses I. 133
Hall, Moses J. 133
Hall, Robert 33
Hall, William 8, 145
Hamilton, John F. 117
Hammond, John E. 105
Hamrick, Isaac 123
Hamrick, William C. 105
Hannah, Harvey 132
Harder, Austin W. 127
Hardison, Joseph R. 32
Hardy, Curtis 55
Hare, William H. 46
Harling, James 53
Harman, T. H. 37
Haroldson, J. 13
Harper, George W. 50
Harper, Higdon 96
Harper, James N. 112
Harrelson, James 13
Harring, D. P. 25
Harrington, Thomas B. 104
Harris, E. 35
Harris, E. E. 35
Harris, Francis A. 32
Harris, J.P. 64
Harris, John N. 87
Harris, William 123
Harrison, Christopher C. 80
Harriss, Charles E. 55
Hartman, Thomas 37
Hartsell, Nimrod 21
Harvel, John 76
Harvell, John 76
Harwood, Redding 87
Hauser, Isaac G. 137, 138, 139
Hauser, Philip 19
Hauser, Philip A. 19
Hauser, Philip Alexander 19
Hauss, David 135
Hauss, Eli 135
Hauss, Joseph 135
Hauss, Peter and Barbara 135
Hauss, William T. 135
Hauss, William Theodare 135
Hawley, Ransom G. 64
Hayes, Abner Berge 77
Hayes, Joseph 105

Haynes, Myamin 124
Hays, A. B. 77
Hays, Calvin 46
Hazelwood, Asa 97
Headrick, Moses L. 138
Hearn, David W. 105
Heart, Wyatt 47
Heavener, Jeremiah 123
Hedgecock, Daniel 42
Heffler, R. H. 20
Heflin, R. H. 20
Hefner, Elcanah R. 105
Hefner, John Marcus 127
Helton, Alfred F. 79
Henderson, J. L. 130
Henderson, John 130
Hendersoon, Thomas M. 55
Hendrix, James Martin 97
Hennesey, M. 15
Hennessey, M. S. 15
Hennessey, Manassas S. 15, 18, 21
Hennessy, M. S. 18
Henry, Thomas 36
Hensley, William J. 21
Hensly, F. 67
Hensly, O. 67
Herbert, John 46
Herren, Cornwell 132
Herring, David P. 25
Herring, James W. 81
Hess, Thomas W. 47
Hewitt, J. R. 4
Hicks, Augustus 32
Hicks, John S. 79
Hicks, Quimby 80
Hicks, William 109
Higgins, Joseph W. 112
Hill, R. A. 74
Hill, Reubin R. 96
Hill, Richard A. 74
Hines, Henry L. 32
Hines, Sherwood 127
Hinnant, Ransom 25
Hinnant, Ransom J. 25
Hinnard, P. 25
Hinnart, P. 25
Hinson, Blythe 64
Hinton, Joseph J. 30
Hitchcock, D. 42
Hitchcock, Daniel 42
Hix, John S. 117
Hodge, Richard O. 139

Hoff, W. A. 81
Hoff, William 81
Hoff, William A. 81
Hofler, Charles 21
Holeman, S. J. 40
Holland, Henry B. 54
Holland, Ingram A. 15, 16, 17
Holland, J. A. 15, 16, 17
Holland, Marion L. 97
Holleman, Silas J. 40
Hollinsworth, James M. 68
Holloway, James 97
Holmes, B. 110, 125
Holmes, Rufus 110, 125
Holterson, Elijah H. 44
Holterton, E. H. 44
Holyfield, Isaac 138
Holyfield, John 64
Honeycutt, R. C. 142
Hood, Benedict B. 139
Hooks, Andrew 105
Hooser, Isaac 137
Hooser, J. G. 137
Hoosier, P. A. 19
Hootman, John 21
Hopper, John M. B. 139
Horn, John L. Van 96
Horne, J.B. 33
Horne, Henry R. 8, 145
Horney, E. P. 66
Horney, Eli P. 66
Horton, Richard 13
Horton, W. H. 85
Horton, William A. 85
Houghstetler, J. B. 65
Hovis, B. Monroe 55
Howard, James E.M. 46
Howard, W. J. 7
Howard, William J. 7
Howell, Robert P. 47
Howlett, Asa 31
Hudgins, James H. 96
Hufstutler, Benson 65
Hughes, Aaron 46
Hughes, Berry E. 87
Hughes, Freeman 90
Hughes, Freeman H. 90
Huneycut, Ambrose 55
Hunsucker, Jonas 96
Hunt, Samuel G. 32
Hunt, Sylvester 31
Hunter, Hugh M. 97

Additional Information and Amendments to the North Carolina Troops 1861-1865

Hurley, Freeman 97
Hurlocker, Monroe 117
Huser, Isaac G. 137
Huss, David 135
Huss, David C. 135
Huss, Elias Calvin 135
Huss, Eli C. 135
Huss, Joseph 135
Huss, Joseph H. 135
Huss, Peter 135
Huss, William T. 135
Hussey, Buchanan 42
Hussey, Bucharon 42
Hutchinson, William 116
Hutchinson, William E. 116

I

Ingle, J. L 65
Ingle, John L. 65
Inman, William A. 79
Irving, Rufus 77
Ivey, W.L. 87

J

Jackson, Benjamin B. 30
Jackson, Henry A. 132
Jackson, S. 13
Jackson, Shadrach 13
Jackson, Shadrack 14
Jackson, T. J. 110
Jackson, Thomas J. 110
Jackson, W. K. 123
Jackson, William K. 123
James, W. A. 29
Jamison, James P. 65
Jarvis, Bryant 55
Jarvis, Foster 46
Jean, M. 109
Jean, Nathaniel 109, 112
Jenkins, Robert 43
Jennings, S.W. 87
Jernigan, J.J. 46
Jestive, L. 121
Jimmison, James P. 65
Jinkins, William S. 42
Johnson, Elias 96
Johnson, Eli 79
Johnson, George 79
Johnson, John H. 94
Johnson, Josiah 46
Johnson, Thomas 94
Johnson, Thomas J. 46, 94

Johnson, W. H. 58
Johnson, William 57
Johnson, Willie 55
Johnston, George A. 59
Johnston, William G. 57
Johnston, Wm A. 57
Joiner, E. H. 64
Joines, Linville 127
Jones, Ambrose 122, 131
Jones, Amos 122, 131
Jones, Council B. 32
Jones, D. W. 50
Jones, Daniel McLean 86
Jones, David W. 50
Jones, George S. 139
Jones, James 100
Jones, James A. 123
Jones, John W. 112
Jones, Joshua 117
Jones, Matthew 33
Jones, Peter Daniel 46
Jones, Thomas 132
Jones, Thomas J. 46
Jones, William T. 5
Joyce, J. 63
Joyce, Joshua 63
Joyner, James 110
Joyner, James H. 6
Justice, Louis 121

K

Keeler, Levy S. 102, 137
Keen, Wiley 105
Keener, E. 102, 137
Keller, J. A. 102, 137
Keller, John J. 55
Keller, L. S. 102, 137
Keller, Levy S. 101, 135, 136
Kellum, Bryant 103, 105
Kelly, Daniel M. 33
Kelly, David W. 87
Kelly, William D. 87
Kemp, Walker 102, 137
Kendall, James S. 75
Kendall, Jas. S. 75
Kendall, Julius A. 116
Kendrick, Benjamin F. 121
Kendrick, Benjamin Franklin 121
Kennerly, A.M. 127
Keptley, W. H. 101, 102, 136, 137
Keptley, William Henry 101, 102, 136, 137
Kerley, Elisha 96

Kershaw, Geo W. 102, 137
Keyser, Jas. 57, 58
Kimse, Jos. H. 102, 137
Kindall, J. A. 116
King, David D. 33
King, S. M. 142
King, W.H. 87
King, William 114, 121
King, William H. 79
King, William J. 114, 121
Kinin, R. 104
Kinnian, Robert 104, 105
Kinsey, James W. 96
Kinston, M. 49
Kirby, M. R. 102, 137
Kirk, George E. 117
Kirkendoff, G. W. 18, 122
Kirkland, Stephen H. 87
Kiser, James 57
Kiser, John H. 123
Kittle, J.B. 123
Koon, G. W. 57
Koone, George W. 57
Koons, A. J. 111
Koonts, H. F. 101, 102, 136, 137
Koonts, Henry F. 101, 102, 136, 137
Koonts, J. H. 102, 137
Koontz, A. J. 111
Kriminger, George G. 96
Kuykendall, William G, 18, 122

L

Lackey, James Allen 105
Lancaster, B. S. 104
Lancaster, Bedford S. 104
Lancaster, L.L. 10
Lance, John B. 74
Lane, D. E. 138
Lane, William 12, 28, 29
Lanier, J. W. 99
Lanier, James N. 105
Lantz, Jacob 125
Latta, James G. 51
Latta, Joseph W. 51
Latta, Sampson 51
Latta, Simpson 51
Layton, Isaac W. 64
Lazenby, Reason S. 139
Ledford, Isaac 127
Lee, John B. 112
Lee, John Thomas 124
Leicester, Johnathan J. 46

Lenair, Ivy W. 99
Lenhardt, J. W. 113
Lenhardt, Joseph 113
Leonard, Alexander 102
Leonard, Caleb 79
Leonard, Jr., Alexander 102
Leonard, Jr., Joseph J. 132
Lew, W. F. 99
Lewallen, Dawson 33
Lewis, James A. 46
Lewis, John P. 139
Lewis, N. 70, 90, 91
Lewis, Noah 70, 90, 91
Lewis, Thomas M. 46
Lewis, William H. 79
Lewis, William T. 99
Leyden, Joseph T. 132
Liles, Kinchen 47
Lilly, Gabriel R. 60
Liverman, William T. 85
Livingston, John 8, 145
Lockhart, John P. 13
Lofton, Isaac N. 10
Loggett, W. 111, 112
Long, W. W. 59
Long, Wallace W. 59
Long, William A. 139
Long, William L. 92
Lovejoy, George S. 52
Lovelace, William G. 123
Lovelace, Willis G. 123
Lovins, William W. 107, 143
Low, Gideon 18, 129
Lowder, Archibald C. 117
Lowder, B. F. 14
Lowe, Gideon 18, 129
Lowrance, Carlos Elphonse 127
Lowrance, Henry Clay 127
Lowrie, P. J. 49
Lowrie, Patrick Johnson 49
Lowry, J. W. 10
Loyd, Thomas 24, 32
Lucas, Henry 123
Lunsford, E. M. 20

M

Macon, Ahigah 99
Macon, Ahijah 99
Macon, Thomas and Rosanna 99
MaCoy, Daniel 131
Macoy, Daniel 122
Madison, A. 36

Madison, Albert 36
Mahone, William 12, 28
Malpass, Thaddeus D. 64
Maner, James M. 75, 79
Manger, M. 143
Mann, Isaac 87
Markes, Joseph J. N. 6
Marlow, D. F. 120
Marlow, David 120
Marshall, Asbury 112
Marshall, Laurister L. 119
Martin, Alex 103
Martin, Allen 32
Martin, C. Dudley 51
Martin, Clarence D. 51
Martin, Ezekiel 116
Martin, J. B. 78, 143
Martin, John B. 78
Martin, John C. 21
Martin, Samuel 40
Martin, Thomas 110
Matheny, George M. 64
Mathews, William H.H. 127
Matthews, Nathan 87
Matthews, Robert 85
Maxwell, Alexander T. 33
May, J. D. 28, 66
May, John D. 28, 66
May, John Henry 61
May, Jonathan 87
May, William R. 32
Mayberry, Isaac S. 80
Maynard, J. 75
McAllister, E. 74, 75
McAllister, Joseph 95
McAlpin, Evander 139
McArthur, J. A. 113
McArthur, Peter 139
McCall, John C. 117
McCall, Z. T. 65
McCall, Zachary Taylor 65
McCan, Alfred P. 32
McCarter, Philip 64
McClellan, William 41
McClellan, William A. 41
McClenahan, J. T. 54
McClenahan, James T. 54
McClenahan, James Taylor 54
McCloud, N. 15
McCollum, Charles 87
McCollum, Daniel 146
McCoy, Daniel 122, 131

McCracken, R. B. 94
McCracken, R. H. 94
McCullen, William S. 11
McCullin, William S. 11
McCullom, D. 146
McDaniel, E. 65
McDaniel, Elisha P. M. 65
McDonald, D. C. 29
McDonald, Daniel C. 29
McEachern, Neill 4
McEwen, T. M. R. 20
McGalliard, James A. 123
McGee, E. A. 43
McGee, P. A. 43
McGee, Paschal A. 43, 47
McGee, Paschell 43
McGee, William H. 43
McGeehee, Paschal A. 43
McGinn, Robert F. 55
McGinness, J. P. 74
McGinnis, Sidney A. 55
McGinnis, Thomas M. 74
McGlamery, B. H. 65
McGlamery, Benjamin H. 65
McHome, W. 12, 28
McHone, W. 12, 28
McIntosh, Daniel J. 47
McIver, K. 15
McIver, K. H. 84
McIver, Kenneth 16
McKay, James 1
McKay, James A. 1
McKeel, William Henry 132
McKenzie, Dr. W. W. 35
McKenzie, William M. 35
McKethan, Sanborn 8, 145
McKinney, J. 143
McKinnon, Hosea 79
McKinnon, Charles E. 8, 145
McKnight, John W. 117
McLean, Hugh C. 79
McLellan, Alexander 64
McLeod, J. 16
McLeod, Neill 15
McMannen, William E. 39
McManning, William E. 38
McMercer, Saul 114
McMillan, Daniel 105
McMillan, William James 10
McNeil, William H. 60
McNeill, Hector L. 139
McNeill, William H. 60

McNeill, Archibald 8, 145
McNeill, Duncan 8, 145
McNeill, Malcolm D., Sr. 8, 145
McPherson, Martin 13
McPhetres, W.A. 47
McQuay, Seaborn 50
Meador, William T. 112
Meaiton, Thomas B. 110, 112
Meares, Henry L. 108
Medley, -John 54
Melton, A. J. 14
Melton, Alexander 102
Melton, Andew J. 14
Melton, William 64
Melver, Kenneth H. 84
Melvin, W. 5, 6
Melvin, William 5, 6
Melvin, William Snowden 5, 6
Mercer, F. 114
Mercer, John Picket 114
Mercer, Miles V. 114
Mercer, Miles Vanburen 114
Mercer, Saul McRibben 114
Merritt, Alexander R. 117
Merritt, William L.F. 105
Merrs, H. L. 108
Messer, Reuben 26
Messer, Reubon 26
Mickey, C. 92
Mickey, Constantine 92
Midgett, James T.(or J.) 20, 130
Miles, William B. 47
Millaway, A. E. 107
Miller, Amos 55
Miller, Charles 121
Miller, Charles W. 121
Miller, Thomas 96
Milling, John A. 79
Milloway, Andrew E. 107
Mills, John Sr. 123
Mills, T. D. 75, 143
Mills, Tilman D. 75
Millsaps, George W. 41
Milsaks, G. W. 41
Mims, Thomas J. 12
Mitchell, John C. 32
Mitchell, William 131
Mitchell, William N. 131
Mize, John 79
Modlin, Jordan 31
Monroe, Daniel R. 138
Monroc, Hugh B. 113

Montague, Dr. Latney J. 71
Montague, Henry Walter 19
Montague, L. J. 71
Montague, W. H. 19
Montague, Walter H. 19
Moody, David E. 55
Moody, Thomas W., Jr. 8, 145
Mooney, George W. 123
Mooneyham, William 127
Moore, Duncan 23
Moore, George W. 47
Moore, Joespeh E. 55
Moore, Walter J. 55
Moore, William H. 124
Moore, Jr., George W. 32
Morgan, Martin 117
Moring, Ferdinand D. 138
Morris, D. 111
Morris, Daniel 111
Morris, Isaac W. 96
Morris, Monroe 55
Morrison, R. H. 143
Morrow, R. Alexander 81
Morrow, Richard A. 81
Morton, Ezekiel 116
Motsinger, A.F. 111
Motsinger, A. Frank 111
Motsinger, Abram F. 111
Mull, David 99
Mull, William E. 99, 100
Munday, William F. 117
Murray, William G. 20, 130
Myers, Andrew J. 47

N

Nailand, William 96
Nash, Frederick K. 64
Neal, Thomas 124
Neally, Isaiah 61
Neel, J. 61
Neese, Elias 32
Nelson, James R. 12
Nelson, John Wesley 78, 80
Nelson, W. P. 78
Nelson, Washington P. 78
Nelson, William R. 97
Newbern, James E. 96
Newsom, James D. 81
Newson, James C. 81
Nichols, J. 143
Nichols, J. G. 65
Nichols, Joseph G. 65

Nickens, Jonathan H. 46
Norton, Andrew 8, 145
Norton, Loderick 9, 145
Norton, William 9, 145
Nunn, Benjamin F. 81
Nunn, Benjamin Franklin 81

O

O'Brien, Dr. John and Elizabeth 11
O'Brien, Hugh 11
O'Brien, M. 11
O'Brien, MacCenas 11
O'Brien, MacEnas 11
O'Brien, Marcenas? 11
O'Neal, David R. 20, 21, 130
Oakley, Marine 107, 108
Oakly, M. 107, 143
Odom, David M. 96
Oliver, Cornelius L. 79
Oliver, Jabez B. 87
Olmstead, James W. 135, 138
Orr, N.C.H. 55
Osborne, J. 32
Osborne, L. 112
Overby, R. W. 3
Overby, Robert 3
Overcash, P.A. 127
Overman, William 80
Overton, James B 96
Owen, William H. 36
Owens, G.M. 47
Owens, George F. 123
Owens, W. 36

P

Padgett, Andrew 123
Page, Bryant 117
Page, John 90
Paris, Nelson 24
Parish, Elias 80
Parish, William A. 138
Parker, John M. 112
Parker, Sampson S. 79
Parks, W. H. 103
Parks, William H. 103
Parrish, James 86
Parrish, John L. 24
Parrish, Nelson 33
Parrish, Parham P. 87
Parrish, Uriah R. 21
Partin, C. C. 7
Partin, G. W. 143

Pate, Alexander 9, 145
Pate, Eldridge 9, 145
Patterson, E. S. 20
Patterson, John 44
Patterson, M. A. 94
Patterson, Neill A. 94
Pattishall, Z. G. 146
Pattishall, Zachariah G. 146
Paul, William Cornelius 32
Payne, William R. 80
Pearson, Solomon G. 79
Pearson, Thomas S. 123
Peele, William E. 21
Peele, John 9, 145
Pendergrass, J.R. 87
Penninger, Henry 47
Perdue, Charles 10
Perkins, John 131
Perkins, John R. 122, 131
Perry, L. H. 4, 51
Perry, Levi H. 4, 51
Perry, W. S. 95
Perry, William 95
Perry, Jr., Willie 54
Person, W. M. 78, 143
Persons, William M. 78
Petway, Joseph L. 46
Phelps, Elisha 55
Phibbs, Robert J. 32
Philips, Willis 76
Phillips, Elias 2
Phillips, Lewis S. 33
Phillips, Lyas (Elias) 2
Phillips, William 79
Phillips, Willis R. 76
Picket, John 114
Pickett, Joseph 31
Piner, J. M. 30, 83
Piner, James 83
Piner, James J. 30, 83, 84
Piner, James M. 30, 33
Piner, John J. 30, 83
Pinson, George W. 96
Pippins, Milus B. 97
Pitman, Calvin W. 73
Pittman, Calvin W. 73
Pittman, Robert M. 123
Pittman, W. T. 7
Pittman, William T. 7
Pitts, J.M. 89, 115
Pitts, John Minett 89, 115
Pleasants, Albert B. 31
Poore, Thomas 64

Pope, D. W. 115
Pope, Doctor W. 115
Pope, E. T. 108
Pope, Elijah T. 108
Porter, Travis L. 33
Porterfield, Alexander 138
Poteet, W. G. 65
Poteet, William 65
Potts, William T. 117
Powell, D. E. 109
Powell, Durrell E. 109
Powell, George W. 64
Powell, Haynes L. 137
Powell, Pinkney 80
Pratt, William R. 117
Prestwood, Fabius 80
Prevatt, H. Purdie 139
Prevett, Abner 46
Prevo, W. Henry B. 114
Price, Jackson 123
Price, Needham 79
Price, Moses 9, 145
Price, Zachariah 9, 145
Priddy, William B. 127
Pridgen, Josiah J. 87
Provo, Henry W. B. 114
Puett, Elisha 21
Pugh, Wiley M. 138
Pyner, J. 30, 83

Q

Quinn, William C. 143

R

Rackley, Hardy 21
Ralph, J. B. 38
Ralph, John B. 38
Ralph, M. 82
Randall, Willis 117
Randolph, Matthew F. 33
Rankin, Robert D. 1
Rankin, Robert G. 1
Raper, Calvin 123
Rash, Asa 123
Rash, Payton 16, 126
Rash, Peyton 16, 17, 126
Rawls, Joseph R. 58
Ray, Henry 16
Ray, John S. 105
Rayl, Thomas A. 11
Reardon, Daniel C. 96
Redwine, John 138

Reece, J. F. 129
Reece, James 129
Reevs, Laomi 33
Register, B. T. 42
Register, Benjamin T. 42
Reid, John L. 95
Rhoads, B. 3
Rhodes, Battle 3
Rhyne, John C. 57, 58, 64
Rial, Charles W. 47
Rich, J. A. 75
Rich, Joseph A. 75
Richards, Albert 26
Ricks, John E. 96
Rierson, J. W. 119
Rierson, John W. 119
Rightsel, M. 78
Rightsell, Millan 78
Ritchey, Pleasant 46
Ritchie, William N. 127
Robason, McG 58
Robason, Noah 27, 84
Roberson, McG. 58
Roberson, R. H. 83
Roberts, John N. 64
Roberts, P. W. 52
Roberts, Philetus W. 51
Roberts, Romulus G. 138
Roberts, W. A. 35
Roberts, W. J. 35
Roberts, William J. 35
Robertson, N. 26, 84
Robertson, N. P. 26, 84
Robertson, Noah P. 26, 84
Robeson, Albert 10
Robinson, Harmon R. 83
Robinson, J. B. 115
Robinson, Jeremiah 115
Robinson, Jeremiah B. 115
Robinson, John 28
Robinson, Joseph B. 115
Robinson, R. H. 83
Robinson, Samuel S. 64
Robintson, W. P. 26
Rodgers, John H. 79
Rogers, Captain 144
Rogers, Jacob M. 53
Rogers, John W. 21
Rogers, R. R. 76, 143
Rogers, Robert 75
Rogerson, David L. 58
Rogerson, William B. 144

Additional Information and Amendments to the North Carolina Troops 1861-1865

Rollins, S. R. 113
Rollins, Summie R. 113
Roper, Amos W. 64
Rose, William 21
Roseman, George W. 138
Ross, Henry E. 32
Rousley, William R. 46
Routh, Jesse 69
Rowan, Richard T. 94
Rowan, Richard Thomas 94
Rowe, W. L. 30
Rowe, Wiley 27
Rowe, Wiley A. 27
Rowe, William L. 30
Royal, Thomas 11
Royster, A. D. 110
Royster, Arkansas Delaware 110
Rudd, Lorenzo D. 21
Ruffin, Thomas 21
Russell, Eli 97
Russell, J. A. 146
Russell, J. F. 127
Russell, John A. 146
Russell, John J. 139
Russell, Jordan F. 127
Ryan, J. C. 57, 58

S

Sadler, William 62
Samm 31
Sands, Benjamin F. 142
Sapp, F. W. 12, 66
Sapp, Francis W. 12, 66
Sapt, F. W. 66
Sasser, John 19
Saunders, Aaron 112
Saunders, Richard A. 46
Savage, D. 89, 115
Savage, David 90, 115
Savage, David W. 89, 115
Sawyer, Ebenezer W. 132
Sawyer, Robinson A. 96
Sawyer, William 20, 122, 130, 131
Scarborough, M. G. 86
Scarborough, Melvin G. 86
Scarlett, Felix 52
Scarlett, Samuel H. 112
Scott, T. G. 72, 120
Scott, Theophilus G. 72, 120
Scott, William 111
Seagle, B. F. 65
Seagle, Benjamin F. 65

Seagle, J. M. 65
Seagle, Jacob M. 65
Searles, Chesley 112
Sedberry, John A. 87
Self, Lemuel S. 96
Setser, W.E. 77
Setser, W. Eli 77
Setzer, Eli 77
Setzer, W. A. & Eliza 77
Setzer, William A. & Eliza J. 77
Setzer, William Eli 77
Sexton, Augustine G. 87
Shadgate, Charles 146
Shadgett, Charles 146
Shadgett, Charles W. 146
Shamel, Jacob W. 47
Sharp, Michael R. 112
Sharp, Oscar D. 32
Shaver, Abraham 47
Shaw, John A. 117
Shearea, Robert F. 143
Shearer, Robert F. 143
Sheaver, Robert T. 143
Shell, Slighter B. 79
Shepard, Jackson L. 33
Shepherd, William H. 112
Sherill, Asaph W. 133
Sherrill, Asaph Wilson 133
Shields, Allen 41, 76
Shields, Allen R. 41, 76
Shields, K. 41, 76, 77
Shipp, John S. 71
Shipp, Wm. T. and H. M. 71
Shivers, William S. 132
Shoe, Nimrod 112
Sibbet, John 60
Sibbit, John 60
Sifford, John Frank 117
Sigman, Benjamin 127
Sigman, Elijah 55
Sigman, Reuben 109
Sigmon, R. 109
Sigmon, Reuben 112
Sikes, Murdock M. 14
Simmons, Elisha 87
Simmons, Ephriam B. 33
Simpson, Even 113, 117
Simpson, James W. 33
Skipper, Murdock 112
Small, Abner R. 42
Small, T. 107
Small, Thomas 107

Smallwood, Jacob H. 47
Smart, Thomas R. 47
Smith, Amos W. 10
Smith, Angus 33
Smith, Henry D. 127
Smith, J. A. 29, 137
Smith, James 17, 96
Smith, James B. 17
Smith, Jesse D. 21
Smith, Johnnie H. 86
Smith, John H. 73, 86
Smith, John Henry 73
Smith, John L. 80
Smith, John S. 55
Smith, Leroy 20, 117, 130
Smith, S. A. 85
Smith, Samuel A. 85
Smith, Silas 124
Smith, W. D. 45
Smith, W. R. 70, 71
Smith, Wellington D. 45, 47
Smith, William E. 1
Smith, William R. 70, 71
Smith, Woody M. 105
Smith, Cameron 9, 145
Smith, Clement 9, 145
Snead, Israel 145
Snead, Israel: 9
Snead, Joshua Jordan 9, 145
Snider, Lewis W. 105
Snipes, John W. 87
Snipes, Manly 139
Snipes, Nelson 117
Sollice, D. Vaughn 87
Southerland, C. C. 28
Southerland, Jere H. 21
Sparrow, S. P. 20, 130
Speas, W. H. 16
Spece, W. H. 16
Speck, J. J. 54
Spencer, William H. 20, 130
Spruill, Asbury 89
Spruill, Benj. A. 89
Spruill, Benjamin Asbury 89
Spruill, Henry W. and Jasper 89
Spurle, H.W. 32
Sr., Perry G. Putman, 96
Stafford, S. H. 120
Stafford, Samuel H. 120, 123
Stafford, Z. J. 120
Stafford, Zadok J. 120
Stafford, Zadok J. & Hanah 120

Stallings, J.G. 79
Stallings, J. G. 65
Stalls, Miles B. 96
Staly, Alfred M. 138
Stanback, George L. 52
Stancell, Samuel T. 54
Stanfield, John O. 21
Stanley, Atlas J. 80
Starr, John C. 64
Stearns, A. L. 95
Stearns, Ambrose Lee 95
Stephens, W. L. 85
Stevenson, Joseph C.G. 97
Stewart, Samuel A. 55
Stier, William 55
Stiles, Charles 100
Stinson, W. C. 14
Stinson, William C. 14
Stocks, Henry 132
Stoker, Robert 87
Stone, Alexander 55
Stone, William A. 112
Stone, William Jackson 33
Stone, William Turner 46
Storgeal, J. 71, 72, 95
Stough, Allison 96
Stowe, Wilson L. 105
Strayhorn, F. 110
Strayhorn, Franklin 110, 112
Strickland, Isaac 62, 143
Strickland, Jacob 6, 84
Strickland, John D. 124
Strickland, Nathaniel 6
Stricklin, Isaac 62
Stroup, Lafayette 117
Stroup, Robert B. 117
Sturgill, James 71, 72, 95
Sudderth, G. H. 78
Sudderth, George 78
Sudderth, George Murray 78
Sullivan, M. 73
Sullivan, Michael 74
Summerlin, Charles H. 32
Summers, Adolphus C. 96
Summers, J. A. 65
Summers, Julius A. 65
Sumner, William H. 21
Suther, David S. 79
Sutton, Elias 33
Swanson, Simeon 105
Sykes, M. M. 14

Additional Information and Amendments to the North Carolina Troops 1861-1865

T

Taber, Alexander 122
Taber, Calvin C. 38, 122
Tabor, Calvin C. 38, 122
Tallah, J. J. 68
Tallah, John J. 68
Talley, Jonas 133
Tanner, C. 40, 41, 62
Tanner, Calton 40, 62
Tanner, Lee 146
Taylor, A. F. 89
Taylor, Alfred A. 33
Taylor, Archibald 89
Taylor, Charles 132
Taylor, Henry E. 21
Taylor, James H. 120
Taylor, McGilbert 32
Taylor, William 58
Taylor, James P. 9, 145
Taylor, Thomas H. 9, 145
Teague, Losson L. 20
Teal, William R. 21
Terry, Edward G. 10
Thigpen, Amos 33
Thomas, Benjamin 32
Thomas, J. M 143
Thomas, J. M. 59
Thomas, W. J. 103
Thomas, William G. 103
Thompson, Duncan A. 94
Thompson, Duncan Alexander 94
Thompson, E. C. 92
Thompson, Emanuel C. 92
Thompson, Josiah J. 124
Thompson, W.H. 105
Thomson, George W. 105
Thrower, John Dallas 138
Thurman, J. M. 133
Thurman, John M. 133
Tillett, Jonathan 132
Tillman, Jeremiah 46
Todd, Aquilla 46
Todd, John L. 96
Tomberlin, James E. 132
Tomkins, M. D. 21
Towery, Jackson 2, 143
Tramwell, E.B. 112
Travis, Thomas B. 46
Trent, James L. 64
Triplett, W. T. 76
Triplett, William T. 76
Tripp, Furnifold 47

Trotter, John M. 63
Tucker, Arthur 105
Turner, David W. 124
Turner, J.C. 46
Turner, J. A. 19
Turner, John A. 19
Tuttle, Abraham 92
Tuttle, Abraham H. 92
Tyson, George W. 67, 90

U

Upchurch, Thomas 47
Usher, James B. 144

V

Vanover, John 79
Vestal, J. W. 27
Vestall, J. W. 27
Vickers, Linsey 31

W

Wade, Robert H. 79
Wagner, A. B. 63, 77
Wagner, Aaron and Susannah 63, 77
Wagner, Alex 63
Wagner, Archibald B. 62, 63, 77
Wagner, John 77
Wagoner, Archibald B. 63, 77
Wagoner, J. M. 60
Wagoner, John 60
Wagoner, William 55
Waldrape, T. D. 73, 93
Waldrop, Jaron D. 72, 73, 93
Waldrop, T. D. 73, 93
Waldrop, Theron D. 72, 93
Walker, D. D. 65
Walker, David 65
Walker, David N. 112
Walker, Jefferson H. 127
Walker, John 79
Walker, John H. 114
Walker, Mary 114
Walker, Robert 112
Wall, John Richard Francis 117
Wallace, James P. 139
Wallace, William 108
Ward, Daniel 115
Ward, W.H. 112
Warner, W. C. 143
Warren, Emory E. 96
Washburn, J. 66

Washburn, Jacob 66
Washburn, John 79
Waters, Harrison 46
Waters, Thomas 60
Waters, David 9, 145
Waters, John 9, 145
Watson, Apollas 64
Weason, William 29
Weathers, J. D. 27
Weathers, James D. 27
Weathers, Rufus P. 55
Weatherspoon, James P. 139
Weaver, John 79
Webb, C. 19
Webb, Curtis A. 19
Webb, Noah R. 105
Webb, Lewis (Louis) H. 9, 145
Welborn, Wisdom P. 33
Wescott, John W. 87
Weseley, W. H. 91
Wesley, Collie 52
Wesley, William 91
Wesley, William H. H. 91
West, Charles E. 21
West, Thomas 108
West, Thomas Upton 108
Westbrook, Young J. 46
Whitaker, William Franklin 79
White, Clinton 32
White, Dr. W. Edward 41
White, Elam Franklin 97
White, Michael 123
White, William Ed. 41
Whitehead, James G. 21
Whitehurst, William M. 132
Whitesell, Daniel 110, 111
Whitesell, Eli 32
Whitey, John 109
Whitfield, George V. 96
Whitman, J. B. 38
Whitman, John A. 38
Whitsel, Daniel 110
Whitt, Reuben P. 75
Wicker, Matthew D. 105
Wiggins, Alfred S. 14
Wiggins, T. B. 54
Wiggins, Thomas B. 54
Wilborn, John 123
Wilburn, Miles 63
Wilkerson, A. 108
Wilkerson, Samuel 24, 59
Wilkinson, Allen 108

Wilkinson, Samuel 24, 59
Willard, William 33
Willets, William J. 10
Williams, David A. 47
Williams, Elias 31
Williams, F. F. 14
Williams, George W. 32
Williams, James 2
Williams, James W. 2
Williams, John B. 96
Williams, Levi Branson 21
Williams, Marshall 80
Williams, Nathan C. 87
Williams, Richard 107
Williams, Richard D. 107
Williams, T. F. 14
Williams, Thomas A. 93
Williams, W. H. 143
Williams, William W. 2
Willis, John 41
Willoughby, Rayford 80
Wilson, Hugh 111
Wilson, J. W. 16
Wilson, John W. 16
Wilson, Lafayette 79
Wilson, Robert Leroy 55
Wilson, William 111
Winecoff, David R. 43
Winker, D. R. 43
Winnekoffer, D. R. 43
Winstead, George W. 35
Winstead, W. 35
Winston, N. David 138
Withers, A. 27
Withers, James D. 27
Witherspoon, Lawson Alexander 96
Womble, William N. 85
Wombles, John W. 85
Wood, Icem 82
Wood, Isom 82
Wood, P. B. 141
Wood, Perry 55
Wood, Peter B. 141
Woods, Joseph 117
Woolard, Wiley 10
Woolen, George H. 87
Worley, Eliphalet 47
Worley, R. K. 141
Worly, Robert K. 141, 146
Worsley, Littleberry and Harrett 91
Worsley, William H. 91
Worsley, William H. H. 91

Wright, A. Spinks 108
Wright, Alfred 108
Wright, C. T. 94
Wright, George W. 96
Wright, James 47
Wright, John 139
Wright, Nathaniel 123, 131
Wright, Thomas C. 94
Wright, Willis F. 32
Wright, Cameron G. 9, 145
Wright, George P. 9, 145
Wright, James 9, 145
Wright, Thomas M. 9, 145
Wyatt, W. A. 81, 143
Wyatt, Wyley A. 81

Y

Yancey, John Dallas 124
Yates, James W. 64
Yates, M. D. 43
Yates, Merrit D. 43
Yeates, G. T. 116
Yeates, George Thomas 116
Young, F.M. 32
Yount, E. M. 72
Yount, Eli 72
Yount, Eli M. 72
Yount, Samuel 72

LaVergne, TN USA
04 May 2010

181464LV00001B/4/P